Renal Diet
Cookbook

314 Wholesome, Mouthwatering, Healthy and Quick Recipes with Low Sodium, Potassium, And Phosphorus for Chronic Kidney Disease

Anna Ray

MEDICAL DISCLAIMER

All content on this book is created and published online for informational purposes only. It is not intended to be a substitute for professional medical advice and should not be relied on as health or personal advice.

Always seek the guidance of your doctor or other qualified health professional with any questions you may have regarding your health or a medical condition. Never disregard the advice of a medical professional, or delay in seeking it because of something you have read on this book.

If you think you may have a medical emergency, call your doctor, go to the nearest hospital emergency department, or call the emergency services immediately. If you choose to rely on any information provided by this book, you do so solely at your own risk.

External (outbound) links to other websites or educational material (e.g. pdf's etc...) that are not explicitly created by Your Health are followed at your own risk. Under no circumstances the author is responsible for the claims of third party websites or educational providers.

TABLE OF CONTENTS

INTRODUCTION

Renal diets are often recommended for people with chronic kidney disease (CKD). A renal diet is one that limits the amount of sodium, protein, potassium, phosphorus and animal protein. It contains less than 60 g of total solids per day to help decrease the amount of fluid retained by the body. This diet also includes more fluids during meals to dilute this food intake in order to help avoid problems from too much salt intake.

Normal kidney function depends on healthy blood vessels, which deliver nutrients to the cells, and remove waste products from the blood. When these blood vessels are not working properly, waste products can build up in your blood. This leaky blood vessel problem is called "hypertension" (high blood pressure). The excess fluid (edema) can swell the feet, ankles, or abdomen with fluid. Swelling in the tissue outside of the kidneys can also occur; this is called "ascites" and may cause problems breathing if it becomes severe. Other indications that may be experienced are queasiness and vomiting, weight gain or loss without trying, weakness and fatigue, burning while urinating or feeling like you have to urinate often.

Most treatments of kidney disease are focused on slowing the loss of kidney function. These may include medications to control blood pressure or medication to control fluid retention. In some advanced cases dialysis or a kidney transplant may be considered.

Dropping sodium consumption is a significant part of a diet for people with CKD because sodium causes the kidneys to retain extra water which makes them work harder. High blood pressure is often caused by too much sodium in the diet, so it follows that reducing sodium will reduce blood pressure, and slow the progression of high blood pressure in this population.

Sodium is found certainly in roughly all foods, and is added to others during processing or cook preparation. For instance, table salt (sodium chloride) is a good source of sodium, and bread, salad dressings and soups often contain large amounts of sodium.

Canned foods are also high in sodium because salt is used to preserve them. Because many people with CKD have difficulty controlling their blood pressure or preventing fluid retention from salt, restricting their intake of sodium can help them manage these problems. In fact, restricting your intake of sodium to 1500 mg per day or less may reduce the need for dialysis by 50%.

The renal diet is designed for people with chronic kidney disease who are already on dialysis. It has no place in the diet of people who can eat and absorb nutrients on their own. It should be changed when the patient's health improves and the medications that are used to treat them are changed accordingly. If a patient has a seizure from an overdose of medications or from a low potassium level, this diet may cause seizures as well as death.

In people with chronic kidney disease, it is important to check the serum potassium level periodically (monthly or as directed) as it is important to keep this level within normal limits. The amount of potassium that can be taken depends on the current serum potassium level. When the serum potassium level is below 5 mEq per L, no additional potassium is allowed aside from what is in foods. When the serum potassium level is above 5 mEq/L, up to 40 mEq of supplemental dietary potassium per day may be added to ensure adequate intake while at the same time avoiding hyperkalemia.

It's critical to talk about your diet with your doctor if you have renal illness. The kidneys are in charge of eliminating waste from the bloodstream and producing urine. Waste goods for example urea and creatinine can build up in the bloodstream if they aren't operating properly, causing harm to other regions of the body.

Chronic kidney disease (CKD) is incurable because damage to portions of our kidneys is often irreversible. The good news is that by accepting a new lifestyle and eating habits, you can slow down the disease's progression into crucial phases. The foods we eat have an undeniable impact on the health of our body organs, especially our kidneys. Switching to a kidney-friendly diet is the best thing you can do if you have chronic renal disease. The renal diet is a frequent term for this type of diet.

Although chronic kidney disease (CKD) cannot be cured, the renal diet can help patients keep their kidney functions and delay kidney failure for years. The renal diet has a huge influence on our kidneys in that it lessens their burden, allowing them to endure longer.

UNDERSTANDING THE BASICS OF KIDNEY DISEASE

Chronic Kidney Disease (CKD)

CKD or chronic kidney disease is the stage of kidney damage where it fails to filter the blood properly. The term chronic can be used to refer to gradual and long-term damage to an organ. Chronic kidney disease is therefore developed after a slow yet progressive damage to the kidneys. The symptoms of this disease only appear when the toxic wastes start to build up in the body. Therefore, such a stage should be prevented at all costs. Hence, early diagnosis of the disease proves to be significant. The sooner the patient realizes the gravity of the situation, the better measures he can take to curb the problem.

What about after we are affected by diseases? Well, even then, we make sure that we spend less time pondering about and trying to change what we cannot and more time on how to take care of ourselves. By focusing on our own actions, we gain more confidence, motivation, and knowledge. We realize that the ability to make changes, however big or small, lies within us.

In the case of chronic kidney diseases, we have the power to ensure that the disease does not get worse.

Causes of Kidney Disease

According to the National Kidney Foundation, the main two causes of chronic kidney disease include high blood pressure and diabetes (National Kidney Foundation, n.d.). If you visit a doctor, health expert, or diet consultant, then you will realize that one of the major ways in managing your blood pressure and prevent diabetes is a healthy diet.

As the blood pressure or diabetes levels get worse, so does the amount of waste buildup. The waste goes into your blood faster than the kidneys are able to filter them. At this point, your kidneys are like an overworked employee at a firm; there is so much work still remaining but only a small amount of time to get finished during a particular period. The kidneys begin to deteriorate over time. The filters begin to leak, unable to hold on to the waste buildup anymore. Only a small percentage of the entire waste gets filtered properly, with the rest entering the bloodstream. For some, the time it takes for kidney failure might be months while for others, the kidneys could worsen across a span of years. It all depends on numerous factors like diet, lifestyle choices, and even genetics.

Pretty soon, you might feel like your kidney functions have been kidnapped; they don't seem to be functioning well anymore or they barely exist. But that is not the case. Think of the example of the overworked employee that we used earlier. At some point, the employee could collapse out of dehydration or exhaustion. In a similar way, the kidney disease causes the organs to fail, which causes numerous problems such as low energy, high exhaustion levels, sleep difficulties, poor appetite, swollen ankles and feet, and the need to urinate more often, especially at night.

Sign And Symptoms Of Kidney Disease

The good thing is that we can prevent the chronic stage of renal disease by identifying the early signs of any form of kidney damage. Even when a person feels minor changes in his body, he should consult an expert to confirm if it might lead to something serious. The following are a few of the early symptoms of renal damage:

- Tiredness or drowsiness
- Muscle cramps
- Loss of appetite
- Changes in the frequency of urination
- Swelling of hands and feet
- A feeling of itchiness
- Numbness
- The darkness of skin
- Trouble in sleeping
- Shortness of breath
- The feeling of nausea or vomiting

These symptoms can appear in combination with one another. These are general signs of body malfunction, and they should never be ignored. And if they are left unnoticed, they can lead to worsening of the condition and may appear as:

- Back pain
- Abdominal pain
- Fever
- Rash
- Diarrhea
- Nosebleeds
- Vomiting

After witnessing any of these symptoms, a person should immediately consult a health expert and prepare himself or herself for the required lifestyle changes.

The Five Stages of Kidney Disease

Chronic kidney disease is categorized into five stages, each one characterized by a certain degree of damage done to the kidneys and rate of glomerular filtration, which is the rate at which filtration takes place in the kidneys. These help us understand just how well the kidneys are functioning.

Stage 1

The first stage is the least severe and actually comes close to a healthy state of your kidneys. Most people will never be aware if they have entered stage 1 of chronic kidney disease, or CKD. In many cases, if people discover stage 1 CKD, then it is because they were being tested for diabetes or high blood pressure. Otherwise, people can find out about stage 1 CKD if they discover protein or blood in the urine, signs of kidney damage in an ultrasound, a computerized tomography (CT) scan or through magnetic resonance imaging (MRI). If people have a family history of polycystic kidney disease (PKD), then there are chances that they might have CKD as well.

Stage 2

In this stage, there is a mild decrease in the glomerular filtration rate. People don't usually notice any symptoms at this stage as well. The reasons for discovering any signs of CKD are the same as with the reasons provided in stage 1.

So, what's the difference between stage 1 and stage 2? It all lies in the glomerular filtration rate, or GFR for short. The GFR is measured in milliliters/minute.

In stage 1, the glomerular filtration rate (GFR) is around 90 ml/min. The normal range of the GFR is from 90 ml/min to 120 ml/min. So, as you can see, stage 1 CKD shows a GFR at the lower end of the range. Because it falls so close to a normal rate, it easily goes unnoticed. At stage 2, the GFR falls to between 60-89 ml/min. You might become concerned with the range stage 2 falls in, but your kidneys are actually resilient. Even if they are not functioning at 100 percent, your kidneys are capable of doing a good job. So good that you might not notice anything was out of the ordinary.

Even though the differences between stage 1 and 2 are minuscule, they cannot be combined because the chances of someone showing certain symptoms of CKD when in stage 2 are greater.

Stage 3

At this stage, the kidneys suffer moderate damage. In order to properly gauge the level of damage, this stage is further divided into two: stage 3A and stage 3B. The reason for the division is because even though the severity of the disease worsens from 3A to 3B, the damage to the kidneys is still within moderate levels.

Each of the divisions are characterized by their GFR.

- 3A has a GFR between 45-59 ml/min
- 3B has a GFR between 30-44 ml/min

When patients reach stage 3, they begin to experience other symptoms of CKD, which include the below:

- Increase in fatigue
- Shortness of breath and swelling of extremities, also called edema
- Slight kidney pain, where the pain is felt in the lower back area
- Change in the color of urine

Stage 4

At stage 4, the kidney disease becomes severe. The GFR falls down to 15-30 ml/min. As the waste buildup increases the patient might experience nausea and vomiting, a buildup of urea in the blood that could cause bad breath, and find themselves having trouble doing everyday tasks such as reading a newspaper or trying to write up an email.

It is important to see a nephrologists' (a doctor who specializes in kidney problems) when the patient reaches stage 4.

Stage 5

At stage 5, the kidneys have a GFR of less than 15 ml/min. This is a truly low rate that causes the waste buildup to reach a critical point. The organs have reached an advanced stage CKD, causing them to lose almost all their abilities in order to function normally.

Best advice to Avoid Dialysis

Some people often think that you have to stop working or retire from your job the moment you start taking dialysis. But that's not necessarily true.

It is very much possible to keep working even after you start dialysis. In fact, it is recommended that you try to continue working in order to stay happier and healthier.

If your company provides health insurance, then you can even keep enjoying the benefits of insurance while you work. It will help you bear the costs of your dialysis as well.

There are some types of dialysis that provide more flexible treatment options, allowing you to have more time during the day for your job.

Nocturnal (Night-Time) dialysis, either at home or hospital, is perfect for these.

However, if you do start working during your dialysis, you should understand your limits. While you are working, it is possible that you might feel bit weak or tired.

If you are following peritoneal dialysis, then you are going to need a clean place to do all your exchanges.

Alternatively, if you are on Hemo, then it is strictly prohibited for you to lift heavy objects or put excess pressure on your vascular access arm.

Depending on your dialysis type, you must talk to your social worker/doctor to adjust your dialysis routine and talk to your employer in order to reach an agreement.

Worst case scenario, if you are unable to work, you still have some options! Various federal and private programs will help you to have a stable income while keeping your insurance for your dialysis program.

Talk to your personal social worker in order to apply for these facilities.

The minerals that maintain the internal concentration balance inside the kidneys obviously come from our diet. Salt, the everyday ingredient of our lives, is one of the purest and most direct sources of sodium. There are also other sources of potassium and calcium. By deliberately limiting the intake of such ingredients in our diet, we can manage all our renal problems and even prevent further damage to the kidney cells. Food has a profound impact on your health, and its importance can never be denied. A comprehensive renal diet provides a concrete plan to keep the kidneys healthy and working.

WHAT IS A RENAL DIET

A renal diet is an eating plan that is followed to assist reduce the amount of waste products in the blood. The renal diet is designed to put the least amount of labor or stress on the kidneys while yet delivering energy and essential nutrients.

A renal diet adheres to a few basic principles. The first is that it must be a well-balanced, nutritious, and long-term diet that is high in whole grains, vitamins, fibers, carbs, omega-3 fats, and fluids. Protein intake should be sufficient, but not excessive.

Blood accumulates are kept to a minimal. Electrolyte levels in the blood are checked on a regular basis, and the diet is adjusted as needed. It's critical to follow your doctor's and dietitian's recommendations.

Protein intake is necessary to rebuild tissues on a daily basis, but it should be restricted to a bare minimum. The body must break down excess proteins into nitrates and carbohydrates. Nitrates are not used by the body and must be eliminated through the kidneys.

Carbohydrates are a vital source of energy and should be consumed in sufficient quantities. The best grains are whole grains. Refined carbs should be avoided.

Table salt should only be used in cooking. Excess salt causes fluid retention by overworking the kidneys. Processed meats, a variety of dishes, sausages, and snacks should all be avoided.

Because phosphorus is required for physiological function and cannot be removed by dialysis, it must be monitored and consumption reduced, but not fully eliminated.

Phosphorus-rich foods include dairy products, darker drinks like colas, and legumes. If blood levels of this rise, potassium-rich foods such as citrus fruits, dark, leafy green lettuce, carrots, and apricots may need to be avoided.

Omega 3 fats are an important part of a balanced diet. Fish is a great source of protein. Omega fats are essential for the human body. Trans-fats and hydrolyzed fats should be avoided.

Fluids should be sufficient, but in cases of fluid retention, they may need to be restricted.

A good renal diet might help you preserve your kidney function longer. The constraints placed on protein and table salt ingestion are the key differences between a renal diet and any balanced diet plan. As indications and symptoms of buildup emerge, hydration and potassium restrictions may become necessary.

This diet is prepared in multiple circumstances and is useful in various stages of the condition. In other cases, the diet is designed for diabetics who want to avoid kidney disease. Diabetes and renal disease patients have difficulty eating the right foods.

The goal of a diabetic meal plan is to keep blood sugar levels within a safe range. This can be accomplished simply by eating often during the day, without skipping any, and eating low-glycemic carbohydrate items.

Including a variety of these carbohydrates in each meal can help the body maintain a healthy blood sugar level that is neither too high nor too low.

Brown rice, sweet potatoes, and whole-grain bread are examples of low-glycemic foods. Whole-grain bread and sweet potatoes, on the other hand, should not be utilized in a diabetic renal diet since they are high in potassium.

People with kidney problems should consume fewer potassium, phosphorus, and sodium-rich meals. A blood sugar-lowering diet for diabetics can also be a diet that is good for kidney problems. Because sodium is included in many foods, patients should read labels carefully.

Dietitians advise against drinking diet coffee pops because they contain salt, which is harmful to renal patients.

THE IMPORTANCE OF DIET FOR KIDNEY DISEASE

There are many benefits to adapting to the renal diet, whether or not you have kidney disease or related conditions. It's a good way to eat and live, especially if you may be susceptible to kidney infections and other issues that impact the function of this vital organ. This includes making changes early and paying close attention to your symptoms and any changes you notice, as these may indicate the progression in the disease itself or a positive change in your kidneys' function. Keeping an eye on the slightest changes can make a significant difference in improving your health and taking charge of your well-being.

How Eating Well Can Make a Difference

The renal diet focuses primarily on supporting kidney health because, in doing so, you'll improve many other aspects of your health, as well. It can also be customized to fit all levels of kidney disease, from early stages and minor infections to more significant renal impairment and dialysis. Preventing the later stages is the main goal, though reaching this stage can still be treated with careful consideration of your dietary choices. In addition to medical treatment, the diet provides a way for you to gain control over your own health and progression. It can mean the difference between a complete renal failure or a manageable chronic condition, where you can lead a regular, enjoyable life despite having kidney issues.

Eating Well is a Natural and Medicine-Free Way to Help Your Kidneys

Whether or not the medication is a part of your treatment plan, your diet takes on a significant role in the health of your kidneys. Some herbs and vitamins can boost the medicinal properties found in foods and give your kidneys additional support while limiting other ingredients, which, in excess, can lead to complete renal failure if there are already signs of kidney impairment. Your kidneys thrive on fresh, unprocessed foods that make it easier for your body to break down, digest, and process nutrients. Choosing natural options also eliminates or reduces the amount of sodium and refined sugars you consume, so you don't have to continuously monitor how many grams of salt or sugar is in your foods.

If you have limited access to fresh fruits or vegetables, choose frozen as the next best option, as they will have retained all or most of the nutrients in their original state. Canned vegetables and fruits are often processed, though these can be added when no other options are available. To reduce the amount of sodium they contain, rinse canned vegetables in the water at least twice before adding them to your meal or dish. Canned fruit is often preserved in a thick or sugary syrup, which should be drained and rinsed before serving to reduce the sugar content. Always read the ingredients of the package or can before you consider adding it to your grocery cart, and only choose these options where fresh or frozen selections are unavailable.

Unless directed by a physician or medical specialist, don't reduce or stop taking medication for your kidneys, even if there are significant improvements to your health as a result of dietary changes and/or medical improvements, and there is an increase in kidney function noted. While diet should be a central part of your lifestyle, keep the medication as part of this treatment goal just the same. Any sudden or significant changes in your treatment plan can thwart any progress made and may cause further damage in the long term. Consider your food and meal choices in the renal diet as part of a whole, which also includes exercise, medical treatment(s), and living well.

Advantages Of Renal Diet

A renal diet is especially useful during the first stages of kidney dysfunction and leads to the following advantages:

- Prevents excess fluid and waste build-up
- Prevents the progression of renal dysfunction stages
- Decreases the likelihood of developing other chronic health problems e.g., heart disorders
- Has a mild antioxidant function in the body, which keeps inflammation and inflammatory responses under control.

The above-mentioned benefits are noticeable once the patient follows the diet for at least a month and then continuing it for longer periods, to avoid the stage where dialysis is needed. The severity of the diet is contingent on the current stage of renal/kidney disease, if, for example, you are in the 3rd or 4th stage, you should follow a stricter diet and be attentive for the food, which is allowed or prohibited.

Renal diet helps in weight loss by restricting the amount of salt and fluids that you take. It maintains certain amount of sodium and potassium in the body. This diet also reduces the tendency of high blood pressure and swelling because of decreased fluid intake.

Chronic renal failure lowers the efficiency of kidneys over time, therefore your ability to process nutrients is also reduced. The renal diet helps in limiting foods that are difficult to digest as well as those that may result an allergic reaction to happen.

FOODS TO AVOID AND SUGGESTED VALUE LIMIT ABOUT SODIUM, PHOSPHORUS AND POTASSIUM

These foods are known to have high levels of potassium, sodium, or phosphorus:

Soda – Soda is believed to contain up to 100 mg of additive phosphorus per 200 ml.

Avocados - 1 cup contains up to 727 mg of potassium.

Canned foods – Canned foods contain high amounts of sodium, so make sure that you avoid using these, or at least opt for low-sodium versions.

Whole wheat bread – 1 ounce of bread contains 57 mg phosphorus and 69 mg potassium, which is higher compared to white bread.

Brown rice – 1 cup of brown rice contains 154 mg potassium, while 1 cup of white rice only has 54 mg potassium.

Bananas – 1 banana contains 422 mg of potassium.

Dairy – Dairy products are high in potassium, phosphorus, and calcium. You can still consume dairy products, but you have to limit it. Use dairy milk alternatives like almond milk and coconut milk.

Processed Meats – Processed meats are not advisable for people with kidney problems because of their high content of additives and preservatives.

Pickled and cured foods – These are made using large amounts of salt.

Apricots – 1 cup contains 427 mg potassium.

Potatoes and sweet potatoes – 1 potato contain 610 mg potassium. You can double boil potatoes and sweet potatoes to reduce potassium by 50 percent.

Tomatoes – 1 cup tomato sauce contains up to 900 mg potassium.

Instant meals – Instant meals are known for extremely high amounts of sodium.

Spinach – Spinach contains up to 290 mg potassium per cup. Cooking helps reduce the amount of potassium.

Raisins, prunes, and dates – Dried fruits have concentrated nutrients, including potassium. 1 cup of prunes contain up to 1,274 mg potassium.

Chips – Chips are known to have high amounts of sodium.

These are the main foods to avoid, but I suggest you to check by yourself each ingredient you use for more details. For more information see the medical disclaimer at the beginning.

Since the Renal Diet is generally a Low Sodium, Low Phosphorus program, there are certain health benefits that you will enjoy from this diet. (Apart from improving your kidney health). Some of the crucial ones are as follows:

- It helps to lower blood pressure
- It helps to lower your LDL cholesterol
- It helps to lower your risk of having a heart attack
- It helps to prevent heart failure
- It decreases the possibility of having a stroke
- It helps to protect your vision
- It helps to improve your memory
- It helps to lower the possibility of dementia
- It helps to build stronger bones

List of Juices and Drinks

Natural and salt-free drinks are best to maintain the internal balance of the kidneys. The more you drink water and other fluids, the more of the toxins and minerals get released out of the kidneys without damaging nephrons. Following is some of the fluids you must drink on a kidney-friendly diet:

- Water
- Cranberry juice
- Apple cider
- Grape juice
- Lemonade
- Fruit Juices You can also try fresh juices from the following fruits:
- Apples
- Berries
- Cherries
- Fruit cocktail, drained
- Grapes
- Peaches
- Pears, fresh or canned, drained
- Pineapples
- Plums
- Tangerines
- Watermelons

A Kidney-Friendly Lifestyle

Once a kidney is damaged there is no one-time solution or magic to undo all the damage. It requires constant management and a whole new lifestyle to provide a healthy environment for your kidneys. For healthy kidneys, you just need to keep the following in mind:

- Upgrade your vegetable intake to 5–9 vegetables per day.

- Reduce the salt intake in your diet.
- Cut down the overall protein intake.
- Remove all the triggers of heart diseases, like fats and sugar, from your diet.
- Do not consume pesticides and other environmental contaminants.
- Try to consume fresh food; homemade is the best.
- Avoid using food additives, as they contain high amounts of potassium, sodium, and phosphorous.
- Drink lots of sodium-free drinks, especially water.
- Choose to be more active and exercise regularly.
- Do not smoke in order to avoid toxicity.
- Obesity can create a greater risk of kidney diseases, so control your weight.
- Do not take painkillers excessively, such as Ibuprofen, as they can also damage your kidneys.

1. Asparagus Frittata

Preparation Time: 5 minutes
Cooking Time: 30 minutes
Servings: 2 servings
Ingredients:

- 10 medium asparagus spears, ends trimmed
- 2 teaspoons extra-virgin olive oil, divided
- Freshly ground black pepper
- 4 large eggs
- ½ teaspoon onion powder
- ¼ cup chopped parsley

Directions:

1. heat the oven to 350°F.
2. Mix the asparagus with 1 teaspoon of olive oil and season with pepper. Place to a baking pan and roast, stirring occasionally, for 20 minutes, until the spears are browned and tender.
3. In a small bowl, beat the eggs with the onion powder and parsley. Season with pepper.
4. Cut the asparagus spears into 1-inch pieces and arrange in a medium skillet. Drizzle with the remaining oil, and shake the pan to distribute.
5. Pour the egg mixture into the skillet, and cook over medium heat. When the egg is well set on the bottom and nearly set on the top, cover it with a plate, invert the pan so the frittata is on the plate, and then slide it back into the pan with the cooked-side up. Continue to cook for about 30 more seconds, until firm.

Nutrition: Calories: 102; Total Fat: 8g; Saturated Fat: 2g; Cholesterol: 104mg; Carbohydrates: 4g; Fiber: 2g; Protein: 6g; Phosphorus: 103mg; Potassium: 248mg; Sodium: 46mg

2. Poached Eggs with Cilantro Butter

Preparation Time: 5 minutes
Cooking Time: 10 minutes
Servings: 2 servings
Ingredients:

- 2 tablespoons unsalted butter
- 1 tablespoon chopped parsley
- 1 tablespoon chopped cilantro
- 4 large eggs
- Dash vinegar
- Freshly ground black pepper

Directions:

1. In a small pan over low heat, melt the butter. Add the parsley and cilantro, and cook for about 1 minute, stirring constantly. Remove from the heat, and pour into a small dish.
2. In a small saucepan, bring about 3 inches of water to a simmer. Add the dash of vinegar.
3. Crack 1 egg into a cup or ramekin. Using a spoon, create a whirlpool in the simmering water, and then pour the egg into the water. Use the spoon to draw the white together until just starting to set. Repeat with the remaining eggs. Cook for 4 to 7 minutes, depending on how set you like your yolk.
4. With a slotted spoon, remove the eggs.
5. Serve the eggs topped with 1 tablespoon of the herbed butter and some pepper.

Nutrition: Calories: 261; Total Fat: 22g; Saturated Fat: 7g; Cholesterol: 429mg; Carbohydrates: 1g; Fiber: 0g; Protein: 14g; Phosphorus: 226mg; Potassium: 173mg; Sodium: 164mg

3.Blueberry Breakfast Smoothie

Preparation Time: 10 minutes
Cooking Time: 10 Minutes
Servings: 1
Ingredients:

- 1/3 cup vanilla almond milk – no sugar added
- 2 tablespoons protein powder of your choice
- ¼ cup of Greek yogurt - look for brands with low sodium and low potassium
- 3 strawberries - fresh, sliced
- 6 raspberries
- 1 cup blueberries – frozen or fresh
- 1 tablespoon cereal – avoid whole grain due to high levels of potassium

Direction:

1. First, you need to blend one cup of blueberries in a food processor, blending the fruit on low speed for around a minute.

2. After a minute, add almond milk, protein powder and Greek yogurt to blended blueberries and blend the mixture for another minute or until the blueberry smoothie turns into a homogeneous mass.
3. Pour the smoothie in a bowl, add cereals, raspberries, sliced strawberries, and serve.

Nutrition: Potassium 270 mg Sodium 108 mg Phosphorus 114 mg Calories 225

4. Cheese Coconut Pancakes

Preparation Time: 10 minutes
Cooking Time: 5 minutes
Servings: 1

Ingredients:

- 2 eggs
- 1 packet stevia
- 1/2 tsp cinnamon
- 2 oz cream cheese
- 1 tbsp coconut flour
- 1/2 tsp vanilla

Directions:

1. Add all ingredients into the bowl and blend until smooth.
2. Spray pan with cooking spray and heat over medium-high heat.
3. Pour batter on the hot pan and make two pancakes.
4. Cook pancake until lightly brown from both the sides.
5. Serve and enjoy.

Nutrition: Calories 386 Fat 30 g Carbohydrates 12 g Sugar 1 g Protein 16 g Cholesterol 389 mg Phosphorus: 110mg Potassium: 117mg Sodium: 75mg

5. Coconut Breakfast Smoothie

Preparation Time: 5 minutes
Cooking Time: 5 minutes
Servings: 1

Ingredients:

- 1/4 cup whey protein powder
- 1/2 cup coconut milk
- 5 drops liquid stevia
- 1 tbsp coconut oil
- 1 tsp vanilla
- 2 tbsp coconut butter
- 1/4 cup water
- 1/2 cup ice

Directions:

1. Add all ingredients into the blender and blend until smooth.
2. Serve and enjoy.

Nutrition: Calories 560 Fat 45 g Carbohydrates 12 g Sugar 4 g Protein 25 g Cholesterol 60 mg Phosphorus: 160mg Potassium: 127mg Sodium: 85mg

6. Turkey and Spinach Scramble on Melba Toast

Preparation Time: 5 minutes
Cooking Time: 15 minutes
Servings: 2
Ingredients:

- 1 tsp. Extra virgin olive oil
- 1 cup Raw spinach
- ½ clove, minced Garlic
- 1 tsp. grated Nutmeg
- 1 cup Cooked and diced turkey breast
- 4 slices Melba toast
- 1 tsp. Balsamic vinegar

Directions:
1. Heat a skillet over medium heat and add oil.
2. Add turkey and heat through for 6 to 8 minutes.
3. Add spinach, garlic, and nutmeg and stir-fry for 6 minutes more.
4. Plate up the Melba toast and top with spinach and turkey scramble.
5. Drizzle with balsamic vinegar and serve.

Nutrition: Calories: 301 Fat: 19g Carbs: 12g Protein: 19g Sodium: 360mg Potassium: 269mg Phosphorus: 215mg

7. Cheesy Scrambled Eggs with Fresh Herbs

Preparation Time: 15 minutes
Cooking Time: 10 minutes
Servings: 4
Ingredients:

- 3 Eggs
- 2 Egg whites
- ½ cup Cream cheese
- ¼ cup Unsweetened rice milk
- 1 tbsp. green part only Chopped scallion
- 1 tbsp. Chopped fresh tarragon
- 2 tbsps. Unsalted butter
- Ground black pepper to taste

Directions:
1. Whisk the eggs, egg whites, cream cheese, rice milk, scallions, and tarragon. Mix until smooth.
2. Melt the butter in a skillet.
3. Put egg mixture and cook for 5 minutes or until the eggs are thick and curds creamy.
4. Season with pepper and serve.

Nutrition: Calories: 221 Fat: 19g Carbs: 3g Protein: 8g Sodium: 193mg Potassium: 140mg Phosphorus: 119mg

8. Mexican Style Burritos

Preparation Time: 5 minutes
Cooking Time: 15 minutes
Servings: 2
Ingredients:

- 1 tbsp. Olive oil
- 2 Corn tortillas
- ¼ cup chopped red onion
- ¼ cup chopped red bell peppers
- ½, deseeded and chopped red chili
- 2 Eggs
- 1 lime juice
- 1 tbsp. chopped Cilantro

Directions:
1. Place the tortillas in medium heat for 1 to 2 minutes on each side or until lightly toasted.
2. Remove and keep the broiler on.
3. Heat the oil in a skillet and sauté onion, chili, and bell peppers for 5 to 6 minutes or until soft.
4. Crack the eggs over the top of the onions and peppers.
5. Place skillet under the broiler for 5 to 6 minutes or until the eggs are cooked.
6. Serve half the eggs and vegetables on top of each tortilla and sprinkle with cilantro and lime juice to serve.

Nutrition: Calories: 202 Fat: 13g Carbs: 19g Protein: 9g Sodium: 77mg Potassium: 233mg Phosphorus: 184mg

9. Bulgur, Couscous, and Buckwheat Cereal

Preparation Time: 10 minutes
Cooking Time: 25 minutes
Servings: 4
Ingredients:
- 2 ¼ cups Water
- 1 ¼ cups Vanilla rice milk
- 6 Tbsps. Uncooked bulgur
- 2 Tbsps. Uncooked whole buckwheat
- 1 cup Sliced apple
- 6 Tbsps. Plain uncooked couscous
- ½ tsp. Ground cinnamon

Directions:
1. Heat the water and milk in the saucepan over medium heat. Let it boil.
2. Put the bulgur, buckwheat, and apple.
3. Reduce the heat to low and simmer, occasionally stirring until the bulgur is tender, about 20 to 25 minutes.
4. Remove the saucepan and stir in the couscous and cinnamon—cover for 10 minutes.
5. Put the cereal before serving.

Nutrition: Calories: 159 Fat: 1g Carbs: 34g Protein: 4g Sodium: 33mg Potassium: 116m Phosphorus: 130mg

10. Blueberry Muffins

Preparation Time: 15 minutes
Cooking Time: 30 minutes
Servings: 12
Ingredients:
- 2 cups Unsweetened rice milk
- 1 Tbsp. Apple cider vinegar
- 3 ½ cups All-purpose flour
- 1 cup Granulated sugar

- 1 Tbsp. Baking soda substitute
- 1 tsp. Ground cinnamon
- ½ tsp. Ground nutmeg
- Pinch ground ginger
- ½ cup Canola oil
- 2 Tbsps. Pure vanilla extract
- 2 ½ cups Fresh blueberries

Directions:
1. Preheat the oven to 375F.
2. Prepare a muffin pan and set aside.
3. Stir together the rice milk and vinegar in a small bowl. Set aside for 10 minutes.
4. In a large bowl, stir together the sugar, flour, baking soda, cinnamon, nutmeg, and ginger until well mixed.
5. Add oil and vanilla to the milk and mix.
6. Put milk mixture to dry ingredients and stir well to combine.
7. Put the blueberries and spoon the muffin batter evenly into the cups.
8. Bake the muffins for 25 to 30 minutes or until golden and a toothpick inserted comes out clean.
9. Cool for 15 minutes and serve.

Nutrition: Calories: 331 Fat: 11g Carbs: 52g Protein: 6g Sodium: 35mg Potassium: 89mg Phosphorus: 90mg

11. <u>Buckwheat and Grapefruit Porridge</u>

Preparation Time: 5 minutes
Cooking Time: 20 minutes
Servings: 2
Ingredients:
- ½ cup Buckwheat
- ¼ chopped Grapefruit
- 1 Tbsp. Honey
- 1 ½ cups Almond milk
- 2 cups Water

Directions:
1. Let the water boil on the stove. Add the buckwheat and place the lid on the pan.
2. Lower heat slightly and simmer for 7 to 10 minutes, checking to ensure water does not dry out.
3. When most of the water is absorbed, remove, and set aside for 5 minutes.
4. Drain any excess water from the pan and stir in almond milk, heating through for 5 minutes.
5. Add the honey and grapefruit.
6. Serve.

Nutrition: Calories: 231 Fat: 4g Carbs: 43g Protein: 13g Sodium: 135mg Potassium: 370mg Phosphorus: 165mg

12. <u>Egg and Veggie Muffins</u>

Preparation Time: 15 minutes
Cooking Time: 20 minutes
Servings: 4
Ingredients:
- 4 Eggs
- 2 Tbsp. Unsweetened rice milk
- ½ chopped sweet onion

- ½ chopped red bell pepper
- Pinch red pepper flakes
- Pinch ground black pepper

Directions:
1. Preheat the oven to 350F.
2. Spray 4 muffin pans with cooking spray. Set aside.
3. Whisk the milk, eggs, onion, red pepper, parsley, red pepper flakes, and black pepper until mixed.
4. Pour the egg mixture into prepared muffin pans.
5. Bake until the muffins are puffed and golden, about 18 to 20 minutes. Serve.

Nutrition: Calories: 84 Fat: 5g Carbs: 3g Protein: 7g Sodium: 75mg Potassium: 117mg Phosphorus: 110mg

13. <u>Berry Chia with Yogurt</u>

Preparation Time: 35 minutes
Cooking Time: 5 minutes
Servings:4
Ingredients:
- ½ cup chia seeds, dried
- 2 cup Plain yogurt
- 1/3 cup strawberries, chopped
- ¼ cup blackberries
- ¼ cup raspberries
- 4 teaspoons Splenda

Directions:
1. Mix up together Plain yogurt with Splenda, and chia seeds.
2. Transfer the mixture into the serving ramekins (jars) and leave for 35 minutes.

40

3. After this, add blackberries, raspberries, and strawberries. Mix up the meal well.
4. Serve it immediately or store it in the fridge for up to 2 days.

Nutrition: Calories: 150 Fat: 5g Carbs: 19g Protein: 6.8g Sodium: 65mg Potassium: 226mg Phosphorus: 75mg

14. <u>Arugula Eggs with Chili Peppers</u>

Preparation Time: 7 minutes
Cooking Time: 10 minutes
Servings: 4
Ingredients:

- 2 cups arugula, chopped
- 3 eggs, beaten
- ½ chili pepper, chopped
- 1 tablespoon butter
- 1 oz Parmesan, grated

Directions:

1. Toss butter in the skillet and melt it.
2. Add arugula and sauté it over medium heat for 5 minutes. Stir it from time to time.
3. Meanwhile, mix up together Parmesan, chili pepper, and eggs.
4. Pour the egg mixture over the arugula and scramble well.
5. Cook for 5 minutes more over medium heat.

Nutrition: Calories: 218 Fat: 15g Carbs: 2.8g Protein: 17g Sodium: 656mg Potassium: 243mg Phosphorus: 310mg

15. <u>Eggplant Chicken Sandwich</u>

Preparation Time: 10 minutes
Cooking Time: 15 minutes
Servings: 2
Ingredients:

- 1 eggplant, trimmed
- 10 oz chicken fillet
- 1 teaspoon Plain yogurt
- ½ teaspoon minced garlic
- 1 tablespoon fresh cilantro, chopped
- 2 lettuce leaves
- 1 teaspoon olive oil
- ½ teaspoon salt
- ½ teaspoon chili pepper
- 1 teaspoon butter

Directions:

1. Slice the eggplant lengthwise into 4 slices.
2. Rub the eggplant slices with minced garlic and brush with olive oil.
3. Grill the eggplant slices on the preheated to 375F grill for 3 minutes from each side.
4. Meanwhile, rub the chicken fillet with salt and chili pepper.
5. Place it in the skillet and add butter.
6. Roast the chicken for 6 minutes from each side over medium-high heat.
7. Cool the cooked eggplants gently and spread one side of them with Plain yogurt.
8. Add lettuce leaves and chopped fresh cilantro.

9. After this, slice the cooked chicken fillet and add over the lettuce.
10. Cover it with the remaining sliced eggplant to get the sandwich shape. Pin the sandwich with the toothpick if needed.

Nutrition: Calories: 276 Fat: 11g Carbs: 41g Protein: 13.8g Sodium: 775mg Potassium: 532mg Phosphorus: 187mg

16. <u>Apple Pumpkin Muffins</u>

Preparation time: 15 minutes
Cooking time: 20 minutes
Servings: 12
Ingredients
- 1 cup all-purpose flour
- 1 cup wheat bran
- 2 teaspoons phosphorus powder
- 1 cup pumpkin purée
- ¼ cup honey
- ¼ cup olive oil
- 1 egg
- 1 teaspoon vanilla extract
- ½ cup cored diced apple

Directions
1. Preheat the oven to 400°f.
2. Line 12 muffin cups with paper liners.
3. Stir together the flour, wheat bran, and baking powder, mix this in a medium bowl.
4. In a small bowl, whisk together the pumpkin, honey, olive oil, egg, and vanilla.
5. Stir the pumpkin mixture into the flour mixture until just combined.
6. Stir in the diced apple.
7. Spoon the batter in the muffin cups.
8. Bake for about 20 minutes, or until a toothpick inserted in the center of a muffin comes out clean.

Nutrition per serving: (1 muffin): calories: 125; total fat: 5g; saturated fat: 1g; cholesterol: 18mg; sodium: 8mg; carbohydrates: 20g; fiber: 3g; phosphorus: 120mg; potassium: 177mg; protein: 2g

17. <u>Chorizo Bowl with Corn</u>

Preparation Time: 10 minutes
Cooking Time: 15 minutes
Servings: 4

Ingredients:
- 9 oz chorizo
- 1 tablespoon almond butter
- ½ cup corn kernels
- ¾ cup heavy cream
- 1 teaspoon butter
- ¼ teaspoon chili pepper
- 1 tablespoon dill, chopped

Directions:
1. Chop the chorizo and place it in the skillet.

2. Add almond butter and chili pepper.
3. Roast the chorizo for 3 minutes.
4. After this, add corn kernels.
5. Add butter and chopped the dill. Mix up the mixture well—Cook for 2 minutes.
6. Close the lid and simmer for 10 minutes over low heat.
7. Transfer the cooked meal into the serving bowls.

Nutrition: Calories: 286 Fat: 15g Carbs: 26g Protein: 13g Sodium: 228mg Potassium: 255mg Phosphorus: 293mg

18. <u>Panzanella Salad</u>

Preparation Time: 10 minutes
Cooking Time: 5 minutes
Servings: 4
Ingredients:

- 2 cucumbers, chopped
- 1 red onion, sliced
- 2 red bell peppers, chopped
- ¼ cup fresh cilantro, chopped
- 1 tablespoon capers
- 1 oz whole-grain bread, chopped
- 1 tablespoon canola oil
- ½ teaspoon minced garlic
- 1 tablespoon Dijon mustard
- 1 teaspoon olive oil
- 1 teaspoon lime juice

Directions:
1. Pour canola oil into the skillet and bring it to boil.
2. Add chopped bread and roast it until crunchy (3-5 minutes).
3. Meanwhile, in the salad bowl, combine sliced red onion, cucumbers, bell peppers, cilantro, capers, and mix up gently.
4. Make the dressing: mix up together lime juice, olive oil, Dijon mustard, and minced garlic.
5. Put the dressing over the salad and stir it directly before serving.

Nutrition: Calories: 224.3 Fat: 10g Carbs: 26g Protein: 6.6g Sodium: 401mg Potassium: 324.9mg Phosphorus: 84mg

19. <u>Poached Asparagus and Egg</u>

Preparation time: 3 minutes
Cooking Time: 15 minutes
Servings: 1

Ingredients:
- 1 egg
- 4 spears asparagus
- Water

Directions:
1. Half-fill a deep saucepan with water set over high heat. Let the water come to a boil.

2. Dip asparagus spears in water. Cook until they turn a shade brighter, about 3 minutes. Remove from saucepan and drain on paper towels. Keep warm—lightly season before serving.
3. Use a slotted spoon to lower the egg into boiling water gently.
4. Cook for only 4 minutes. Remove from pan immediately. Place on egg holder.
5. Slice off the top. The egg should still be fluid inside.
6. Place asparagus spears on a small plate and serve egg on the side.
7. Dip asparagus into the egg and eat while warm.

Nutrition: Calories: 178 Fat: 13g Carbs: 1g Protein: 7.72g Calories 178 Sodium: 71mg Potassium: 203mg Phosphorus: 124mg

20. Egg Drop Soup

Preparation Time: 5 minutes
Cooking Time: 10 minutes
Servings:4
Ingredients:

- ¼ cup minced fresh chives
- 4 cups unsalted vegetable stock
- 4 whisked eggs

Directions:
1. Pour unsalted vegetable stock into the oven set over high heat. Bring to a boil. Lower heat.
2. Pour in the eggs. Stir until ribbons form into the soup.
3. Turn off the heat immediately. The residual heat will cook eggs through.
4. Cool slightly before ladling the desired amount into individual bowls. Garnish with a pinch of parsley, if using.
5. Serve immediately.

Nutrition: Calories: 73 Fat: 3g Carbs: 1g Protein: 7g Sodium: 891mg Potassium: 53mg Phosphorus: 36mg

21. Breakfast Salad from Grains and Fruits

Preparation Time: 5 minutes
Cooking Time: 15 minutes
Servings: 6
Ingredients:

- 1 8-oz low fat vanilla yogurt
- 1 mango
- 1 Red delicious apple
- 1 Granny Smith apple
- ¾ cup bulgur
- ¼ teaspoon salt
- 3 cups water

Direction:
1. On high fire, place a large pot and bring water to a boil.
2. Add bulgur and rice. Lower fire to a simmer and cooks for ten minutes while covered.
3. Turn off fire, set aside for 2 minutes while covered.
4. In baking sheet, transfer and evenly spread grains to cool.
5. Meanwhile, peel mango and cut into slices. Chop and core apples.
6. Once grains are cool, transfer to a large serving bowl along with fruits.
7. Add yogurt and mix well to coat.

8. Serve and enjoy.

Nutrition: Calories: 187; Carbs: 4g; Protein: 6g; Fats: g; Phosphorus: 60 mg; Potassium: 55 mg; Sodium: 117mg

22. French Toast with Applesauce

Preparation Time: 5 minutes
Cooking Time: 15 minutes
Servings: 6
Ingredients:

- ¼ cup unsweetened applesauce
- ½ cup almond milk
- 1 teaspoon ground cinnamon
- 2 eggs
- 2 tablespoon white sugar

Directions:

1. Mix well applesauce, sugar, cinnamon, almond milk and eggs in a mixing bowl.
2. Soak the bread, one by one into applesauce mixture until wet.
3. On medium fire, heat a nonstick skillet greased with cooking spray.
4. Add soaked bread one at a time and cook for 2-3 minutes per side or until lightly browned.
5. Serve and enjoy.

Nutrition: Calories: 57; Carbs: 6g; Protein: 4g; Fats: 4g; Phosphorus: 69mg; Potassium: 88mg; Sodium: 43mg

23. Bagels Made Healthy

Preparation Time: 5 minutes
Cooking Time: 25 minutes
Servings: 8
Ingredients:

- 2 teaspoon yeasts
- 1 ½ tablespoon olive oil
- 1 ¼ cups bread flour
- 2 cups whole wheat flour
- 1 tablespoon vinegar
- 2 tablespoon honeys
- 1 ½ cups warm water

Directions:

1. In a bread machine, mix all ingredients, and then process on dough cycle.
2. Once done or end of cycle, create 8 pieces shaped like a flattened ball.
3. In the center of each ball, make a hole using your thumb then create a donut shape.
4. In a greased baking sheet, place donut-shaped dough then covers and let it rise about ½ hour.
5. Prepare about 2 inches of water to boil in a large pan.
6. In a boiling water, drop one at a time the bagels and boil for 1 minute, then turn them once.
7. Remove them and return them to baking sheet and bake at 350oF (175oC) for about 20 to 25 minutes until golden brown.

Nutrition : Calories : 221 ; Carbs: 42g; Protein: 7g; Fats: g; Phosphorus: 130mg; Potassium: 166mg; Sodium: 47mg

24. Cornbread with Southern Twist

Preparation Time: 15 minutes
Cooking Time: 60 minutes
Servings: 8
Ingredients:

- 2 tablespoons shortening
- 1 ¼ cups skim almond milk
- ¼ cup egg substitute
- 4 tablespoons sodium free baking powder
- ½ cup flour
- 1 ½ cups cornmeal

Directions:

1. Prepare 8 x 8-inch baking dish or a black iron skillet then add shortening.
2. Put the baking dish or skillet inside the oven on 425oF, once the shortening has melted that means the pan is hot already.
3. In a bowl, add almond milk and egg then mix well.
4. Take out the skillet and add the melted shortening into the batter and stir well.
5. Pour all mixed ingredients into skillet.
6. For 15 to 20 minutes, cook in the oven until golden brown.

Nutrition: Calories: 166; Carbs: 35g; Protein: 5g; Fats: 1g; Phosphorus: 79mg; Potassium: 122mg; Sodium: 34mg

25. Grandma's Pancake Special

Preparation Time: 5 minutes
Cooking Time: 15 minutes
Servings: 3
Ingredients:

- 1 tablespoon oil
- 1 cup almond milk
- 1 egg
- 2 teaspoons sodium free baking powder
- 2 tablespoons sugar
- 1 ¼ cups flour

Directions:

1. Mix together all the dry ingredients such as the flour, sugar and baking powder.
2. Combine oil, almond milk and egg in another bowl. Once done, add them all to the flour mixture.
3. Make sure that as your stir the mixture, blend them together until slightly lumpy.
4. In a hot greased griddle, pour-in at least ¼ cup of the batter to make each pancake.
5. To cook, ensure that the bottom is a bit brown, then turn and cook the other side, as well.

Nutrition: Calories: 167; Carbs: 50g; Protein: 11g; Fats: 11g; Phosphorus: 176mg; Potassium: 215mg; Sodium: 70mg

26. Pasta with Indian Lentils

Preparation Time: 5 minutes
Cooking Time: 0 minutes
Servings: 6

Ingredients:

- ¼-½ cup fresh cilantro (chopped)
- 3 cups water
- 2 small dry red peppers (whole)
- 1 teaspoon turmeric
- 1 teaspoon ground cumin
- 2-3 cloves garlic (minced)
- 1 can (15 ounces) cubed Red bell peppers (with juice)
- 1 large onion (chopped)
- ½ cup dry lentils (rinsed)
- ½ cup orzo or tiny pasta

Directions:

1. In a skillet, combine all ingredients except for the cilantro then boil on medium-high heat.
2. Ensure to cover and slightly reduce heat to medium-low and simmer until pasta is tender for about 35 minutes.
3. Afterwards, take out the chili peppers then add cilantro and top it with low-fat sour cream.

Nutrition: Calories: 175; Carbs: 40g; Protein: 3g; Fats: 2g; Phosphorus: 139mg; Potassium: 513mg; Sodium: 61mg

27. Pineapple Bread

Preparation Time: 20 Minutes
Cooking Time: 1 Hour
Servings: 10
Ingredients:

- 1/3 cup Swerve
- 1/3 cup butter, unsalted
- 2 eggs
- 2 cups flour
- 3 teaspoons baking powder
- 1 cup pineapple, undrained
- 6 cherries, chopped

Directions:

1. Whisk the Swerve with the butter in a mixer until fluffy.
2. Stir in the eggs, then beat again.
3. Add the baking powder and flour, then mix well until smooth.
4. Fold in the cherries and pineapple.
5. Spread this cherry-pineapple batter in a 9x5 inch baking pan.
6. Bake the pineapple batter for 1 hour at 350 degrees F.
7. Slice the bread and serve.

Nutrition: Calories 197, Total Fat 7.2g, Sodium 85mg, Dietary Fiber 1.1g, Sugars 3 g, Protein 4g, Calcium 79mg, Phosphorous 316mg, Potassium 227mg

28. Parmesan Zucchini Frittata

Preparation Time: 10 minutes

Cooking Time: 35 minutes
Servings: 6
Ingredients:

- 1 tablespoon olive oil
- 1 cup yellow onion, sliced
- 3 cups zucchini, chopped
- ½ cup Parmesan cheese, grated
- 8 large eggs
- 1/2 teaspoon black pepper
- 1/8 teaspoon paprika
- 3 tablespoons parsley, chopped

Directions:

1. Toss the zucchinis with the onion, parsley, and all other ingredients in a large bowl.
2. Pour this zucchini-garlic mixture in an 11x7 inches pan and spread it evenly.
3. Bake the zucchini casserole for approximately 35 minutes at 350 degrees F.
4. Cut in slices and serve.

Nutrition: Calories 142, Total Fat 9.7g, Saturated Fat 2.8g, Cholesterol 250mg, Sodium 123mg, Carbohydrate 4.7g, Dietary Fiber 1.3g, Sugars 2.4g, Protein 10.2g, Calcium 73mg, Phosphorous 375mg, Potassium 286mg

29. Garlic Mayo Bread

Preparation Time: 10 minutes
Cooking Time: 5 minutes
Servings: 16
Ingredients:

- 3 tablespoons vegetable oil
- 4 cloves garlic, minced
- 2 teaspoons paprika
- Dash cayenne pepper
- 1 teaspoon lemon juice
- 2 tablespoons Parmcsan cheese, grated
- 3/4 cup mayonnaise
- 1 loaf (1 lb.) French bread, sliced
- 1 teaspoon Italian herbs

Directions:

1. Mix the garlic with the oil in a small bowl and leave it overnight.
2. Discard the garlic from the bowl and keep the garlic-infused oil.
3. Mix the garlic-oil with cayenne, paprika, lemon juice, mayonnaise, and Parmesan.
4. Place the bread slices in a baking tray lined with parchment paper.
5. Top these slices with the mayonnaise mixture and drizzle the Italian herbs on top.
6. Broil these slices for 5 minutes until golden brown.
7. Serve warm.

Nutrition: Calories 217, Total Fat 7.9g, Sodium 423mg, Dietary Fiber 1.3g, Sugars 2g, Protein 7g, Calcium 56mg, Phosphorous 347mg, Potassium 72mg

30. Strawberry Topped Waffles

Preparation Time: 15 minutes

Cooking Time: 20 minutes
Servings: 5
Ingredients:

- 1 cup flour
- 1/4 cup Swerve
- 1 ¾ teaspoons baking powder
- 1 egg, separated
- ¾ cup almond milk
- ½ cup butter, melted
- ½ teaspoon vanilla extract
- Fresh strawberries, sliced

Directions:

1. Prepare and preheat your waffle pan following the instructions of the machine.
2. Begin by mixing the flour with Swerve and baking soda in a bowl.
3. Separate the egg yolks from the egg whites, keeping them in two separate bowls.
4. Add the almond milk and vanilla extract to the egg yolks.
5. Stir the melted butter and mix well until smooth.
6. Now beat the egg whites with an electric beater until foamy and fluffy.
7. Fold this fluffy composition in the egg yolk mixture.
8. Mix it gently until smooth, then add in the flour mixture.
9. Stir again to make a smooth mixture.
10. Pour a half cup of the waffle batter in a preheated pan and cook until the waffle is done.
11. Cook more waffles with the remaining batter.
12. Serve fresh with strawberries on top.

Nutrition: Calories 342, Total Fat 20.5g, Sodium 156mg, Dietary Fiber 0.7g, Sugars 3.5g, Protein 4.8g, Calcium 107mg, Phosphorous 126mg, Potassium 233mg

31. Cheese Spaghetti Frittata

Preparation Time: 10 minutes
Cooking Time: 10 minutes
Servings: 6
Ingredients:

- 4 cups whole-wheat spaghetti, cooked
- 4 teaspoons olive oil
- 3 medium onions, chopped
- 4 large eggs
- 1/2 cup almond milk
- 1/3 cup Parmesan cheese, grated
- 2 tablespoons fresh parsley, chopped
- 2 tablespoons fresh basil, chopped
- 1/2 teaspoon black pepper

Directions:

1. Set a suitable non-stick skillet over moderate heat and add in the olive oil.
2. Place the spaghetti in the skillet and cook by stirring for 2 minutes on moderate heat.
3. Whisk the eggs with almond milk, parsley, and black pepper in a bowl.
4. Pour this almond milky egg mixture over the spaghetti and top it all with basil, cheese.
5. Cover the spaghetti frittata again with a lid and cook for approximately 8 minutes on low heat.

6. Slice and serve.

Nutrition: Calories 230, Total Fat 7.8g, Sodium 77mg, Dietary Fiber 5.6g, Sugars 4.5g, Protein 11.1g, Calcium 88mg, Phosphorous 368 mg, Potassium 214mg,

32. <u>Shrimp Bruschetta</u>

Preparation Time: 15 minutes
Cooking Time: 10 minutes
Servings: 4
Ingredients:

- 13 oz. shrimps, peeled
- ½ teaspoon Splenda
- ¼ teaspoon garlic powder
- 1 teaspoon fresh parsley, chopped
- ½ teaspoon olive oil
- 1 teaspoon lemon juice
- 4 whole-grain bread slices
- 1 cup water, for cooking

Directions:

1. In the saucepan, pour water and bring it to boil.
2. Add shrimps and boil them over the high heat for 5 minutes.
3. After this, drain shrimps and chill them to the room temperature.
4. Mix up together shrimps with Splenda, garlic powder, and fresh parsley.
5. Add lemon juice and stir gently.
6. Preheat the oven to 360f.
7. Coat the slice of bread with olive oil and bake for 3 minutes.
8. Then place the shrimp mixture on the bread. Bruschetta is cooked.

Nutrition: Calories 199, Fat 3.7, Fiber 2.1, Carbs 15.3, Protein 24.1 Calcium 79mg, Phosphorous 316mg, Potassium 227mg Sodium: 121 mg

33. <u>Strawberry Muesli</u>

Preparation Time: 10 minutes
Cooking Time: 30 minutes
Servings: 4
Ingredients:

- 2 cups Greek yogurt
- 1 ½ cup strawberries, sliced
- 1 ½ cup Muesli
- 4 teaspoon maple syrup
- ¾ teaspoon ground cinnamon

Directions:

1. Put Greek yogurt in the food processor.
2. Add 1 cup of strawberries, maple syrup, and ground cinnamon.
3. Blend the ingredients until you get smooth mass.
4. Transfer the yogurt mass in the serving bowls.
5. Add Muesli and stir well.
6. Leave the meal for 30 minutes in the fridge.

7. After this, decorate it with remaining sliced strawberries.

Nutrition: Calories 149, Fat 2.6, Fiber 3.6, Carbs 21.6, Protein 12 Calcium 69mg, Phosphorous 216mg, Potassium 227mg Sodium: 151 mg

34. <u>Yogurt Bulgur</u>

Preparation Time: 10 minutes
Cooking Time: 15 minutes
Servings: 3
Ingredients:
- 1 cup bulgur
- 2 cups Greek yogurt
- 1 ½ cup water
- ½ teaspoon salt
- 1 teaspoon olive oil

Directions:
1. Pour olive oil in the saucepan and add bulgur.
2. Roast it over the medium heat for 2-3 minutes. Stir it from time to time.
3. After this, add salt and water.
4. Close the lid and cook bulgur for 15 minutes over the medium heat.
5. Then chill the cooked bulgur well and combine it with Greek yogurt. Stir it carefully.
6. Transfer the cooked meal into the serving plates. The yogurt bulgur tastes the best when it is cold.

Nutrition: Calories 274, Fat 4.9, Fiber 8.5, Carbs 40.8, Protein 19.2 Calcium 39mg, Phosphorous 216mg, Potassium 237mg Sodium: 131 mg

35. <u>Breakfast Casserole</u>

Preparation Time: 10 minutes
Cooking Time: 60 Minutes
Servings: 8
Ingredients:

- 200 grams of ground lean beef – fresh and grass-fed if possible
- 4 slices of bread – white, cut in cubes
- 5 eggs
- 1 teaspoon of mustard – dry
- ½ teaspoon garlic powder with no added sodium

Direction:

1. Preheat your oven to 350 degrees F as you are preparing ingredients for breakfast casserole.
2. Cube bread sliced and place it aside while you are taking care of the ground beef. As you prepare the beef, add a tablespoon of olive oil to the skillet and add the beef.
3. Cook the beef with occasional stirring as you are breaking the meat parts to bits. Once the meat is browned, set aside and add garlic powder, stirring it well to combine.
4. Beat the five eggs in a bowl, combine all ingredients in the egg bowl, and mix to get a homogenous mass out of the egg mixture. Pour the mixture into the mildly greased baking dish and place it in the oven. Bake for 50 minutes or until ready.

Nutrition: Potassium 176 mg Sodium 201 mg Phosphorus 119 mg Calories 220

36. Cauliflower Tortilla

Preparation Time: 15 minutes
Cooking Time: 25 Minutes
Servings: 4
Ingredients:

- 4 cups cauliflower
- 1 cup onion – chopped
- 2 garlic cloves – minced
- 1 cup egg substitute - liquefied
- ¼ teaspoon nutmeg
- 1 tablespoon parsley – fresh, chopped
- ½ teaspoon allspice

Direction:

1. Prepare the cauliflower by cutting it into small cubes, then place the cauliflower bits in a bowl with a tablespoon of water and microwave it for 5 minutes until cauliflower is crisped.
2. While you are waiting for the cauliflower bits to get ready in the microwave, you may start preparing the onion.
3. Sauté chopped onions with 2 tablespoons of olive oil until browned, which should take around 5 minutes, then add garlic, nutmeg and allspice to the pan. Stir in and cook for another 1 to 2 minutes then add the cauliflower and egg substitute.
4. Stir in all ingredients to combine the mixture then seal the pan and lower the heat. Cook for another 10 to 15 minutes, until cauliflower tortilla is browned. Serve by slicing the tortilla into 4 pieces.

Nutrition: Potassium 272 mg Sodium 148 mg Phosphorus 78 mg Calories 102

37. Eggs Benedict

Preparation Time: 20 minutes
Cooking Time: 35 Minutes
Servings: 4
Ingredients:

- 2 pieces of toasted bread - white flour
- 4 eggs
- 3 egg yolks
- 1 tablespoon lemon juice
- ½ teaspoon of cayenne pepper
- ½ teaspoon of paprika
- 1 tablespoon apple cider vinegar
- 2 tablespoons of unsalted butter

Direction:

1. Slice the two toasted bread pieces in two, so you can end up with four pieces where each piece represents one serving.
2. Take a large skillet or a pot and pour one cup of water in it. Add a tablespoon of vinegar and bring the water to boil. When the water starts to boil, break four eggs, one at the time, and poach the eggs by covering the skillet. Eggs should be done between 3 and 5 minutes of poaching, depending on how you like your eggs cooked.
3. Next place poached eggs on top of bread pieces. Take a skillet and add the butter to melt it then add cayenne and paprika to the melted butter. Beat the egg yolks over medium heat then add the eggs to the mixture with butter. Add lemon juice and whisk it into the egg and butter mixture. Once the sauce reaches an adequate thickness, remove from the heat and pour over the eggs and toasted bread.

Nutrition: Potassium 146 mg Sodium 206 mg Phosphorus 114 mg Calories 316

38. Italian Apple Fritters

Preparation Time: 5 minutes
Cooking Time: 8 minutes
Servings: 4
Ingredients:

- 2 large apples, seeded, peeled, and thickly sliced in circles
- 3 tbsp. of corn flour
- ½ tsp. of water
- 1 tsp. of sugar
- 1 tsp. of cinnamon
- Vegetable oil (for frying)
- Sprinkle of icing sugar or honey

Directions:

1. Combine the corn flour, water, and sugar to make your batter in a small bowl.
2. Deep the apple rounds into the corn flour mix.
3. Heat enough vegetable oil to cover half of the pan's surface over medium to high heat.
4. Add the apple rounds into the pan and cook until golden brown.
5. Transfer into a shallow dish with absorbing paper on top and sprinkle with cinnamon and icing sugar.

Nutrition: Calories: 183 Carbohydrate: 17.9g Protein: 0.3g Sodium: 2g Potassium: 100mg Phosphorus: 12.5mg Dietary Fiber: 1.4g Fat: 14.17g

39. Tofu and Mushroom Scramble

Preparation Time: 5 minutes
Cooking Time: 4 minutes
Servings: 2
Ingredients:

- ½ cup of sliced white mushrooms
- 1/3 cup of medium-firm tofu, crumbled
- 1 tbsp. of chopped shallots
- 1/3 tsp. of turmeric
- 1 tsp. of cumin
- 1/3 tsp. of smoked paprika
- ½ tsp. of garlic salt
- Pepper
- 3 tbsp. of vegetable oil

Directions:

1. Heat the oil frying pan, set it on a medium, and saute the sliced mushrooms with the shallots until softened (around 3–4 minutes) over medium to high heat.
2. Add the tofu pieces and toss in the spices and the garlic salt. Toss lightly until tofu and mushrooms are nicely combined.

Nutrition: Calories: 220 Carbohydrate: 2.59g Protein: 3.2g Sodium: 288 mg Potassium: 133.5mg Phosphorus: 68.5mg Dietary Fiber: 1.7g Fat: 23.7g

40. Egg Fried Rice

Preparation Time: 10 minutes

Cooking Time: 20 minutes
Servings: 6
Ingredients:

- 1 tablespoon of olive oil
- 1 tablespoon of grated peeled fresh ginger
- 1 teaspoon of minced garlic
- 1 cup of chopped carrots
- 1 scallion, white and green parts, chopped
- 2 tablespoons of chopped fresh cilantro
- 4 cups of cooked rice
- 1 tablespoon of low-sodium soy sauce
- 4 eggs, beaten

Directions:

1. Heat the olive oil.
2. Add the ginger and garlic, and sauté until softened, about 3 minutes.
3. Add the carrots, scallion, and cilantro, and sauté until tender, about 5 minutes.
4. Stir in the rice and soy sauce, and sauté until the rice is heated over 5 minutes.
5. Move the rice over to one side of the skillet, and pour the eggs into the space.
6. Scramble the eggs, then mix them into the rice.
7. Serve hot.
8. Low-sodium tip: Soy sauces, even low-sodium versions, are very salty. If you have the time, making your substitution sauce is simple and effective, even if it does not taste quite the same. Many versions of this diet-friendly sauce are online, with ingredients like vinegar, molasses, garlic, and herbs.

Nutrition: Calories: 204 Total fat: 6g Saturated fat: 1g Cholesterol: 141mg Sodium: 223mg Carbohydrates: 29g Fiber: 1g Phosphorus: 120mg Potassium: 147mg Protein: 8g

41. <u>Quick Thai Chicken and Vegetable Curry</u>

Preparation Time: 15 minutes
Cooking Time: 20 minutes
Servings: 4
Ingredients:

- 1 ½ cups cauliflower florets
- 1 clove garlic, minced
- 1 cup light coconut almond milk
- 1 cup low sodium chicken broth
- 1 lb chicken breasts
- 1 medium bell pepper, julienned
- 1 medium onion, halved and sliced
- 1 tbsp fish sauce or low sodium soy sauce
- 1 tbsp fresh ginger, minced
- 1 tbsp lime juice
- 1 tsp light brown sugar
- 1 tsp red curry paste
- 2 tsp canola oil
- Lime wedges

Directions:

1. Heat oil in a skillet. Sauté the onion and bell pepper for four minutes or until soft.
2. Add the ginger, garlic, and curry paste. Mix then add the chicken. Sauté for two minutes before adding the coconut almond milk, broth, brown sugar, and fish sauce.
3. Add the cauliflowers and reduce the heat to medium-low. Boil and stir the mixture occasionally until the chicken is cooked through.
4. Serve immediately with lime wedges.

Nutrition: Calories: 394 Carbs: 11g Protein: 29g Fat: 28g Phosphorus: 316mg Potassium: 745mg Sodium: 252mg

42. Cajun Stuffed Peppers

Preparation Time: 10 minutes
Cooking Time: 45 minutes
Servings: 6
Ingredients:

- 1 cup of chopped roasted red peppers
- 6 fresh bell peppers
- 1/2 lb. of ground beef
- 1/2 lb. of ground pork
- 1/4 cup of hot water
- 1 medium onion chopped
- 3 cups of cooked white rice
- 1/2 tsp. of black pepper
- 1/2 tsp. of lemon pepper
- 1 tbsp. of dried thyme
- 1 tbsp. of minced garlic

Directions:

1. Preheat oven to 350°F.
2. Take a large pot of water to a boil and drop in the bell peppers.
3. Boil the peppers for 5 minutes. Remove and drain.
4. Arrange the peppers by removing the stem and removing the seeds.
5. In a large skillet, cook the ground meat over medium heat until it is browned.
6. Add the hot water, roasted red peppers, onions, garlic, and spices.
7. Cook for 5 minutes.
8. Add rice and stir to combine and cook for 3 minutes. Remove from the heat and stuff the bell peppers. Put the stuffed peppers in a baking sheet and bake, uncovered, for 30 minutes.
9. Serve with a garnish of roasted red peppers.

Nutrition: Calories: 173.5 Protein: 8.8g Sodium: 27.7mg Phosphorus: 8.0mg Potassium: 166.1mg

43. Mexican Chorizo Sausage

Preparation Time: 10 minutes
Cooking Time: 15 minutes
Servings: 1
Ingredients:

- 2 pounds of boneless pork but coarsely ground
- 3 tbsp. of red wine vinegar
- 2 tbsp. of smoked paprika
- ½ tsp of cinnamon
- ½ tsp of ground cloves
- ¼ tsp of coriander seeds
- ¼ tsp ground ginger
- 1 tsp of ground cumin
- 3 tbsp. of brandy

Directions:

1. In a large mixing bowl, combine the ground pork with the seasonings, brandy, and vinegar and mix with your hands well.
2. Place the mixture into a large Ziploc bag and leave in the fridge overnight.
3. Form into 15-16 patties of equal size.
4. Heat the oil in a large pan and fry the patties for 5-7 minutes on each side, or until the meat inside is no longer pink and there is a light brown crust on top.
5. Serve hot.

Nutrition: Calories: 134 Carbohydrate: 0 g Protein: 10 g Fat: 7 g Sodium: 40 mg Potassium: 138 mg Phosphorus: 128 mg

44. <u>Eggplant Casserole</u>

Preparation Time: 10 minutes
Cooking Time: 25 – 30 minutes
Servings: 4
Ingredients:

- 3 cups of eggplant, peeled and cut into large chunks
- 2 egg whites
- 1 large egg, whole
- ½ cup of unsweetened vegetable
- ¼ tsp of sage
- ½ cup of breadcrumbs
- 1 tbsp. of margarine, melted
- 1/4 tsp garlic salt

Directions:

1. Preheat the oven at 350F/180C.
2. Place the eggplants chunks in a medium pan, cover with a bit of water and cook with the lid covered until tender. Drain from the water and mash with a tool or fork.
3. Beat the eggs with the non-dairy vegetable cream, sage, salt, and pepper. Whisk in the eggplant mush.
4. Combine the melted margarine with the breadcrumbs.
5. Bake in the oven for 20-25 minutes or until the casserole has a golden-brown crust.

Nutrition: Calories: 186 Carbohydrate: 19 g Protein: 7 g Fat: 9 g Sodium: 503 mg Potassium: 230 mg Phosphorus: 62 mg

45. Pizza with Chicken and Pesto

Preparation Time: 10 minutes
Cooking Time: 25 minutes
Servings: 4
Ingredients:

- 1 ready-made frozen pizza dough
- 2/3 cup cooked chicken, chopped
- 1/2 cup of mango bell pepper, diced
- 1/2 cup of green bell pepper, diced
- 1/4 cup of purple onion, chopped
- 2 tbsp. of green basil pesto
- 1 tbsp. of chives, chopped
- 1/3 cup of parmesan or Romano cheese, grated
- 1/4 cup of mozzarella cheese
- 1 tbsp. of olive oil

Directions:

1. Thaw the pizza dough according to instructions on the package.
2. Heat the olive oil in a pan and sauté the peppers and onions for a couple of minutes. Set aside
3. Once the pizza dough has thawed, spread the Bali pesto over its surface.
4. Top with half of the cheese, the peppers, the onions, and the chicken. Finish with the rest of the cheese.
5. Bake at 350F/180C for approx. 20 minutes (or until crust and cheese are baked).
6. Slice in triangles with a pizza cutter or sharp knife and serve.

Nutrition: Calories: 225 Carbohydrate: 13.9 g Protein: 11.1 g Fat: 12 g Sodium: 321 mg Potassium: 174 mg Phosphorus: 172 mg

46. Shrimp Quesadilla

Preparation Time: 10 minutes
Cooking Time: 10 minutes
Servings: 2
Ingredients:

- 5 oz. of shrimp, shelled and deveined
- 4 tbsp. of Mexican salsa
- 2 tbsp. of fresh cilantro, chopped
- 1 tbsp. of lemon juice
- 1 tsp of ground cumin
- 1 tsp of cayenne pepper
- 2 tbsp. of unsweetened soy yogurt or creamy tofu
- 2 medium corn flour tortillas
- 2 tbsp. of low-fat cheddar cheese

Directions:

1. Mix the cilantro, cumin, lemon juice, and cayenne in a Ziploc bag to make your marinade.
2. Put the shrimps and marinate for 10 minutes.
3. Heat a pan over medium heat with some olive oil and toss in the shrimp with the marinade. Let cook for a couple of minutes or as soon as shrimps have turned pink and opaque.
4. Add the soy cream or soft tofu to the pan and mix well. Remove from the heat and keep the marinade aside.

5. Heat tortillas in the grill or microwave for a few seconds.
6. Place 2 tbsp. of salsa on each tortilla. Top one tortilla with the shrimp mixture and add the cheese on top.
7. Stack one tortilla against each other (with the spread salsa layer facing the shrimp mixture).
8. Transfer this on a baking tray and cook for 7-8 minutes at 350F/180C to melt the cheese and crisp up the tortillas.
9. Serve warm.

Nutrition: Calories: 255 Carbohydrate: 21 g Fat: 9 g Protein: 24 g Sodium: 562 g Potassium: 235 mg Phosphorus: 189 mg

47. <u>Grilled Corn on the Cob</u>

Preparation Time: 5 minutes
Cooking Time: 20 minutes
Servings: 4
Ingredients:
- 4 frozen corn on the cob, cut in half
- ½ tsp of thyme
- 1 tbsp. of grated parmesan cheese
- ¼ tsp of black pepper

Directions:
1. Combine the oil, cheese, thyme, and black pepper in a bowl.
2. Place the corn in the cheese/oil mix and roll to coat evenly.
3. Fold all 4 pieces in aluminum foil, leaving a small open surface on top.
4. Place the wrapped corns over the grill and let cook for 20 minutes.
5. Serve hot.

Nutrition: Calories: 125 Carbohydrate: 29.5 g Protein: 2 g Fat: 1.3 g Sodium: 26 g Potassium: 145 mg Phosphorus: 91.5 mg

48. <u>Couscous with Veggies</u>

Preparation Time: 10 minutes
Cooking Time: 10 minutes
Servings: 5
Ingredients:

- ½ cup of uncooked couscous
- ¼ cup of white mushrooms, sliced
- ½ cup of red onion, chopped
- 1 garlic clove, minced
- ½ cup of frozen peas
- 2 tbsp. of dry white wine
- ½ tsp of basil
- 2 tbsp. of fresh parsley, chopped
- 1 cup water or vegetable stock
- 1 tbsp. of margarine or vegetable oil

Directions:

1. Thaw the peas by setting them aside at room temperature for 15-20 minutes.
2. In a medium pan, heat the margarine or vegetable oil.
3. Add the onions, peas, mushroom, and garlic and sauté for around 5 minutes. Add the wine and let it evaporate.
4. Add all the herbs and spices and toss well. Take off the heat and keep aside.
5. In a small pot, cook the couscous with 1 cup of hot water or vegetable stock. Bring to a boil, take off the heat, and sit for a few minutes with a lid covered.
6. Add the sauté veggies to the couscous and toss well.
7. Serve in a serving bowl warm or cold.

Nutrition: Calories: 110.4 Carbohydrate: 18 g Protein: 3 g Fat: 2 g Sodium: 112.2 mg Potassium: 69.6 mg Phosphorus: 46.8 mg

49. <u>Easy Egg Salad</u>

Preparation Time: 5 minutes
Cooking Time: 8 minutes
Servings: 4
Ingredients:

- 4 large eggs
- ½ cup of sweet onion, chopped
- ¼ cup of celery, chopped
- 1 tbsp. of yellow mustard
- 1 tsp of smoked paprika
- 3 tbsp. of mayo

Directions:

1. Hard boil the eggs in a small pot filled with water for approx. 7-8 minutes. Leave the eggs in the water for an extra couple of minutes before peeling.
2. Peel the eggs and chop finely with a knife or tool.
3. Combine all the chopped veggies with the mayo and mustard. Add in the eggs and mix well.
4. Sprinkle with some smoked paprika on top.
5. Serve cold with pitta, white bread slices, or lettuce wraps.

Nutrition: Calories: 127 Carbohydrate: 6 g Protein: 7 g Fat: 13 g Sodium: 170.7 mg Potassium: 87.5 mg Phosphorus: 101 mg

50. Dolmas Wrap

Preparation Time: 10 minutes
Cooking Time: 5 minutes
Servings: 2
Ingredients:

- 2 whole wheat wraps
- 6 dolmas (stuffed grape leaves)
- 1 cucumber, chopped
- 2 oz. Greek yogurt
- ½ teaspoon minced garlic
- ¼ cup lettuce, chopped
- 2 oz. Feta, crumbled

Directions:

1. In the mixing bowl combine together, cucumber, Greek yogurt, minced garlic, lettuce, and Feta.
2. When the mixture is homogenous transfer it in the center of every wheat wrap.
3. Arrange dolma over the vegetable mixture.
4. Carefully wrap the wheat wraps.

Nutrition: calories 341, fat 12.9, fiber 9.2, carbs 52.4, protein 13.2 Phosphorus: 110mg Potassium: 117mg Sodium: 75mg

51. Salad al Tonno

Preparation Time: 15 minutes
Cooking Time: 0 minutes
Servings: 2
Ingredients:

- 1 ½ cup lettuce leaves, teared
- ½ cup cherry red bell peppers, halved
- ½ teaspoon garlic powder
- ½ teaspoon salt
- ½ teaspoon ground black pepper
- 1 tablespoon lemon juice
- 6 oz. tuna, canned, drained

Directions:

1. Chop the tuna roughly and put it in the salad bowl.
2. Add cherry red bell peppers, lettuce leaves, salt, garlic powder, ground black pepper. Lemon juice, and olive oil.
3. Give a good shake to the salad.
4. Salad can be stored in the fridge for up to 3 hours.

Nutrition: calories 235, fat 12, fiber 1, carbs 6.5, protein 23.4 Phosphorus: 120mg Potassium: 217mg Sodium: 75mg

52. Arlecchino Rice Salad

Preparation Time: 10 minutes
Cooking Time: 15 minutes
Servings: 3

Ingredients:

- ½ cup white rice, dried
- 1 cup chicken stock
- 1 zucchini, shredded
- 2 tablespoons capers
- 1 carrot, shredded
- 1 tablespoon apple cider vinegar
- ½ teaspoon salt
- 2 tablespoons fresh parsley, chopped
- 1 tablespoon canola oil

Directions:

1. Put rice in the pan.
2. Add chicken stock and boil it with the closed lid for 15-20 minutes or until rice absorbs all water.
3. Meanwhile, in the mixing bowl combine together shredded zucchini, capers, carrot.
4. Add fresh parsley.
5. Make the dressing: mix up together canola oil, salt, and apple cider vinegar.
6. Chill the cooked rice little and add it in the salad bowl to the vegetables.
7. Add dressing and mix up salad well.

Nutrition: calories 183, fat 5.3, fiber 2.1, carbs 30.4, protein 3.8 Phosphorus: 110mg Potassium: 117mg Sodium: 75mg

53. Sauteed Chickpea and Lentil Mix

Preparation Time: 10 minutes
Cooking Time: 50 minutes
Servings: 4
Ingredients:

- 1 cup chickpeas, half-cooked
- 1 cup lentils
- 5 cups chicken stock
- ½ cup fresh cilantro, chopped
- 1 teaspoon salt
- ½ teaspoon chili flakes
- ¼ cup onion, diced

Directions:

1. Place chickpeas in the pan.
2. Add water, salt, and chili flakes.
3. Boil the chickpeas for 30 minutes over the medium heat.
4. Then add diced onion, lentils. Stir well.
5. Close the lid and cook the mix for 15 minutes.
6. After this, add chopped cilantro, stir the meal well and cook it for 5 minutes more.
7. Let the cooked lunch chill little before serving.

Nutrition: calories 370, fat 4.3, fiber 23.7, carbs 61.6, protein 23.2 Phosphorus: 110mg Potassium: 117mg Sodium: 75mg

54. Crazy Japanese Beef Croquettes

Preparation Time: 10 minutes

Cooking Time: 20 minutes
Servings: 10
Ingredients:

- 3 medium russet carrots, peeled and chopped
- 1 tablespoon almond butter
- 1 tablespoon vegetable oil
- 3 onions, diced
- ¾ pound ground beef
- 4 teaspoons light coconut aminos
- All-purpose flour for coating
- 2 eggs, beaten
- Panko bread crumbs for coating
- ½ cup oil, frying

Directions:

1. Take a saucepan and place it over medium-high heat; add carrots and sunflower seeds water, boil for 16 minutes.
2. Remove water and put carrots in another bowl, add almond butter and mash the carrots.
3. Take a frying pan and place it over medium heat, add 1 tablespoon oil and let it heat up.
4. Add onions and stir fry until tender.
5. Add coconut aminos to beef to onions.
6. Keep frying until beef is browned.
7. Mix the beef with the carrots evenly.
8. Take another frying pan and place it over medium heat; add half a cup of oil.
9. Form croquettes and coat them with flour, then eggs and finally breadcrumbs.
10. Fry patties until golden on all sides.
11. Enjoy!

Nutrition: Calories: 239 Fat: 4g Carbohydrates: 20g Protein: 10g Phosphorus: 120mg Potassium: 107mg Sodium: 75mg

55. <u>Traditional Black Bean Chili</u>

Preparation Time: 10 minutes
Cooking Time: 4 hours
Servings: 4
Ingredients:

- 1 ½ cups red bell pepper, chopped
- 1 cup yellow onion, chopped
- 1 ½ cups mushrooms, sliced
- 1 tablespoon olive oil
- 1 tablespoon chili powder
- 2 garlic cloves, minced
- 1 teaspoon chipotle chili pepper, chopped
- ½ teaspoon cumin, ground
- 16 ounces canned black beans, drained and rinsed
- 2 tablespoons cilantro, chopped
- 1 cup red bell peppers, chopped

Directions:

1. Add red bell peppers, onion, dill, mushrooms, chili powder, garlic, chili pepper, cumin, black beans, and red bell peppers to your Slow Cooker.
2. Stir well.
3. Place lid and cook on HIGH for 4 hours.
4. Sprinkle cilantro on top.
5. Serve and enjoy!

Nutrition: Calories: 211 Fat: 3g Carbohydrates: 22g Protein: 5g Phosphorus: 90mg Potassium: 107mg Sodium: 75mg

56. <u>Green Palak Paneer</u>

Preparation Time: 5 minutes
Cooking Time: 10 minutes
Servings: 4
Ingredients:
- 1-pound green lettuce
- 2 cups cubed paneer (vegan)
- 2 tablespoons coconut oil
- 1 teaspoon cumin
- 1 chopped up onion
- 1-2 teaspoons hot green chili minced up
- 1 teaspoon minced garlic
- 15 cashews
- 4 tablespoons almond milk
- 1 teaspoon Garam masala
- Flavored vinegar as needed

Directions:
1. Add cashews and almond milk to a blender and blend well.
2. Set your pot to Sauté mode and add coconut oil; allow the oil to heat up.
3. Add cumin seeds, garlic, green chilies, ginger and sauté for 1 minute.
4. Add onion and sauté for 2 minutes.
5. Add chopped green lettuce, flavored vinegar and a cup of water.
6. Lock up the lid and cook on HIGH pressure for 10 minutes.
7. Quick-release the pressure.
8. Add ½ cup of water and blend to a paste.
9. Add cashew paste, paneer and Garam Masala and stir thoroughly.
10. Serve over hot rice!

Nutrition: Calories: 367 Fat: 26g Carbohydrates: 21g Protein: 16g Phosphorus: 110mg Potassium: 117mg Sodium: 75mg

57. <u>Cucumber Sandwich</u>

Preparation Time: 1 hour
Cooking Time: 5 minutes
Servings: 2
Ingredients:
- 6 tsp. of cream cheese
- 1 pinch of dried dill weed

- 3 tsp. of mayonnaise
- .25 tsp. dry Italian dressing mix
- 4 slices of white bread
- .5 of a cucumber

Directions:
1. Prepare the cucumber and cut it into slices.
2. Mix cream cheese, mayonnaise, and Italian dressing. Chill for one hour.
3. Distribute the mixture onto the white bread slices.
4. Place cucumber slices on top and sprinkle with the dill weed.
5. Cut in halves and serve.

Nutrition: Calories: 143 Fat: 6g Carbs: 16.7g Protein: 4g Sodium: 255mg Potassium: 127mg Phosphorus: 64mg

58. <u>Pizza Pitas</u>

Preparation Time: 10 minutes
Cooking Time: 10 minutes
Servings: 1
Ingredients:
- 33 cup of mozzarella cheese
- 2 pieces of pita bread, 6 inches in size
- 2 cloves of garlic (minced)
- .25 cups of onion, chopped small
- .25 tsp. of red pepper flakes
- .25 cup of bell pepper, chopped small
- 2 ounces of ground pork, lean
- No-stick oil spray
- .5 tsp. of fennel seeds

Directions:
1. Preheat oven to 400.
2. Put the garlic, ground meat, pepper flakes, onion, and bell pepper in a pan. Sauté until cooked.
3. Grease a flat baking pan and put pitas on it. Use the mixture to spread on the pita bread.
4. Spread and top with cheese.
5. Bake for five to eight minutes, until the cheese is bubbling.

Nutrition: Calories: 284 Fat: 10g Carbs: 34g Protein: 16g Sodium: 795mg Potassium: 706mg Phosphorus: 416mg

59. <u>Lettuce Wraps with Chicken</u>

Preparation Time: 10 minutes
Cooking Time: 15 minutes
Servings: 4
Ingredients:
- 8 lettuce leaves
- .25 cups of fresh cilantro
- .25 cups of mushroom
- 1 tsp. of five spices seasoning
- .25 cups of onion
- 6 tsp. of rice vinegar
- 2 tsp. of hoisin

- 6 tsp. of oil (canola)
- 3 tsp. of oil (sesame)
- 2 tsp. of garlic
- 2 scallions
- 8 ounces of cooked chicken breast

Directions:
1. Mince together the cooked chicken and the garlic. Chop up the onions, cilantro, mushrooms, and scallions.
2. Use a skillet overheat, combine chicken to all remaining ingredients, minus the lettuce leaves. Cook for fifteen minutes, stirring occasionally.
3. Place .25 cups of the mixture into each leaf of lettuce.
4. Wrap the lettuce around like a burrito and eat.

Nutrition: Calories: 84 Fat: 4g Carbs: 9g Protein: 5.9g Sodium: 618mg Potassium: 258mg Phosphorus: 64mg

60. Turkey Pinwheels

Preparation Time: 10 minutes
Cooking Time: 15 minutes
Servings: 6
Ingredients:
- 6 toothpicks
- 8 oz. of spring mix salad greens
- 1 ten-inch tortilla
- 2 ounces of thinly sliced deli turkey
- 9 tsp. of whipped cream cheese
- 1 roasted red bell pepper

Directions:
1. Cut the red bell pepper into ten strips about a quarter-inch thick.
2. Spread the whipped cream cheese on the tortilla evenly.
3. Add the salad greens to create a base layer and then lay the turkey on top of it.
4. Space out the red bell pepper strips on top of the turkey.
5. Tuck the end and begin rolling the tortilla inward.
6. Use the toothpicks to hold the roll into place and cut it into six pieces.
7. Serve with the swirl facing upward.

Nutrition: Calories: 206 Fat: 9g Carbs: 21g Protein: 9g Sodium: 533mg Potassium: 145mg Phosphorus: 47mg

61. Chicken Tacos

Preparation Time: 5 minutes
Cooking Time: 20 minutes
Servings: 4
Ingredients:
- 8 corn tortillas
- 1.5 tsp. of Sodium-free taco seasoning
- 1 juiced lime
- .5 cups of cilantro
- 2 green onions, chopped
- 8 oz. of iceberg or romaine lettuce, shredded or chopped
- .25 cup of sour cream

- 1 pound of boneless and skinless chicken breast

Directions:
1. Cook chicken, by boiling, for twenty minutes. Shred or chop cooked chicken into fine bite-sized pieces.
2. Mix the seasoning and lime juice with the chicken.
3. Put chicken mixture and lettuce in tortillas.
4. Top with the green onions, cilantro, and sour cream.

Nutrition: Calories: 260 Fat: 3g Carbs: 36g Protein: 23g Sodium: 922mg Potassium: 445mg Phosphorus: 357mg

62. Tuna Twist

Preparation Time: 10 minutes
Cooking Time: 30 minutes
Servings: 4
Ingredients:

- 1 can of unsalted or water packaged tuna, drained
- 6 tsp. of vinegar
- .5 cup of cooked peas
- .5 cup celery (chopped)
- 3 tsp. of dried dill weed
- 12 oz. cooked macaroni
- .75 cup of mayonnaise

Directions:
1. Stir together the macaroni, vinegar, and mayonnaise together until blended and smooth.
2. Stir in remaining ingredients.
3. Chill before serving.

Nutrition: Calories: 290 Fat: 10g Carbs: 32g Protein: 16g Sodium: 307mg Potassium: 175mg Phosphorus: 111mg

63. Ciabatta Rolls with Chicken Pesto

Preparation Time: 10 minutes
Cooking Time: 20 minutes
Servings: 2
Ingredients:

- 6 tsp. of Greek yogurt
- 6 tsp. of pesto
- 2 small ciabatta rolls
- 8 oz. of a shredded iceberg or romaine lettuce
- 8 oz. of cooked boneless and skinless chicken breast, shredded
- .125 tsp. of pepper

Directions:
1. Combine the shredded chicken, pesto, pepper, and Greek yogurt in a medium-sized bowl.
2. Slice and toast the ciabatta rolls.
3. Divide the shredded chicken and pesto mixture in half and make sandwiches with the ciabatta rolls.
4. Top with shredded lettuce if desired.

Nutrition: Calories: 374 Fat: 10g Carbs: 40g Protein: 30g Sodium: 522mg Potassium: 360mg Phosphorus: 84mg

64. Marinated Shrimp Pasta Salad

Preparation Time: 15 minutes
Cooking Time: 5 hours
Servings: 1
Ingredients:

- 1/4 cup of honey
- 1/4 cup of balsamic vinegar
- 1/2 of an English cucumber, cubed
- 1/2 pound of fully cooked shrimp
- 15 baby carrots
- 1.5 cups of dime-sized cut cauliflower
- 4 stalks of celery, diced
- 1/2 large yellow bell pepper (diced)
- 1/2 red onion (diced)
- 1/2 large red bell pepper (diced)
- 12 ounces of uncooked tri-color pasta (cooked)
- 3/4 cup of olive oil
- 3 tsp. of mustard (Dijon)
- 1/2 tsp. of garlic (powder)
- 1/2 tsp. pepper

Directions:

1. Cut vegetables and put them in a bowl with the shrimp.
2. Whisk together the honey, balsamic vinegar, garlic powder, pepper, and Dijon mustard in a small bowl. While still whisking, slowly add the oil and whisk it all together.
3. Add the cooked pasta to the bowl with the shrimp and vegetables and mix it.
4. Toss the sauce to coat the pasta, shrimp, and vegetables evenly.
5. Cover and chill for a minimum of five hours before serving. Stir and serve while chilled.

Nutrition: Calories: 205 Fat: 13g Carbs: 10g Protein: 12g Sodium: 363mg Potassium: 156mg Phosphorus: 109mg

65. Peanut Butter and Jelly Grilled Sandwich

Preparation Time: 5 minutes
Cooking Time: 5 minutes
Servings: 1
Ingredients:

- 2 tsp. butter (unsalted)
- 6 tsp. butter (peanut)
- 3 tsp. of flavored jelly
- 2 pieces of bread

Directions:

1. Put the peanut butter evenly on one bread. Add the layer of jelly.
2. Butter the outside of the pieces of bread.
3. Add the sandwich to a frying pan and toast both sides.

Nutrition: Calories: 300 Fat: 7g Carbs: 49g Protein: 8g Sodium: 460mg Potassium: 222mg Phosphorus: 80mg

66. Grilled Onion and Pepper Jack Grilled Cheese Sandwich

Preparation Time: 5 minutes
Cooking Time: 5 minutes
Servings: 2
Ingredients:

- 1 tsp. of oil (olive)
- 6 tsp. of whipped cream cheese
- 1/2 of a medium onion
- 2 ounces of pepper jack cheese
- 4 slices of rye bread
- 2 tsp. of unsalted butter

Directions:

1. Set out the butter so that it becomes soft. Slice up the onion into thin slices.
2. Sauté onion slices. Continue to stir until cooked. Remove and put it to the side.
3. Spread one tablespoon of the whipped cream cheese on two of the slices of bread.
4. Then add grilled onions and cheese to each slice. Then top using the other two bread slices.
5. Spread the softened butter on the outside of the slices of bread.
6. Use the skillet to toast the sandwiches until lightly brown and the cheese is melted.

Nutrition: Calories: 350 Fat: 18g Carbs: 34g Protein: 13g Sodium: 589mg Potassium: 184mg Phosphorus: 226mg

67. Aromatic Carrot Cream

Preparation Time: 15 minutes
Cooking Time: 25 minutes
Servings: 4
Ingredients:

- 1 tablespoon olive oil
- ½ sweet onion, chopped
- 2 teaspoons fresh ginger, peeled and grated
- 1 teaspoon fresh garlic, minced
- 4 cups water
- 3 carrots, chopped
- 1 teaspoon ground turmeric
- ½ cup coconut almond milk

Directions:
1. Heat the olive oil into a big pan over medium-high heat.
2. Add the onion, garlic and ginger. Softly cook for about 3 minutes until softened.
3. Include the water, turmeric and the carrots. Softly cook for about 20 minutes (until the carrots are softened).
4. Blend the soup adding coconut almond milk until creamy.
5. Serve and enjoy!

Nutrition: Calories 112 Fat 10 g Cholesterol 0 mg Carbohydrates 8 g Sugar 5 g Fiber 2 g Protein 2 g Sodium 35 mg Calcium 32 mg Phosphorus 59 mg Potassium 241 mg

68. Mushrooms Velvet Soup

Preparation Time: 40 minutes
Cooking Time: 40 minutes
Servings: 6
Ingredients:
- 1 teaspoon olive oil
- ½ teaspoon fresh ground black pepper
- 3 medium (85g) shallots, diced
- 2 stalks (80g) celery, chopped
- 1 clove garlic, diced
- 12-ounces cremini mushrooms, sliced
- 5 tablespoons flour
- 4 cups low sodium vegetable stock, divided
- 3 sprigs fresh thyme
- 2 bay leaves
- ½ cup regular yogurt

Directions:
1. Heat oil in a large pan.
2. Add ground pepper, shallots and celery. Cook over medium-high heat.
3. Sauté for 2 minutes until golden.
4. Add garlic and stir.
5. Include the sliced mushrooms. Stir and cook until the mushrooms give out their liquid.
6. Sprawl the flour on the mushrooms and toast for about 2 min.
7. Add one cup of hot stock, thyme sprigs and bay leaves. Stir and add the second cup of stock
8. Stir until well combined.
9. Add the remaining cups of stock.
10. Slowly cook for 15 minutes.
11. Take out bay leaves and thyme sprigs.
12. Blend until mixture is smooth.

13. Include the yogurt and stir well.
14. Slowly cook for 4 minutes.
15. Serve and enjoy!

Nutrition: Calories 126 Fat 8 g Cholesterol 0 mg Carbohydrate 14 g Sugar 4 g Fiber 2 g Protein 3 g Sodium 108 mg Calcium 55 mg Phosphorus 70 mg Potassium 298 mg

69. <u>Pumpkin Bites</u>

Preparation Time: 10 minutes
Cooking Time: 5 minutes
Servings: 12
Ingredients:
- 8 oz cream cheese
- 1 tsp vanilla
- 1 tsp pumpkin pie spice
- 1/4 cup coconut flour
- 1/4 cup erythritol
- 1/2 cup pumpkin puree
- 4 oz butter

Directions:
1. Add all ingredients into the mixing bowl and beat using hand mixer until well combined.
2. Scoop mixture into the silicone ice cube tray and place it in the refrigerator until set.
3. Serve and enjoy.

Nutrition: Calories 149 Fat 14.6 g Carbohydrates 8.1 g Sugar 5.4 g Protein 2 g Cholesterol 41 mg Phosphorus: 66mg Potassium: 77mg Sodium: 55mg

70. <u>Feta Bean Salad</u>

Preparation Time: 5 minutes
Cooking Time: 20 minutes
Servings: 2
Ingredients:
- 1 tbsp of olive oil
- 2 egg whites (boiled)
- 1 cup of green beans (8 oz)
- 1 tbsp of onion
- 1/2 red chili
- 1/8 cup of cilantro
- 1 1/2 tbsp lime juice
- 1/4 tbsp of black pepper

Directions:
1. Remove the ends off the green beans and cut them into small pieces.
2. Chop the onion, cilantro, and chili and mix it.
3. Use a steamer to cook green beans for 5- 10 minutes and rinse with cold water once done.
4. Place all the mixed dry ingredients together in two serving bowls.
5. Chop the egg whites up and place them on top of the salad with crumbled feta.
6. Drizzle a pinch of olive oil with black pepper on top.

Nutrition: Calories: 255 Fat: 24g Carbs: 8g Protein: 5g Sodium: 215.6mg Potassium: 211mg Phosphorus: 125mg

71. Seafood Casserole

Preparation Time: 20 minutes
Cooking Time: 45 minutes
Servings: 1
Ingredients:

- 2 cups, peeled and diced into 1-inch pieces Eggplant
- Butter, for greasing the baking dish
- 1 tbsp. Olive oil
- ½, chopped sweet onion
- 1 tsp. Minced garlic
- 1 chopped Celery stalk
- ½ boiled and chopped red bell pepper
- 3 tbsps. Freshly squeezed lemon juice
- 1 tsp. Hot sauce
- ¼ tsp. Creole seasoning mix
- ½ cup, uncooked White rice
- 1 large Egg
- 4 ounces cooked shrimp
- 6 ounces Queen crab meat

Directions:

1. Preheat the oven to 350f.
2. Boil the eggplant in a saucepan for 5 minutes. Drain and set aside.
3. Grease a 9-by-13-inch baking dish with butter and set aside.
4. Heat the olive oil in a large skillet over medium heat.
5. Sauté the garlic, onion, celery, and bell pepper for 4 minutes or until tender.
6. Add the sautéed vegetables to the eggplant, along with the lemon juice, hot sauce, seasoning, rice, and egg.
7. Stir to combine.
8. Fold in the shrimp and crab meat.
9. Spoon the casserole mixture into the casserole dish, patting down the top.
10. Bake for 25 to 30 minutes or until casserole is heated through and rice is tender. Serve warm.

Nutrition: Calories: 118 Fat: 4g Carbs: 9g Protein: 12g Sodium: 235mg Potassium: 199mg Phosphorus: 102mg

72. Eggplant and Red Pepper Soup

Preparation Time: 20 minutes
Cooking Time: 40 minutes
Servings: 1
Ingredients:

- 1 small, cut into quarters sweet onion
- 2, halved Small red bell peppers
- 2 cups Cubed eggplant
- 2 cloves, crushed Garlic
- 1 tbsp. Olive oil
- 1 cup Chicken stock
- Water
- ¼ cup Chopped fresh basil

- Ground black pepper

Directions:
1. Preheat the oven to 350f.
2. Put the onions, red peppers, eggplant, and garlic in a baking dish.
3. Drizzle the vegetables with the olive oil.
4. Cook vegetables for 30 minutes or until they are slightly charred and soft.
5. Cool the vegetables slightly and remove the skin from the peppers.
6. Puree the vegetables with a hand mixer (with the chicken stock).
7. Transfer the soup to a medium pot and add enough water to reach the desired thickness.
8. Heat the soup to a simmer and add the basil.
9. Season with pepper and serve.

Nutrition: Calories: 61 Fat: 2g Carbs: 9g Protein: 2g Sodium: 98mg Potassium: 198mg Phosphorus: 33mg

73. <u>Ground Beef and Rice Soup</u>

Preparation time: 15 minutes
cooking time: 40 minutes
Servings: 1
Ingredients:
- ½ pound Extra-lean ground beef
- ½, chopped Small sweet onion
- 1 tsp. Minced garlic
- 2 cups Water
- 1 cup Low-sodium beef broth
- ½ cup, uncooked Long-grain white rice
- 1, chopped Celery stalk
- ½ cup, cut into – 1-inch pieces Fresh green beans
- 1 tsp. Chopped fresh thyme
- Ground black pepper

Directions:
1. Sauté the ground beef in a saucepan for 6 minutes or until the beef is completely browned.
2. Drain off the excess fat and add the onion and garlic to the saucepan.
3. Sauté the vegetables for about 3 minutes, or until they are softened.
4. Add the celery, rice, beef broth, and water.
5. Let it boil, reduce the heat to low, and simmer for 30 minutes or until the rice is tender.
6. Add the green beans and thyme and simmer for 3 minutes.
7. Remove the soup from the heat and season with pepper.

Nutrition: Calories: 154 Fat: 7g Carbs: 14g Protein: 9g Sodium: 133mg Potassium: 179mg Phosphorus: 76mg

74. <u>Baked Flounder</u>

Preparation Time: 20 minutes
Cooking Time: 5 minutes
Servings: 4
Ingredients:
- ¼ cup Homemade mayonnaise
- Juice of 1 lime
- Zest of 1 lime

- ½ cup Chopped fresh cilantro
- 4 (3-ounce) Flounder fillets
- Ground black pepper

Directions:
1. Preheat the oven to 400f.
2. In a bowl, stir together the cilantro, lime juice, lime zest, and mayonnaise.
3. Prepare foil on a clean work surface.
4. Place a flounder fillet in the center of each square.
5. Top the fillets evenly with the mayonnaise mixture.
6. Season the flounder with pepper.
7. Fold the foil's sides over the fish, and place on baking sheet.
8. Bake for 4 - 5 minutes.
9. Unfold the packets and serve.

Nutrition: Calories: 92 Fat: 4g Carbs: 2g Protein: 12g Sodium: 267mg Potassium: 137mg Phosphorus: 208mg

75. Persian Chicken

Preparation Time: 10 minutes
Cooking Time: 20 minutes
Servings: 5
Ingredients:
- ½, chopped sweet onion
- ¼ cup Lemon juice
- 1 tbsp. Dried oregano
- 1 tsp. Minced garlic
- 1 tsp. Sweet paprika
- ½ tsp. Ground cumin
- ½ cup Olive oil
- 5 Boneless, skinless chicken thighs

Directions:
1. Put the cumin, paprika, garlic, oregano, lemon juice, and onion in a food processor and pulse to mix the ingredients.
2. Put olive oil until the mixture is smooth.
3. Put chicken thighs in a large Ziploc and add the marinade for 2 hours.
4. Remove the thighs from the marinade.
5. Preheat the barbecue to medium.
6. Grill the chicken for about 20 minutes, turning once, until it reaches 165F.

Nutrition: Calories: 321 Fat: 21g Carbs: 3g Protein: 22g Sodium: 86mg Potassium: 220mg Phosphorus: 131mg

76. Beef Chili

Preparation Time: 10 minutes
Cooking Time: 30 minutes
Servings: 2
Ingredients:
- 1 diced Onion
- 1 diced red bell pepper
- 2 cloves, minced Garlic

- 6 oz. Lean ground beef
- 1 tsp. Chili powder
- 1 tsp. Oregano
- 2 tbsps. Extra virgin olive oil
- 1 cup Water
- 1 cup Brown rice
- 1 tbsp. Fresh cilantro to serve

Directions:
1. Soak vegetables in warm water.
2. Boil pan of water and add rice for 20 minutes.
3. Meanwhile, add the oil to a pan and heat on medium-high heat.
4. Add the pepper, onions, and garlic and sauté for 5 minutes until soft.
5. Remove and set aside.
6. Add the beef to the pan and stir until browned.
7. Put and stir vegetables back into the pan.
8. Now add the chili powder and herbs and the water, cover, and turn the heat down a little to simmer for 15 minutes.
9. Meanwhile, drain the water from the rice and the lid and steam while the chili is cooking.
10. Serve hot with the fresh cilantro sprinkled over the top.

Nutrition: Calories: 459 Fat: 22g Carbs: 36g Protein: 22g Sodium: 33mg Potassium: 360mg Phosphorus: 332mg

77. **Pork Meatloaf**

Preparation Time: 10 minutes
Cooking Time: 50 minutes
Servings: 1
Ingredients:
- 1-pound lean ground beef
- ½ cup Breadcrumbs
- ½ cup Chopped sweet onion
- 1 Egg
- 2 tbsps. Chopped fresh basil
- 1 tsp. Chopped fresh thyme
- 1 tsp. Chopped fresh parsley
- ¼ tsp. Ground black pepper
- 1 tbsp. Brown sugar
- 1 tsp. White vinegar
- ¼ tsp. Garlic powder

Directions:
1. Preheat the oven to 350f.
2. Mix well the breadcrumbs, beef, onion, basil, egg, thyme, parsley, and pepper.
3. Stir the brown sugar, vinegar, and garlic powder in a small bowl.
4. Put the brown sugar mixture evenly over the meat.
5. Bake the meatloaf for about 50 minutes or until it is cooked through.
6. Let the meatloaf stand for 10 minutes and then pour out any accumulated grease.

Nutrition: Calories: 103 Fat: 3g Carbs: 7g Protein: 11g Sodium: 87mg Potassium: 190mg Phosphorus: 112mg

78. Chicken Stew

Preparation Time: 20 minutes
Cooking Time: 50 minutes
Servings: 1
Ingredients:

- 1 tbsp. Olive oil
- 1 pound, cut into 1-inch cubes Boneless, skinless chicken thighs
- ½, chopped sweet onion
- 1 tbsp. Minced garlic
- 2 cups Chicken stock
- 1 cup, plus 2 tbsps. Water
- 1 sliced Carrot
- 2 stalks, sliced Celery
- 1, sliced thin Turnip
- 1 tbsp. Chopped fresh thyme
- 1 tsp. Chopped fresh rosemary
- 2 tsp. Cornstarch
- Ground black pepper to taste

Directions:
1. Prepare a large saucepan on medium heat and add the olive oil.
2. Sauté the chicken for 6 minutes or until it is lightly browned, stirring often.
3. Add the onion and garlic, and sauté for 3 minutes.
4. Add 1-cup water, chicken stock, carrot, celery, and turnip and bring the stew to a boil.
5. Simmer for 30 minutes or until cooked and tender.
6. Add the thyme and rosemary and simmer for 3 minutes more.
7. In a small bowl, stir together the 2 tbsps. Of water and the cornstarch
8. add the mixture to the stew.
9. Stir to incorporate the cornstarch mixture and cook for 3 to 4 minutes or until the stew thickens.
10. Remove from the heat once done and season with pepper.

Nutrition: Calories: 141 Fat: 8g Carbs: 5g Protein: 9g Sodium: 214mg Potassium: 192mg Phosphorus: 53mg

79. Apple & Cinnamon Spiced Honey Pork Loin

Preparation time: 20 minutes
Cooking time: 6 hours
Servings: 6
Ingredients

- 1 2-3lb boneless pork loin roast
- ½ teaspoon low-sodium salt
- ¼ teaspoon pepper
- 1 tablespoon canola oil
- 3 medium apples, peeled and sliced
- ¼ cup honey
- 1 small red onion, halved and sliced
- 1 tablespoon ground cinnamon

Directions

1. Season the pork with salt and pepper.
2. Heat the oil in a skillet and brown the pork on all sides.
3. Arrange half the apples in the base of a 4 to 6-quart slow cooker.
4. Top with the honey and remaining apples.
5. Sprinkle with cinnamon and cover.
6. Cover and cook on low for 6-8 hours until the meat is tender.

Nutrition: Calories 290, Fat 10g, Carbs 19g, Protein 29g, Fiber 2g, Potassium 789mg, Sodium 22mg

80. <u>Golden Eggplant Fries</u>

Preparation Time: 10 minutes
Cooking Time: 15 minutes
Servings: 8
Ingredients:

- 2 eggs
- 2 cups almond flour
- 2 tablespoons coconut oil, spray
- 2 eggplants, peeled and cut thinly
- Sunflower seeds and pepper

Directions:
1. Preheat your oven to 400 degrees F.
2. Take a bowl and mix with sunflower seeds and black pepper.
3. Take another bowl and beat eggs until frothy.
4. Dip the eggplant pieces into the eggs.
5. Then coat them with the flour mixture.
6. Add another layer of flour and egg.
7. Then, take a baking sheet and grease with coconut oil on top.
8. Bake for about 15 minutes.
9. Serve and enjoy!

Nutrition: Calories: 212 Fat: 15.8g Carbohydrates: 12.1g Protein: 8.6g Phosphorus: 150mg Potassium: 147mg Sodium: 105mg

81. <u>Very Wild Mushroom Pilaf</u>

Preparation Time: 10 minutes
Cooking Time: 3 hours
Servings: 4
Ingredients:

- 1 cup wild rice
- 2 garlic cloves, minced
- 6 green onions, chopped
- 2 tablespoons olive oil
- ½ pound baby Bella mushrooms
- 2 cups water

Directions:
1. Add rice, garlic, onion, oil, mushrooms and water to your Slow Cooker.
2. Stir well until mixed.
3. Place lid and cook on LOW for 3 hours.
4. Stir pilaf and divide between serving platters.

5. Enjoy!

Nutrition: Calories: 210 Fat: 7g Carbohydrates: 16g Protein: 4g Phosphorus: 110mg Potassium: 117mg Sodium: 75mg

82. <u>Sporty Baby Carrots</u>

Preparation Time: 5 minutes
Cooking Time: 5 minutes
Servings: 4
Ingredients:
- 1-pound baby carrots
- 1 cup water
- 1 tablespoon clarified ghee
- 1 tablespoon chopped up fresh mint leaves
- Sea flavored vinegar as needed

Directions:
1. Place a steamer rack on top of your pot and add the carrots.
2. Add water.
3. Lock the lid and cook at HIGH pressure for 2 minutes.
4. Do a quick release.
5. Pass the carrots through a strainer and drain them.
6. Wipe the insert clean.
7. Return the insert to the pot and set the pot to Sauté mode.
8. Add clarified butter and allow it to melt.
9. Add mint and sauté for 30 seconds.
10. Add carrots to the insert and sauté well.
11. Remove them and sprinkle with bit of flavored vinegar on top.
12. Enjoy!

Nutrition: Calories: 131 Fat: 10g Carbohydrates: 11g Protein: 1g Phosphorus: 130mg Potassium: 147mg Sodium: 85mg

83. <u>Saucy Garlic Greens</u>

Preparation Time: 5 minutes
Cooking Time: 20 minutes
Servings: 4
Ingredients:
- 1 bunch of leafy greens
- Sauce
- ½ cup cashews soaked in water for 10 minutes
- ¼ cup water
- 1 tablespoon lemon juice
- 1 teaspoon coconut aminos
- 1 clove peeled whole clove
- 1/8 teaspoon of flavored vinegar

Directions:
1. Make the sauce by draining and discarding the soaking water from your cashews and add the cashews to a blender.

2. Add fresh water, lemon juice, flavored vinegar, coconut aminos, and garlic.
3. Blitz until you have a smooth cream and transfer to bowl.
4. Add ½ cup of water to the pot.
5. Place the steamer basket to the pot and add the greens in the basket.
6. Lock the lid and steam for 1 minute.
7. Quick-release the pressure.
8. Transfer the steamed greens to strainer and extract excess water.
9. Place the greens into a mixing bowl.
10. Add lemon garlic sauce and toss.
11. Enjoy!

Nutrition: Calories: 77 Fat: 5g Carbohydrates: 0g Protein: 2g Phosphorus: 120mg Potassium: 137mg Sodium: 85mg

84. <u>Garden Salad</u>

Preparation Time: 5 minutes
Cooking Time: 20 minutes
Servings: 6
Ingredients:
- 1-pound raw peanuts in shell
- 1 bay leaf
- 2 medium-sized chopped up red bell peppers
- ½ cup diced up green pepper
- ½ cup diced up sweet onion
- ¼ cup finely diced hot pepper
- ¼ cup diced up celery
- 2 tablespoons olive oil
- ¾ teaspoon flavored vinegar
- ¼ teaspoon freshly ground black pepper

Directions:
1. Boil your peanuts for 1 minute and rinse them.
2. The skin will be soft, so discard the skin.
3. Add 2 cups of water to the Instant Pot.
4. Add bay leaf and peanuts.
5. Lock the lid and cook on HIGH pressure for 20 minutes.
6. Drain the water.
7. Take a large bowl and add the peanuts, diced up vegetables.
8. Whisk in olive oil, lemon juice, pepper in another bowl.
9. Pour the mixture over the salad and mix.
10. Enjoy!

Nutrition: Calories: 140 Fat: 4g Carbohydrates: 24g Protein: 5g Phosphorus: 110mg Potassium: 117mg Sodium: 75mg

85. <u>Beef Bulgogi</u>

Preparation Time: 10 minutes
Cooking Time: 5 minutes
Servings: 4
Ingredients:

- 1-pound flank steak, thinly sliced
- 5 tablespoons Worcestershire sauce
- 2 1/2 tablespoons honey
- 1/4 cup chopped green onion
- 2 tablespoons minced garlic
- 2 tablespoons olive oil
- 1/2 teaspoon ground black pepper

Directions:
1. Place the beef in a shallow dish. Combine Worcestershire sauce, honey, green onion, garlic, olive oil, and ground black pepper in a small bowl. Pour over beef. Cover and refrigerate for at least 1 hour or overnight.
2. Preheat an outdoor grill for high heat, and lightly oil the grate.
3. Quickly grill beef on hot grill until slightly charred and cooked through, 1 to 2 minutes per side

Nutrition: Calories 348, Total Fat 16.5g, Saturated Fat 4.9g, Cholesterol 62mg, Sodium 272mg, Total Carbohydrate 16.6g, Dietary Fiber 0.4g, Total Sugar 14.7g,

86. <u>Creamy Chicken with Cider</u>

Preparation Time: 25 minutes
Cooking Time: 20 minutes
Servings: 4
Ingredients:
- 4 bone-in chicken breasts
- 2 tbsp. of lightly salted butter
- ¾ cup of apple cider vinegar
- 2/3 cup of rich unsweetened coconut almond milk or cream
- Kosher pepper

Directions:
1. Melt the butter in a skillet over medium heat.
2. Season the chicken with the pepper and add to the skillet. Cook over low heat for approx. 20 minutes.
3. Remove the chicken from the heat and set aside in a dish.
4. In the same skillet, add the cider and bring to a boil until most of it has evaporated.
5. Add the coconut cream and let cook for 1 minute until slightly thickened.
6. Pour the cider cream over the cooked chicken and serve.

Nutrition: Calories: 86.76kcal Carbohydrate: 1.88g Protein: 1.5g Sodium: 93.52mg Potassium: 74.65mg Phosphorus: 36.54mg Dietary Fiber: 0.1g Fat: 8.21g

87. <u>Exotic Palabok</u>

Preparation Time: 25 minutes
Cooking Time: 15 minutes
Servings: 6
Ingredients:
- 12 oz. rice noodles.
- 1 ½ cups of medium shrimp, peeled and deveined
- 2/3 cup of white onion, chopped
- 1 spring onion, sliced
- 3 tbsp. of canola oil
- 1-pound, lean ground turkey

- 2 cups of firm tofu, chopped
- 2 packs of shrimp or ordinary gravy mix
- 5 hard-boiled eggs
- 1 lemon
- ½ cup of pork rinds (optional)

Directions:
1. Boil rice noodles until nice and soft. Keep aside.
2. Boil the peeled shrimp for 2-3 minutes in a pot with plain water.
3. In a wok or shallow pan, sauté the garlic and onion with the oil. Add the ground turkey, tofu, and shrimps.
4. Dissolve the gravy mix in water or as per package instructions.
5. Combine the rice noodles, tofu, onions, and the gravy mix with ½ cup of pork rind (optional).
6. Slice the egg and lemons.
7. Serve with egg and lemons on top.

Nutrition: Calories: 305 kcal Carbohydrate: 39.14g Protein: 17.6g Sodium: 536mg Potassium: 243.52 mg Phosphorus: 180.41mg Dietary Fiber: 0.9g

88. <u>Vegetarian Gobi Curry</u>

Preparation Time: 25 minutes
Cooking Time: 15 minutes
Servings: 4
Ingredients:

- 2 cups of cauliflower florets
- 2 tbsp. of unsalted butter
- 1 medium dry white onion, thinly chopped
- ½ cup of green peas (frozen if wish)
- 1 tsp. of fresh ginger, chopped
- 1/2 tsp. of turmeric
- 1 tsp of garam masala
- ¼ tsp. cayenne pepper
- 1 tbsp. of water

Directions:
1. Heat a skillet over medium heat with the butter and sauté the onions until caramelized (golden brown).
2. Add the spices e.g., ginger, garam masala turmeric, and cayenne.
3. Add the cauliflower and the (frozen) peas and stir.
4. Add the water and cover with a lid. Reduce the heat to a low temperature and let cook covered for 10 minutes.
5. Serve with white rice.

Nutrition: Calories: 91.04kcal Carbohydrate: 7.3g Protein: 2.19g Sodium: 39.38mg Potassium: 209.58mg Phosphorus: 42mg Dietary Fiber: 3g Fat: 6.4g

89. <u>Marinated Shrimp and Pasta</u>

Preparation Time: 10 minutes
Cooking Time: 20 minutes
Servings: 10
Ingredients:

- 12 oz. of three-colored penne pasta

- ½ pound of cooked shrimp
- ½ red bell pepper, diced
- ½ cup of red onion, chopped
- 3 stalks of celery
- 12 baby carrots, cut into thick slices
- 1 cup of cauliflower, cut into small round pieces
- ¼ cup of honey
- ¼ cup balsamic vinegar
- ½ tsp. of black pepper
- ½ tsp. garlic powder
- 1 tbsp. of French mustard
- ¾ cup of olive oil

Directions:
1. Cook pasta for around 10 minutes (or according to packaged instructions).
2. While pasta is boiling, cut all your veggies and place into a large mixing bowl. Add the cooked shrimp.
3. In a mixing bowl, add the honey, vinegar, black pepper, garlic powder, and mustard. While you whisk, slowly incorporate the oil and stir well.
4. Add in the drained pasta with the veggies and shrimp and gently combine everything. Pour the liquid marinade over the pasta and veggies and toss to coat everything evenly.
5. Refrigerate for 3-5 hours before serving. Serve chilled.

Nutrition: Calories: 256kcal Carbohydrate: 41g Protein: 6.55g Sodium: 242.04mg Potassium: 131.88mg Phosphorus: 86.03mg Dietary Fiber: 2.28g Fat: 16.88g

90. Steak and Onion Sandwich

Preparation Time: 25 minutes
Cooking Time: 8 minutes

Servings: 4

Ingredients:

- 4 flank steaks (around 4 oz. each)
- 1 medium red onion, sliced
- 1 tbsp. of lemon juice
- 1 tbsp. of Italian seasoning
- 1 tsp. of black pepper
- 1 tbsp. of vegetable oil
- 4 sandwich/burger buns

Directions:

1. Wrap the steak with the lemon juice, the Italian seasoning, and pepper to taste. Cut into 4 pieces Heat the vegetable oil in a medium skillet over medium heat.
2. Cook steaks around 3 minutes on each side until you get a medium to well-done result. Take off and transfer onto a dish with absorbing paper.
3. In the same skillet, sauté the onions until tender and transparent (around 3 minutes).
4. Cut the sandwich bun into half and place 1 piece of steak in each topped with the onions. Serve or wrap with paper or foil and keep in the fridge for the next day.

Nutrition: Calories: 315.26 kcal Carbohydrate: 8.47g Protein: 38.33g Sodium: 266.24mg Potassium: 238.2mg Phosphorus: 364.25mg Dietary Fiber: 0.76g Fat: 13.22g

91. Zesty Crab Cakes

Preparation Time: 25 minutes

Cooking Time: 6 minutes

Servings: 6

Ingredients:

- 9 oz. (250 grams) of crab meat
- 1/3 cup of green or red bell pepper, thinly chopped
- 1/3 cup of low salt crackers, crushed
- ¼ cup of low-fat mayonnaise
- 1 tbsp. of dry mustard
- ½ tsp. of pepper
- 2 tbsp. of lemon juice
- ½ tsp. of lemon zest
- 1 tsp. of garlic powder
- 2 tbsp. of vegetable oil

Directions:

1. Mix all the ingredients except for the oil until uniform. Divide into 6 flat patties (around 5 inches in diameter).
2. Heat the vegetable oil in the skillet and shallow fry the patties for 2-3 minutes on each side (or until golden brown).
3. Serve warm on a dish with absorbing paper.

Nutrition: Calories: 144.42kcal Carbohydrate: 5.12g Protein: 8.47g Sodium: 212.31mg Potassium: 195mg Phosphorus: 127.42mg Dietary Fiber: 1.02g Fat: 9.2g

92. Tofu Hoisin Sauté

Preparation Time: 15 minutes

Cooking Time: 20 minutes
Servings: 4
Ingredients:

- 2 tablespoons of hoisin sauce
- 2 tablespoons of rice vinegar
- 1 teaspoon of cornstarch
- 2 tablespoons of olive oil
- 1 (15-ounce) package extra-firm tofu, cut into 1-inch cubes
- 2 cups of unpeeled cubed eggplant
- 2 scallions, white and green parts, sliced
- 2 teaspoons of minced garlic
- 1 jalapeño pepper, minced
- 2 tablespoons of chopped fresh cilantro

Directions:

1. In a small bowl, whisk together the hoisin sauce, rice vinegar, and cornstarch and set aside.
2. In a large skillet over medium-high heat, heat the olive oil. Add the tofu, and sauté gently until golden brown, about 10 minutes, and transfer to a plate.
3. Reduce the heat to medium. Add the eggplant, scallions, garlic, jalapeño pepper, and sauté until tender and fragrant, about 6 minutes.
4. Stir in the reserved sauce, and toss until the sauce thickens about 2 minutes. Stir in the tofu and cilantro, and serve hot.
5. Low-sodium tip Hoisin sauce is made with soy sauce, containing a hefty amount of sodium per serving. This recipe would still be tasty, while slightly less intensely flavored if you use 1 tablespoon of hoisin sauce instead of 2 tablespoons.

Nutrition: Calories: 105 Total fat: 4g Saturated fat: 1g Cholesterol: 0mg Sodium: 234mg Carbohydrates: 9g Fiber: 2g Phosphorus: 105mg Potassium: 192mg Protein: 8g

93. <u>Zucchini Noodles with Spring Vegetables</u>

Preparation Time: 20 minutes
Cooking Time: 10 minutes
Servings: 6
Ingredients:

- 6 zucchinis, cut into long noodles
- 1 cup of halved snow peas
- 1 cup (3-inch pieces) of asparagus
- 1 tablespoon of olive oil
- 1 teaspoon of minced fresh garlic
- 1 tablespoon of freshly squeezed lemon juice
- 2 tablespoons of chopped fresh basil leaves

Directions:

1. Fill a medium saucepan with water, place over medium-high heat, and bring to a boil.
2. Reduce the heat to medium, and blanch the zucchini ribbons, snow peas, and asparagus by submerging them in the water for 1 minute. Drain and rinse immediately under cold water.
3. Pat the vegetables dry with paper towels, and transfer to a large bowl.
4. Place a medium skillet over medium heat, and add the olive oil. Add the garlic, and sauté until tender, about 3 minutes.
5. Add the lemon juice

6. Add the zucchini mixture, and basil and toss until well combined.
7. Serve immediately.

Nutrition: Calories: 52 Total fat: 2g Saturated fat: 0g Cholesterol: 0mg Sodium: 7mg Carbohydrates: 4g Fiber: 1g Phosphorus: 40mg Potassium: 197mg Protein: 2g

94. <u>Stir-Fried Vegetables</u>

Preparation Time: 15 minutes
Cooking Time: 15 minutes
Servings: 4
Ingredients:

- 2 teaspoons of olive oil
- ½ medium red onion, sliced
- 1 tablespoon of grated peeled fresh ginger
- 2 teaspoons of minced garlic
- 2 cups of broccoli florets
- 2 cups of cauliflower florets
- 1 red bell pepper, diced
- 1 cup of sliced carrots

Directions:

1. In a large skillet over medium-high heat, heat the olive oil.
2. Add the onion, ginger, and garlic and sauté until softened, about 3 minutes.
3. Add the broccoli, cauliflower, bell pepper, carrots, and sauté until tender, about 10 minutes.
4. Serve hot.

Nutrition: Calories: 50 Total fat: 1g Saturated fat: 0g Cholesterol: 0mg Sodium: 26mg Carbohydrates: 6g Fiber: 2g Phosphorus: 36mg Potassium: 198mg Protein: 1g

95. <u>Lime Asparagus Spaghetti</u>

Preparation Time: 5 minutes
Cooking Time: 20 minutes
Servings: 6
Ingredients:

- 1 pound of asparagus spears, trimmed and cut into 2-inch pieces
- 2 teaspoons of olive oil
- 2 teaspoons of minced garlic
- 2 teaspoons of all-purpose flour
- 1 cup of Homemade Rice Almond milk (here, or use unsweetened store-bought) or almond milk
- Juice and zest of ½ lemon
- 1 tablespoon of chopped fresh thyme
- Freshly ground black pepper
- 2 cups of cooked spaghetti
- ¼ cup of grated Parmesan cheese

Directions:

1. Fill a large saucepan with water and bring to a boil over high heat. Add the asparagus and blanch until crisp-tender, about 2 minutes. Drain and set aside.

2. In a large skillet over medium-high heat, heat the olive oil. Add the garlic, and sauté until softened, about 2 minutes. Whisk in the flour to create a paste, about 1 minute. Whisk in the rice almond milk, lemon juice, lemon zest, and thyme.
3. Reduce the heat to medium and cook the sauce, whisking constantly, until thickened and creamy, about 3 minutes.
4. Season the sauce with pepper.
5. Stir in the spaghetti and the asparagus.
6. Serve the pasta topped with the Parmesan cheese.

Nutrition: Calories:127 Total fat: 3g Saturated fat: 1g Cholesterol: 4mg Sodium: 67mg Carbohydrates: 19g Fiber: 2g Phosphorus 109mg Potassium: 200mg Protein: 6g

96. Garden Crustless Quiche

Preparation Time: 25 minutes
Cooking Time: 20 minutes
Servings: 6
Ingredients:

- 6 eggs
- 2 egg whites
- ¼ cup of Homemade Rice Almond milk (here or use unsweetened store-bought)
- ¼ cup of shredded Swiss cheese, divided
- ¼ teaspoon of freshly ground black pepper
- 1 teaspoon of unsalted butter, plus more for the pie plate
- 1 teaspoon of minced garlic
- 1 scallion, white and green parts, chopped
- 1 yellow zucchini, chopped
- ½ cup of shredded stemmed kale

Directions:

1. In a medium bowl, beat the eggs, egg whites, rice almond milk, half the Swiss cheese, and the pepper until well blended, and set aside.
2. Preheat the oven to 350°F.
3. Grease a 9-inch pie plate with butter and set aside.
4. In a medium skillet over medium-high heat, melt 1 teaspoon of butter. Add the garlic and scallion, and sauté until softened, about 2 minutes.
5. Add the zucchini and kale, and sauté until wilted, about 3 minutes.
6. Transfer the vegetables from the skillet to the pie plate and spreading the vegetables evenly across the bottom.
7. Pour the egg mixture into the pie plate, and sprinkle with the remaining half of the Swiss cheese.
8. Bake until the quiche is puffed and lightly browned, 15 to 20 minutes.
9. Serve hot, warm, or cold.
10. Ingredient tip yellow zucchini, sometimes called summer squash, is usually lined up in a bin next to the more common green variety. You can interchange green with yellow in this dish.

Nutrition: Calories: 120 Total fat: 8g Saturated fat: 4g Cholesterol: 221mg Sodium: 93mg Carbohydrates: 3g Fiber: 0g Phosphorus 120mg Potassium: 189mg Protein: 9g

97. Spicy Cabbage Dish

Preparation Time: 10 minutes
Cooking Time: 4 hours

Servings: 4
Ingredients:

- 2 yellow onions, chopped
- 10 cups red cabbage, shredded
- 1 cup plums, pitted and chopped
- 1 teaspoon cinnamon powder
- 1 garlic clove, minced
- 1 teaspoon cumin seeds
- ¼ teaspoon cloves, ground
- 2 tablespoons red wine vinegar
- 1 teaspoon coriander seeds
- ½ cup water

Directions:

1. Add cabbage, onion, plums, garlic, cumin, cinnamon, cloves, vinegar, coriander and water to your Slow Cooker.
2. Stir well.
3. Place lid and cook on LOW for 4 hours.
4. Divide between serving platters.
5. Enjoy!

Nutrition: Calories: 197 Fat: 1g Carbohydrates: 14g Protein: 3g Phosphorus: 115mg Potassium: 119mg Sodium: 75mg

98. <u>Extreme Balsamic Chicken</u>

Preparation Time: 10 minutes
Cooking Time: 35 minutes
Servings: 4
Ingredients:

- 3 boneless chicken breasts, skinless
- Sunflower seeds to taste
- ¼ cup almond flour
- 2/3 cups low-fat chicken broth
- 1 ½ teaspoons arrowroot
- ½ cup low sugar raspberry preserve
- 1 ½ tablespoons balsamic vinegar

Directions:

1. Cut chicken breast into bite-sized pieces and season them with seeds.
2. Dredge the chicken pieces in flour and shake off any excess.
3. Take a non-stick skillet and place it over medium heat.
4. Add chicken to the skillet and cook for 15 minutes, making sure to turn them half-way through.
5. Remove chicken and transfer to platter.
6. Add arrowroot, broth, raspberry preserve to the skillet and stir.
7. Stir in balsamic vinegar and reduce heat to low, stir-cook for a few minutes.
8. Transfer the chicken back to the sauce and cook for 15 minutes more.
9. Serve and enjoy!

Nutrition: Calories: 546 Fat: 35g Carbohydrates: 11g Protein: 44g Phosphorus: 120mg Potassium: 117mg Sodium: 85mg

99. Enjoyable Green lettuce and Bean Medley

Servings: 4
Preparation Time: 10 minutes
Cooking Time: 4 hours
Ingredients:

- 5 carrots, sliced
- 1 ½ cups great northern beans, dried
- 2 garlic cloves, minced
- 1 yellow onion, chopped
- Pepper to taste
- ½ teaspoon oregano, dried
- 5 ounces baby green lettuce
- 4 ½ cups low sodium veggie stock
- 2 teaspoons lemon peel, grated
- 3 tablespoon lemon juice

Directions:

1. Add beans, onion, carrots, garlic, oregano and stock to your Slow Cooker.
2. Stir well.
3. Place lid and cook on HIGH for 4 hours.
4. Add green lettuce, lemon juice and lemon peel.
5. Stir and let it sit for 5 minutes.
6. Divide between serving platters and enjoy!

Nutrition: Calories: 219 Fat: 8g Carbohydrates: 14g Protein: 8g Phosphorus: 210mg Potassium: 217mg Sodium: 85mg

100. Tantalizing Cauliflower and Dill Mash

Preparation Time: 10 minutes
Cooking Time: 6 hours
Servings: 6
Ingredients:

- 1 cauliflower head, florets separated
- 1/3 cup dill, chopped
- 6 garlic cloves
- 2 tablespoons olive oil
- Pinch of black pepper

Directions:

1. Add cauliflower to Slow Cooker.
2. Add dill, garlic and water to cover them.
3. Place lid and cook on HIGH for 5 hours.
4. Drain the flowers.
5. Season with pepper and add oil, mash using potato masher.
6. Whisk and serve.
7. Enjoy!

Nutrition: Calories: 207 Fat: 4g Carbohydrates: 14g Protein: 3g Phosphorus: 130mg Potassium: 107mg Sodium: 105mg

101. Green Tuna Salad

Preparation Time: 10 minutes
Cooking Time: 15 -20 minutes
Servings: 2
Ingredients:

- 5 ounces of tuna (in freshwater only)
- 2-3 cups of lettuce
- 1 cup of baby marrows
- 1/2 cup of red bell pepper
- 1/4 cup of red onion
- 1/4 cup of fresh thyme
- 2 tbsp olive oil
- 1/8 tsp of black pepper
- 2 tbsp of red wine vinegar

Directions:

1. Chop the bell pepper, onion, baby marrow, and thyme into small pieces.
2. Add a 3/4 cup of water to a saucepan and add the bell pepper, onion, baby marrow, and thyme to the pan. Let it boil, steam the vegetables by adding a lid on top of the saucepan—steam for 10 minutes.
3. Remove the vegetables and drain them.
4. Combine the vegetables (once cooled down) with the chopped tuna.
5. Mix olive oil, red wine vinegar, and black pepper to create a salad dressing.
6. Add the mixture on a bed of lettuce and drizzle the dressing on top.

Nutrition: Calories: 210 Fat: 1.5g Carbs: 4g Protein: 43.3g Sodium: 726mg Potassium: 582mg Phosphorus: 296mg

102. Roasted Chicken and Vegetables

Preparation Time: 10 minutes
Cooking Time: 45 minutes

Servings: 2

Ingredients:

- 8 oz chicken strips
- 5 oz green beans
- 2 tbsp sesame seed oil
- 1 tsp of Cajun chicken spice
- ½ tbsp Italian herb dressing

Directions:

1. Heat the oven to 400 degrees-Fahrenheit
2. Fill up a large pot with water until it is ¾ full.
3. Chop off the tips of the green beans.
4. Line a 9 x 13-inch oven tray with parchment paper or spray the oven tray with cooking spray.
5. Place the chicken strips on the tray side, with the green beans
6. Add Cajun chicken spice to the chicken breasts and drizzle sesame seed oil over the chicken and vegetables.
7. Roast for 20 minutes.
8. Drizzle Italian herb dressing on top of the chicken and vegetables and roast for another 5-10 minutes.

Nutrition: Calories: 263 Fat: 6g Sodium: 366mg Potassium: 879mg Phosphorus: 275mg Carbs: 28.6g Protein: 23g

103. <u>Sirloin Medallions, Green Squash, and Pineapple</u>

Preparation Time: 10 minutes
Cooking Time: 40 minutes
Servings: 4
Ingredients:

- 1 lb. of sirloin medallions
- 1 medium baby marrows
- 1 yellow squash
- ½ onion
- 8 oz of thinly sliced pineapple
- 3 tbsp of olive oil
- 2 tsp of ginger
- ½ tsp of salt
- 1 garlic clove

Directions:

1. Retrieve thinly sliced pineapple rings from a can and drain. Set the juice aside.
2. Slice garlic and ginger into fine pieces.
3. Mix the pineapple juice, ginger, garlic, salt, and olive oil together in a bowl to create a dressing for the sirloin medallions.
4. Add the sirloin medallions to the marinade and let it sit for 10-15 minutes.
5. Heat the oven to 450 degrees-Fahrenheit and line 2 oven trays with parchment paper.
6. Chop the squash into little ½-inch circles and place it on the parchment paper—drizzle 1tbsp of olive oil on top of it.
7. Cut the onion into small wedges, add to the tray and drizzle with olive oil.
8. Add pineapple rings next to the squash on the first tray and roast for 6 minutes.
9. Remove the pan and turn the squash and pineapple over. Add the onion onto the tray and roast it for another 5 minutes. Close the fruit and vegetables with foil to lock in the heat and set aside.

10. Remove sirloin medallions from the marinade. Line another oven tray pan with parchment paper and place the sirloin medallions on top.
11. Cook for 5 minutes and flip the sirloin to cook for another 5 minutes on the other side.
12. Serve the sirloin medallions with the vegetables and pineapple on a platter.

Nutrition: Calories: 264 Fat: 12g Carbs: 14g Protein: 25g Sodium: 150mg Potassium: 685mg Phosphorus: 257mg

104.   Chicken and Savory Rice

Preparation Time: 15 minutes
Cooking Time: 45 minutes
Servings: 4
Ingredients:
- 4 medium chicken breasts
- 1 baby marrow (chopped)
- 1 red bell pepper (chopped)
- 3 tbsp olive oil
- 1 onion
- 1 garlic clove (minced)
- ½ tsp of black pepper
- 1 tbsp of cumin
- ¼ tsp cayenne pepper
- 2 cups of brown rice

Directions:
1. Add 2 tbsp of olive oil to medium heat and place the chicken breasts into the pan. Cook for 15 minutes and remove from the pan.
2. Add another tbsp of olive oil to the pan, and add the baby marrow, onion, red pepper, and corn.
3. Sauté the vegetables on medium heat for 10 minutes or until golden brown.
4. Add minced garlic, black pepper, cumin, and cayenne pepper to the vegetables. Stir the vegetables and spices together well.
5. Cut the chicken into cube and add it back to the pan. Mix it with the vegetables for 5 minutes.
6. In a medium pot, fill it up with water until it is 2/3 full. Add the rice to the pot and cook it for 35-40 minutes.
7. Serve the chicken and vegetable mixture on a bed of rice with extra black pepper.

Nutrition: Calories: 374 Fat: 6.2g Carbs: 65g Protein: 15g Sodium: 520mg Potassium: 645mg Phosphorus: 268mg

105.   Salmon and Green Beans

Preparation Time: 10 minutes
Cooking Time: 20 minutes
Servings: 4
Ingredients:
- 3 oz x 4 salmon fillets
- ½ lb. of green beans
- 2 tbsp of dill
- 2 tbsp of coriander
- 2 lemons
- 2 tbsp olive oil
- 4 tbsp of mayonnaise

Directions:

1. Rinse and salmon fillets and wait for it to dry. Don't remove the skin.
2. Wash green beans and chop the tips of the green beans.
3. Heat the oven up to 425 degrees-Fahrenheit.
4. Spray an oven sheet pan with cooking spray and place the salmon fillets on the sheet pan.
5. Chop up the dill and combine it with the mayonnaise.
6. Put mayo mixture on top of the salmon fillets.
7. Place the green beans next to the salmon fillets and drizzle olive oil on top of everything.
8. Place the oven baking sheet in the middle of the oven and cook for 15 minutes.
9. Slice the lemons into wedges and serve with the salmon fillets and green beans.

Nutrition: Calories: 399 Fat: 21g Carbs: 8g Protein: 38g Sodium: 229mg Potassium: 1000mg Phosphorus: 723mg

106. Lentil Veggie Burgers

Preparation Time: 15 minutes
Cooking Time: 10 minutes
Servings: 4
Ingredients:

- 2½ cups cooked white rice
- ½ cup cooked red lentils, drained and rinsed
- 2 eggs, lightly beaten
- 2 tablespoons chopped fresh parsley
- 2 teaspoons chopped fresh basil leaves
- Juice and zest of 1 lime
- 1 teaspoon minced garlic
- 1 tablespoon olive oil

Directions:

1. In a food processor (or blender), pulse the rice, lentils, eggs, parsley, basil, lime juice, lime zest, and garlic until the mixture holds together.
2. Transfer the rice mixture to a medium bowl, and set in the refrigerator until it firms up, about 1 hour.
3. Form the rice mixture into 4 patties.
4. In a large skillet over medium-high heat, heat the olive oil.
5. Add the veggie patties and cook until golden, about 5 minutes. Flip the patties over. Cook the other side for 5 minutes.
6. Transfer the burgers to a paper towel - lined plate.
7. Serve the veggie burgers hot with your favorite toppings.

Nutrition: Calories: 247 Total fat: 7g Saturated fat: 2g Cholesterol: 106mg Sodium: 36mg Carbohydrates: 31g Fiber: 3g Phosphorus 120mg Potassium: 183mg Protein: 8g

107. Baked Cauliflower Rice Cakes

Preparation Time: 20 minutes
Cooking Time: 10 minutes
Servings: 6
Ingredients:

- Olive oil for the pan
- 2 cups of chopped blanched cauliflower
- 2 cups of cooked white basmati rice
- ¼ cup of plain yogurt

- 2 eggs, lightly beaten
- ½ cup of grated Cheddar cheese
- ¼ teaspoon of ground nutmeg
- Freshly ground black pepper

Directions:

1. Preheat the oven to 350°f.
2. Lightly coat 6 cups of a standard muffin tin with olive oil.
3. In a large bowl, mix the cauliflower, rice, yogurt, eggs, cheese, and nutmeg.
4. Season the mixture with pepper.
5. Evenly divide the cauliflower mixture among the 6 prepared muffin cups.
6. Bake until golden and slightly puffy, about 20 minutes.
7. Let them stand for 5 minutes, then run a knife around the edges to loosen.
8. Serve hot, warm, or cold.

Nutrition: Calories: 141 Total fat: 5g Saturated fat: 3g Cholesterol: 82mg Sodium: 98mg Carbohydrates: 18g Fiber: 1g Phosphorus 119mg Potassium: 178mg Protein: 7g

108.   Curried Cauliflower

Preparation time: 5 minutes
Cooking time: 20 minutes
Servings: 4 servings
Ingredients:
- 1 tsp. turmeric
- 1 diced onion
- 1 tbsp. chopped fresh cilantro
- 1 tsp. cumin
- ½ diced chili
- ½ cup water
- 1 minced garlic clove
- 1 tbsp. coconut oil
- 1 tsp. garam masala
- 2 cups cauliflower florets

Directions:
1. Add the oil to a skillet on medium heat.
2. Sauté the onion and garlic for 5 minutes until soft.
3. Add the cumin, turmeric and garam masala and stir to release the aromas.
4. Now add the chili to the pan along with the cauliflower.
5. Stir to coat.
6. Pour in the water and reduce the heat to a simmer for 15 minutes.
7. Garnish with cilantro to serve.

Nutrition: Calories: 108 kcal; Total Fat: 7 g; Saturated Fat: 0 g; Cholesterol: 0 mg; Sodium: 35 mg; Total Carbs: 11 g; Fiber: 0 g; Sugar: 0 g; Protein: 2 g

109.   Chinese Tempeh Stir Fry

Preparation time: 5 minutes
Cooking time: 15 minutes
Servings: 2 servings
Ingredients:
- 2 oz. sliced tempeh
- 1 cup cooked rice
- 1 minced garlic clove
- ½ cup green onions
- 1 tsp. minced fresh ginger
- 1 tbsp. coconut oil
- ½ cup corn

Directions:
1. Heat the oil in a skillet or wok on a high heat and add the garlic and ginger.
2. Sauté for 1 minute.
3. Now add the tempeh and cook for 5-6 minutes before adding the corn for a further 10 minutes.

4. Now add the green onions and serve over rice.

Nutrition: Calories: 304 kcal; Total Fat: 4 g; Saturated Fat: 0 g; Cholesterol: 0 mg; Sodium: 91 mg; Total Carbs: 35 g; Fiber: 0 g; Sugar: 0 g; Protein: 10 g

110. Egg White Frittata with Penne

Preparation time: 15 minutes
Cooking time: 30 minutes
Servings: 4 servings
Ingredients:

- Egg whites- 6
- Rice almond milk – ¼ cup
- Chopped fresh parsley – 1 tbsp.
- Chopped fresh thyme – 1 tsp
- Chopped fresh chives – 1 tsp
- Ground black pepper
- Olive oil – 2 tsp.
- Small sweet onion – ¼, chopped
- Minced garlic – 1 tsp
- Boiled and chopped red bell pepper – ½ cup
- Cooked penne – 2 cups

Directions:

1. Preheat the oven to 350f.
2. In a bowl, whisk together the egg whites, rice almond milk, parsley, thyme, chives, and pepper.
3. Heat the oil in a skillet.
4. Sauté the onion, garlic, red pepper for 4 minutes or until they are softened.
5. Add the cooked penne to the skillet.
6. Pour the egg mixture over the pasta and shake the pan to coat the pasta.
7. Leave the skillet on the heat for 1 minute to set the frittata's bottom and then transfer the skillet to the oven.
8. Bake the frittata for 25 minutes, or until it is set and golden brown.
9. Serve.

Nutrition: Calories: 170 kcal; Total Fat: 3 g; Saturated Fat: 0 g; Cholesterol: 0 mg; Sodium: 90 mg; Total Carbs: 25 g; Fiber: 0 g; Sugar: 0 g; Protein: 10 g

111. Vegetable Fried Rice

Preparation time: 20 minutes
Cooking time: 20 minutes
Servings: 6 servings
Ingredients:

- Olive oil – 1 tbsp.
- Sweet onion – ½, chopped
- Grated fresh ginger – 1 tbsp.
- Minced garlic - 2 tsp
- Sliced carrots   1 cup
- Chopped eggplant – ½ cup
- Peas – ½ cup

- Green beans – ½ cup, cut into 1-inch pieces
- Chopped fresh cilantro – 2 tbsp.
- Cooked rice – 3 cups

Directions:
1. Heat the olive oil in a skillet.
2. Sauté the ginger, onion, and garlic for 3 minutes or until softened.
3. Stir in carrot, eggplant, green beans, and peas and sauté for 3 minutes more.
4. Add cilantro and rice.
5. Sauté, constantly stirring, for about 10 minutes or until the rice is heated through.
6. Serve.

Nutrition: Calories: 189 kcal; Total Fat: 7 g; Saturated Fat: 0 g; Cholesterol: 0 mg; Sodium: 13 mg; Total Carbs: 28 g; Fiber: 0 g; Sugar: 0 g; Protein: 6 g

112. Couscous Burgers

Preparation time: 20 minutes
Cooking time: 10 minutes
Servings: 4 servings
Ingredients:

- chickpeas – ½ cup
- Chopped fresh cilantro – 2 tbsp.
- Chopped fresh parsley
- Lemon juice - 1 tbsp.
- Lemon zest – 2 tsp
- Minced garlic – 1 tsp
- Cooked couscous – 2 ½ cups
- Eggs – 2, lightly beaten
- Olive oil – 2 tbsp.

Directions:
1. Put the cilantro, chickpeas, parsley, lemon juice, lemon zest, and garlic in a food processor and pulse until a paste form.
2. Transfer the chickpea mixture to a bowl, and add the eggs and couscous. Mix well.
3. Chill the mixture in the refrigerator for 1 hour.
4. Form the couscous mixture into 4 patties.
5. Heat olive oil in a skillet.
6. Place the patties in the skillet, 2 at a time, gently pressing them down with the fork of a spatula.
7. Cook for 5 minutes or until golden, and flip the patties over.
8. Cook the other side for 5 minutes and transfer the cooked burgers to a plate covered with a paper towel.
9. Repeat with the remaining 2 burgers.

Nutrition: Calories: 242 kcal; Total Fat: 10 g; Saturated Fat: 0 g; Cholesterol: 0 mg; Sodium: 43 mg; Total Carbs: 29 g; Fiber: 0 g; Sugar: 0 g; Protein: 9 g

113. Marinated Tofu Stir-Fry

Preparation time: 20 minutes
Cooking time: 20 minutes
Servings: 4 servings
Ingredients:
For the tofu:

- Lemon juice – 1 tbsp.
- Minced garlic – 1 tsp
- Grated fresh ginger – 1 tsp
- Pinch red pepper flakes
- Extra-firm tofu- 5 ounces, pressed well and cubed

For the stir-fry:

- Olive oil – 1 tbsp.
- Cauliflower florets – ½ cup
- Thinly sliced carrots – ½ cup
- Julienned red pepper – ½ cup
- Fresh green beans – ½ cup
- Cooked white rice – 2 cups

Directions:

1. In a bowl, mix the lemon juice, garlic, ginger, and red pepper flakes.
2. Add the tofu and toss to coat.
3. Place the bowl in the refrigerator and marinate for 2 hours.
4. To make the stir-fry, heat the oil in a skillet.
5. Sauté the tofu for 8 minutes or until it is lightly browned and heated through.
6. Add the carrots, and cauliflower and sauté for 5 minutes. Stirring and tossing constantly.
7. Add the red pepper and green beans, sauté for 3 minutes more.
8. Serve over white rice.

Nutrition: Calories: 190 kcal; Total Fat: 6 g; Saturated Fat: 0 g; Cholesterol: 0 mg; Sodium: 22 mg; Total Carbs: 30 g; Fiber: 0 g; Sugar: 0 g; Protein: 6 g

114. <u>Curried Veggie Stir-Fry</u>

Preparation Time: 20 minutes
Cooking Time: 10 minutes
Servings: 6
Ingredients:

- 2 tablespoons of extra-virgin olive oil
- 1 onion, chopped
- 4 garlic cloves, minced
- 4 cups of frozen stir-fry vegetables
- 1 cup unsweetened full-fat coconut almond milk
- 1 cup of water
- 2 tablespoons of green curry paste

Directions:

1. In a wok or non-stick, heat the olive oil over medium-high heat. Stir-fry the onion and garlic for 2 to 3 minutes, until fragrant.
2. Add the frozen stir-fry vegetables and continue to cook for 3 to 4 minutes longer, or until the vegetables are hot.
3. Meanwhile, in a small bowl, combine coconut almond milk, water, and curry paste. Stir until the paste dissolves.
4. Add the broth mixture to the wok and cook for another 2 to 3 minutes, or until the sauce has reduced slightly and all the vegetables are crisp-tender.
5. Serve over couscous or hot cooked rice.

Nutrition: Calories: 293 Total fat: 18g Saturated fat: 10g Sodium: 247mg Phosphorus: 138mg Potassium: 531mg Carbohydrates: 28g Fiber: 7g Protein: 7g Sugar: 4g

115. Chilaquiles

Preparation Time: 20 minutes
Cooking Time: 20 minutes
Servings: 4
Ingredients:

- 3 (8-inch) corn tortillas, cut into strips
- 2 tablespoons of extra-virgin olive oil
- 12 tomatillos, papery covering removed, chopped
- 3 tablespoons for freshly squeezed lime juice
- 1/8 teaspoon of salt
- 1/8 teaspoon of freshly ground black pepper
- 4 large egg whites
- 2 large eggs
- 2 tablespoons of water
- 1 cup of shredded pepper jack cheese

Directions:

1. In a dry nonstick skillet, toast the tortilla strips over medium heat until they are crisp, tossing the pan and stirring occasionally. This should take 4 to 6 minutes. Remove the strips from the pan and set aside.

2. In the same skillet, heat the olive oil over medium heat and add the tomatillos, lime juice, salt, and pepper. Cook and frequently stir for about 8 to 10 minutes until the tomatillos break down and form a sauce. Transfer the sauce to a bowl and set aside.
3. In a small bowl, beat the egg whites, eggs, and water and add to the skillet. Cook the eggs for 3 to 4 minutes, stirring occasionally until they are set and cooked to 160°F.
4. Preheat the oven to 400°F.
5. Toss the tortilla strips in the tomatillo sauce and place in a casserole dish. Top with the scrambled eggs and cheese.
6. Bake for 10 to 15 minutes, or until the cheese starts to brown. Serve.

Nutrition: Calories: 312 Total fat: 20g Saturated fat: 8g Sodium: 345mg Phosphorus: 280mg Potassium: 453mg Carbohydrates: 19g Fiber: 3g Protein: 15g Sugar: 5g

116. Roasted Veggie Sandwiches

Preparation Time: 20 minutes
Cooking Time: 35 minutes
Servings: 6
Ingredients:

- 3 bell peppers, assorted colors, sliced
- 1 cup of sliced yellow summer squash
- 1 red onion, sliced
- 2 tablespoons of extra-virgin olive oil
- 2 tablespoons of balsamic vinegar
- 1/8 teaspoon of salt
- 1/8 teaspoon of freshly ground black pepper
- 3 large whole-wheat pita breads, halved

Directions:

1. Preheat the oven to 400°F.

2. Prepare a parchment paper and line it in a rimmed baking sheet.
3. Spread the bell peppers, squash, and onion on the prepared baking sheet. Sprinkle with the olive oil, vinegar, salt, and pepper.
4. Roast for 30 to 40 minutes, turning the vegetables with a spatula once during cooking, until they are tender and light golden brown.
5. Pile the vegetables into the pita breads and serve.

Nutrition: Calories: 182 Total fat: 5g Saturated fat: 1g Sodium: 234mg Phosphorus: 106mg Potassium: 289mg Carbohydrates: 31g Fiber: 4g Protein: 5g Sugar: 6g

117. <u>Pasta Fagioli</u>

Preparation Time: 25 minutes
Cooking Time: 25 minutes
Servings: 6
Ingredients:
- 1 (15-ounce) can low-sodium great northern beans, drained and rinsed, divided
- 2 cups frozen peppers and onions, thawed, divided
- 5 cups low-sodium vegetable broth
- 1/8 teaspoon salt
- 1/8 teaspoon freshly ground black pepper
- 1 cup whole-grain orecchiette pasta
- 2 tablespoons extra-virgin olive oil
- 1/3 cup grated Parmesan cheese

Directions:
1. In a large saucepan, place the beans and cover with water. Bring to a boil over high heat and boil for 10 minutes. Drain the beans.

2. In a food processor or blender, combine 1/3 cup of beans and 1/3 cup of thawed peppers and onions. Process until smooth.
3. In the same saucepan, combine the pureed mixture, the remaining 1 2/3 cups of peppers and onions, the remaining beans, the broth, and the salt and pepper and bring to a simmer.
4. Add the pasta to the saucepan. Make sure to stir it and bring it to boil, reduce the heat to low, and simmer for 8 to 10 minutes, or until the pasta is tender.
5. Serve drizzled with olive oil and topped with Parmesan cheese.

Nutrition: Calories: 245 Total fat: 7g Saturated fat: 2g Sodium: 269mg Phosphorus: 188mgPotassium: 592mg Carbohydrates: 36g Fiber: 7g Protein: 12g Sugar: 4g

118.Roasted Peach Open-Face Sandwich

Preparation Time: 5 minutes
Cooking Time: 15 minutes
Servings: 4
Ingredients:

- 2 fresh peaches, peeled and sliced
- 1 tablespoon of extra-virgin olive oil
- 1 tablespoon of freshly squeezed lemon juice
- 1/8 teaspoon of salt
- 1/8 teaspoon of freshly ground black pepper
- 4 ounces of cream cheese, at room temperature
- 2 teaspoons of fresh thyme leaves

- 4 bread slices

Directions:
1. Preheat the oven to 400°F.
2. Arrange the peaches on a rimmed baking sheet. Brush them with olive oil on both sides.
3. Roast the peaches for 10 to 15 minutes, until they are lightly golden brown around the edges. Sprinkle with lemon juice, salt, and pepper.
4. In a small bowl, combine the cream cheese and thyme and mix well.
5. Toast the bread. Get the toasted bread and spread it with the cream cheese mixture. Top with the peaches and serve.

Nutrition: Calories: 250 Total fat: 13g Saturated fat: 6g Sodium: 376mg Phosphorus: 163mg Potassium: 260mg Carbohydrates: 28g Fiber: 3g Protein: 6g Sugar: 8g

119. Spicy Corn and Rice Burritos

Preparation Time: 10 minutes
Cooking Time: 20 minutes
Servings: 4
Ingredients:
- 3 tablespoons of extra-virgin olive oil, divided
- 1 (10-ounce) package of frozen cooked rice
- 1½ cups of frozen yellow corn
- 1 tablespoon of chili powder
- 1 cup of shredded pepper jack cheese

- 4 large or 6 small corn tortillas

Directions:
1. Put the skillet in over medium heat and put 2 tablespoons of olive oil. Add the rice, corn, and chili powder and cook for 4 to 6 minutes, or until the ingredients are hot.
2. Transfer the ingredients from the pan into a medium bowl. Let cool for 15 minutes.
3. Stir the cheese into the rice mixture.
4. Heat the tortillas using the directions from the package to make them pliable. Fill the corn tortillas with the rice mixture, then roll them up.
5. At this point, you can serve them as is, or you can fry them first. Heat the remaining tablespoon of olive oil in a large skillet. Fry the burritos, seam-side down at first, turning once, until they are brown and crisp, about 4 to 6 minutes per side, then serve.

Nutrition: Calories: 386 Total fat: 21g Saturated fat: 7g Sodium: 510mg Phosphorus: 304mg Potassium: 282mg Carbohydrates: 41g Fiber: 4g Protein: 11g Sugar: 2g

120. <u>Crust less Cabbage Quiche</u>

Preparation Time: 10 minutes
Cooking Time: 40 minutes
Servings: 6
Ingredients:
- Olive oil cooking spray
- 2 tablespoons of extra-virgin olive oil
- 3 cups of coleslaw blend with carrots
- 3 large eggs, beaten
- 3 large egg whites, beaten
- ½ cup of half-and-half
- 1 teaspoon of dried dill weed

- 1/8 teaspoon of salt
- 1/8 teaspoon of freshly ground black pepper
- 1 cup of grated Swiss cheese

Directions:
1. Preheat the oven to 350°F. Spray pie plate (9-inch) with cooking spray and set aside.
2. In a skillet, put an oil and put it in medium heat. Add the coleslaw mix and cook for 4 to 6 minutes, stirring, until the cabbage is tender. Transfer the vegetables from the pan to a medium bowl to cool.
3. Meanwhile, in another medium bowl, combine the eggs and egg whites, half-and-half, dill, salt, and pepper and beat to combine.
4. Stir the cabbage mixture into the egg mixture and pour into the prepared pie plate.
5. Sprinkle with the cheese.
6. Bake for 30 to 35 minutes, or until the mixture is puffed, set, and light golden brown. Let stand for 5 minutes, then slice to serve.

Nutrition: Calories: 203 Total fat: 16g Saturated fat: 6g Sodium: 321mg Phosphorus: 169mg Potassium: 155mg Carbohydrates: 5g Fiber: 1g Protein: 11g Sugar: 4g

121. Vegetable Confetti

Preparation Time: 25 minutes
Cooking Time: 15 minutes
Servings: 1
Ingredients:
- ½ red bell pepper
- ½ green pepper, boiled and chopped

- 4 scallions, thinly sliced
- ½ tsp. of ground cumin
- 3 tbsp. of vegetable oil
- 1 ½ tbsp. of white wine vinegar
- Black pepper to taste

Directions:
1. Join all fixings and blend well.
2. Chill in the fridge.
3. You can include a large portion of slashed jalapeno pepper for an increasingly fiery blend

Nutrition: Calories: 230 Fat: 25g Fiber: 3g Carbs: 24g Protein: 43g

122. <u>Creamy Veggie Casserole</u>

Preparation Time: 25 minutes
Cooking Time: 35 minutes
Servings: 4
Ingredients:
- 1/3 cup extra-virgin olive oil, divided
- 1 onion, chopped
- 2 tablespoons flour
- 3 cups low-sodium vegetable broth
- 3 cups frozen California blend vegetables
- 1 cup crushed crisp rice cereal

Directions:
1. Preheat the oven to 375°F.
2. Next is heat 2 tablespoons of olive oil in a large skillet over medium heat. Add the onion and cook for 3 to 4 minutes, stirring, until the onion is tender.

3. Add the flour and stir for 2 minutes.
4. Add the broth to the saucepan, stirring for 3 to 4 minutes, or until the sauce starts to thicken.
5. Add the vegetables to the saucepan. Simmer and cook until vegetables are tender (for six to eight minutes).
6. When the vegetables are done, pour the mixture into a 3-quart casserole dish.
7. Sprinkle the vegetables with the crushed cereal.
8. Bake for 20 to 25 minutes or until the cereal is golden brown and the filling is bubbling. Let cool for 5 minutes and serve.

Nutrition: Calories: 234 Total fat: 18g Saturated fat: 3g Sodium: 139mg Phosphorus: 21mg Potassium: 210mg Carbohydrates: 16g Fiber: 3g Protein: 3g Sugar: 5g

123. <u>Vegetable Green Curry</u>

Preparation Time: 20 minutes
Cooking Time: 20 minutes
Servings: 6
Ingredients:

- 2 tablespoons extra-virgin olive oil
- 1 head broccoli, cut into florets
- 1 bunch asparagus, cut into 2-inch lengths
- 3 tablespoons water
- 2 tablespoons green curry paste
- 1 medium eggplant
- 1/8 teaspoon salt
- 1/8 teaspoon freshly ground black pepper
- 2/3 cup plain whole-almond milk yogurt

Directions:

1. Put olive oil in a large saucepan in a medium heat. Add the broccoli and stir-fry for 5 minutes. Add the asparagus and stir-fry for another 3 minutes.
2. Meanwhile, in a small bowl, combine the water with the green curry paste.
3. Add the eggplant, curry-water mixture, salt, and pepper. Stir-fry or until vegetables are all tender.
4. Add the yogurt. Heat through but avoid simmering. Serve.

Nutrition: Calories: 113 Total fat: 6g Saturated fat: 1g Sodium: 174mg Phosphorus: 117mg Potassium: 569mg Carbohydrates: 13g Fiber: 6g Protein: 5g Sugar: 7g

124. Spiced Lamb Burgers

Preparation Time: 10 minutes
Cooking Time: 20 minutes
Servings: 2
Ingredients:

- 1 tablespoon extra-virgin olive oil
- 1 teaspoon cumin
- ½ finely diced red onion
- 1 minced garlic clove
- 1 teaspoon harissa spices
- 1 cup arugula
- 1 juiced lemon
- 6-ounce lean ground lamb
- 1 tablespoon parsley
- ½ cup low-fat plain yogurt

Directions:

1. Preheat the broiler on medium to high heat. Mix the ground lamb, red onion, parsley, Harissa spices, and olive oil until combined.
2. Shape 1-inch-thick patties using wet hands. Add the patties to a baking tray and place under the broiler for 7-8 minutes on each side. Mix the yogurt, lemon juice, and cumin and serve over the lamb burgers with arugula's side salad.

125.   Pork Loins with Leeks

Preparation Time: 10 minutes
Cooking Time: 35 minutes
Servings: 2
Ingredients:

- 1 sliced leek
- 1 tablespoon mustard seeds
- 6-ounce pork tenderloin
- 1 tablespoon cumin seeds
- 1 tablespoon dry mustard
- 1 tablespoon extra-virgin oil

Directions:

1. Preheat the broiler to medium-high heat. In a dry skillet, heat mustard and cumin seeds until they start to pop (3-5 minutes). Grind seeds using a pestle and mortar or blender and then mix in the dry mustard.
2. Massage the pork on all sides using the mustard blend and add to a baking tray to broil for 25-30 minutes or until cooked through. Turn once halfway through.
3. Remove and place to one side, then heat-up the oil in a pan on medium heat and add the leeks for 5-6 minutes or until soft. Serve the pork tenderloin on a bed of leeks and enjoy it!

Nutrition: Calories 139 Fat 5g Carbs 2g Phosphorus 278mg Potassium 45mg Sodium 47mg Protein 18g

126. Chinese Beef Wraps

Preparation Time: 10 minutes
Cooking Time: 30 minutes
Servings: 2
Ingredients:

- 2 iceberg lettuce leaves
- ½ diced cucumber
- 1 teaspoon canola oil
- 5-ounce lean ground beef
- 1 teaspoon ground ginger
- 1 tablespoon chili flakes
- 1 minced garlic clove
- 1 tablespoon rice wine vinegar

Directions:

1. Mix the ground meat with the garlic, rice wine vinegar, chili flakes, and ginger in a bowl. Heat-up oil in a skillet over medium heat.
2. Put the beef in the pan and cook for 20-25 minutes or until cooked through. Serve beef mixture with diced cucumber in each lettuce wrap and fold.

Nutrition: Calories 156 Fat 2g Carbs 4 g Phosphorus 1 mg Sodium 54mg Protein 14g Potassium 0mg

127. Spicy Lamb Curry

Preparation Time: 15 minutes
Cooking Time: 2 hours 15 minutes
Servings: 6-8
Ingredients:

- 4 teaspoons ground coriander
- 4 teaspoons ground coriander
- 4 teaspoons ground cumin
- ¾ teaspoon ground ginger
- 2 teaspoons ground cinnamon
- ½ teaspoon ground cloves

- ½ teaspoon ground cardamom
- 2 tablespoons sweet paprika
- ½ tablespoon cayenne pepper
- 2 teaspoons chili powder
- 2 teaspoons salt
- 1 tablespoon coconut oil
- 2 pounds boneless lamb, trimmed and cubed into 1-inch size
- Salt
- ground black pepper
- 2 cups onions, chopped
- 1¼ cups water
- 1 cup of coconut almond milk

Directions:

1. For spice mixture in a bowl, mix all spices. Keep aside. Season the lamb with salt and black pepper.
2. Warm oil on medium-high heat in a large Dutch oven. Add lamb and stir fry for around 5 minutes. Add onion and cook approximately 4-5 minutes.
3. Stir in the spice mixture and cook approximately 1 minute. Add water and coconut almond milk and provide some boil on high heat.
4. Adjust the heat to low and simmer, covered for approximately 1-120 minutes or until the lamb's desired doneness. Uncover and simmer for about 3-4 minutes. Serve hot.

Nutrition: Calories: 466 Fat: 10g Carbohydrates: 23g Protein: 36g Potassium 599 mg Sodium 203 mg Phosphorus 0mg

128. Roast Beef

Preparation Time: 25 minutes
Cooking Time: 55 minutes
Servings: 3
Ingredients:

- Quality rump or sirloin tip roast

- Pepper & herbs

Directions:
1. Place in a roasting pan on a shallow rack. Season with pepper and herbs. Insert meat thermometer in the center or thickest part of the roast.
2. Roast to the desired degree of doneness. After removing from over for about 15 minutes, let it chill. In the end, the roast should be moister than well done.

Nutrition: Calories 158 Protein 24 g Fat 6 g Carbs 0 g Phosphorus 206 mg Potassium 328 mg Sodium 55 mg

129.   Peppercorn Pork Chops

Preparation time: 30 min
Cooking Time: 30 minutes
Servings: 4

Ingredients:
- 1 tablespoon crushed black peppercorns
- 4 pork loin chops
- 2 tablespoons olive oil
- 1/4 cup butter
- 5 garlic cloves
- 1 cup green and red bell peppers
- 1/2 cup pineapple juice

Directions:
1. Sprinkle and press peppercorns into both sides of pork chops.
2. Heat oil, butter and garlic cloves in a large skillet over medium heat, stirring frequently.
3. Add pork chops and cook uncovered for 5–6 minutes.
4. Dice the bell peppers. Add the bell peppers and pineapple juice to the pork chops.
5. Cover and simmer for another 5–6 minutes or until pork is thoroughly cooked.

Nutrition: Calories 317, Total Fat 25.7g, Saturated Fat 10.5g, Cholesterol 66mg, Sodium 126mg, Total Carbohydrate 9.2g, Dietary Fiber 2g, Total Sugars 6.4g, Protein 13.2g, Calcium 39mg, Iron 1mg, Potassium 250mg, Phosphorus 115 mg

130.   Pork Chops with Apples, Onions

Preparation time: 30 min
Cooking Time: 60 minutes
Servings: 4

Ingredients:
- 4 pork chops
- salt and pepper to taste
- 2 onions, sliced into rings
- 2 apples - peeled, cored, and sliced into rings
- 3 tablespoons honey
- 2 teaspoons freshly ground black pepper

Directions:
1. Preheat oven to 375 degrees F.
2. Season pork chops with salt and pepper to taste, and arrange in a medium oven-safe skillet. Top pork chops with onions and apples. Sprinkle with honey. Season with 2 teaspoons pepper.

3. Cover, and bake 1 hour in the preheated oven, pork chops have reached an internal temperature of 145 degrees F.

Nutrition: Calories 307, Total Fat 16.1g, Saturated Fat 6g, Cholesterol 55mg, Sodium 48mg, Total Carbohydrate 26.8g, Dietary Fiber 3.1g, Total Sugars 21.5g, Protein 15.1g, Calcium 30mg, Iron 1mg, Potassium 387mg, Phosphorus 315 mg

131. Baked Lamb Chops

Preparation time: 10 min
Cooking Time: 45 minutes
Servings: 4
Ingredients:
- 2 eggs
- 2 teaspoons Worcestershire sauce
- 8 (5.5 ounces) lamb chops
- 2 cups graham crackers

Directions:
1. Preheat oven to 375 degrees F.
2. In a medium bowl, combine the eggs and the Worcestershire sauce; stir well. Dip each lamb chop in the sauce and then lightly dredge in the graham crackers. Then arrange them in a 9x13-inch baking dish.
3. Bake at 375 degrees F for 20 minutes, turn chops over and cook for 20 more minutes, or to the desired doneness.

Nutrition: Calories176, Total Fat 5.7g, Saturated Fat 1.4g, Cholesterol 72mg, Sodium 223mg, Total Carbohydrate 21.9g, Dietary Fiber 0.8g, Total Sugars 9.2g, Protein 9.1g, Vitamin D 5mcg, Calcium 17mg, Iron 2mg, Potassium 121mg, Phosphorus 85 mg

132. Grilled Lamb Chops with Pineapple

Preparation time: 15 min
Cooking Time: 55 minutes
Servings: 4
Ingredients:
- 1 lemon, zest and juiced
- 2 tablespoons chopped fresh oregano
- 2 cloves garlic, minced
- salt and black pepper to taste
- 8 (3 ounces) lamb chops
- 1/2 cup fresh unsweetened pineapple juice
- 1 cup pineapples

Directions:
1. Whisk together the lemon zest and juice, oregano, garlic, salt, and black pepper in a bowl; pour into a resealable plastic bag. Add the lamb chops, coat with the marinade, squeeze out excess air, and seal the bag.
2. Set aside to marinate.
3. Preheat an outdoor grill for medium-high heat, and lightly oil the grate.
4. Bring the pineapple juice in a small saucepan over high heat.
5. Reduce heat to medium-low, and continue simmering until the liquid has reduced to half of its original volume, about 45 minutes.
6. Stir in the pineapples and set aside.

7. Remove the lamb from the marinade and shake off excess.
8. Discard the remaining marinade.
9. Cook the chops on the preheated grill until they start to firm and are reddish-pink and juicy in the center, about 4 minutes per side for medium rare.
10. Serve the chops drizzled with the pineapple reduction.

Nutrition: Calories 69, Total Fat 1.6g, Saturated Fat 0.5g, Cholesterol 17mg, Sodium 16mg, Total Carbohydrate 8.5g, Dietary Fiber 1.4g, Total Sugars 5.1g, Protein 5.9g, Calcium 37mg, Iron 1mg, Potassium 163mg, Phosphorus 65 mg

133. <u>Lemon and Thyme Lamb Chops</u>

Preparation time: 10 min
Cooking Time: 10 minutes
Servings: 4
Ingredients:
- 1 tablespoon olive oil
- 1/4 tablespoon lemon juice
- 1 tablespoon chopped fresh thyme
- Salt and pepper to taste
- 4 lamb chops

Directions:
1. Stir together olive oil, lemon juice, and thyme in a small bowl. Season with salt and pepper to taste. Place lamb chops in a shallow dish and brush with the olive oil mixture. Marinate in the refrigerator for 1 hour.
2. Preheat grill for high heat.
3. Lightly oil grill grate. Place lamb chops on the grill, and discard marinade. Cook for 10 minutes, turning once, or to the desired doneness

Nutrition: Calories 111, Total Fat 6.7g, Saturated Fat 1.6g, Cholesterol 38mg, Sodium 33mg, Total Carbohydrate 0.5g, Dietary Fiber 0.3g, Total Sugars 0g, Protein 12g, Calcium 19mg, Iron 2mg, Potassium 149mg, Phosphorus 93mg

134. <u>Basil Grilled Mediterranean Lamb Chops</u>

Preparation time: 10 min
Cooking Time: 10 minutes
Servings: 4
Ingredients:
- 4 (8 ounces) lamb shoulder chops
- 2 tablespoons Dijon mustard
- 2 tablespoons balsamic vinegar
- ½ tablespoon garlic powder
- 1/4 teaspoon ground black pepper
- 1/2 cup olive oil
- 2 tablespoons shredded fresh basil, or to taste

Directions:
1. Pat lamb chops dry and arrange in a single layer in a shallow glass baking dish.
2. Whisk Dijon mustard, balsamic vinegar, garlic, and pepper together in a small bowl.
3. Whisk in oil slowly until marinade is smooth.
4. Stir in basil. Pour marinade over lamb chops, turning to coat both sides.
5. Cover and refrigerate for 1 to 4 hours.

6. Bring lamb chops to room temperature, about 30 minutes.
7. Preheat grill for medium heat and lightly oil the grate.
8. Grill lamb chops until browned, 5 to 10 minutes per side.
9. An instant-read thermometer inserted into the center should read at least 145 degrees F.

Nutrition: Calories 270, Total Fat 27.8g, Saturated Fat 4.4g, Cholesterol 19mg, Sodium 109mg, Total Carbohydrate 1.4g, Dietary Fiber 0.4g, Total Sugars 0.4g, Protein 6.1g, Calcium 14mg, Iron 1mg, Potassium 33mg, Phosphorus 30mg

135. <u>Shredded Beef</u>

Preparation time: 10 min
Cooking Time: 5 hr.10 minutes
Servings: 4
Ingredients:
- 1/2 cup onion
- 2 garlic cloves
- 2 tablespoons fresh parsley
- 2-pound beef rump roast
- 1 tablespoon Italian herb seasoning
- 1 teaspoon dried parsley
- 1 bay leaf
- 1/2 teaspoon pepper
- 1/4 teaspoon salt
- 2 tablespoons olive oil
- 1/3 cup vinegar
- 2 to 3 cups water
- 8 hard rolls, 3-1/2-inch diameter, 2 ounces each

Directions:
1. Chop onion, garlic and fresh parsley. Place beef roast in a Crock-Pot. Add chopped onion, garlic and remaining ingredients, except fresh parsley and rolls, to Crock-Pot; stir to combine.
2. Cover and cook on low-heat setting for 8 to 10 hours, or on high setting for 4 to 5 hours, until fork-tender.
3. Remove roast from Crock-Pot.
4. Shred with two forks then return meat to cooking broth to keep warm until ready to serve.
5. Slice rolls in half and top with shredded beef, fresh parsley and 1-2 spoons of the broth.
6. Serve open-face or as a sandwich.

Nutrition: Calories 218, Total Fat 9.7g, Saturated Fat 2.6g, Cholesterol 75mg, Sodium 184mg, Total Carbohydrate 5.1g, Dietary Fiber 0.4g, Total Sugars 0.4g, Protein 26g, Calcium 26mg, Iron 3mg, Potassium 28mg, Phosphorus 30mg

136. <u>Lamb Stew with Green Beans</u>

Preparation time: 30 min
Cooking Time:1 hr.10 minute
Servings: 4
Ingredients:
- 1 tablespoon olive oil
- 1 large onion, chopped
- 1 stalk green onion, chopped

- 1-pound boneless lamb shoulder, cut into 2-inch pieces
- 3 cups hot water
- ½ pound fresh green beans, trimmed
- 1 tablespoon chopped fresh parsley
- 1/2 teaspoon dried mint
- 1/2 teaspoon dried dill weed
- 1 pinch ground nutmeg
- ¼ teaspoon honey
- Salt and pepper to taste

Directions:
1. Heat oil in a large pot over medium heat. Sauté onion and green onion until golden.
2. Stir in lamb, and cook until evenly brown.
3. Stir in water. Reduce heat and simmer for about 1 hour.
4. Stir in green beans. Season with parsley, mint, dill, nutmeg, honey, salt and pepper.
5. Continue cooking until beans are tender.

Nutrition: Calories 81, Total Fat 5.1g, Saturated Fat 1.1g, Cholesterol 19mg, Sodium 20mg, Total Carbohydrate 2.8g, Dietary Fiber 1g, Total Sugars 1g, Protein 6.5g, Calcium 17mg, Iron 1mg, Potassium 136mg, Phosphorus 120mg

137. Grilled Lamb Chops with Fresh Mint

Preparation time: 15 min
Cooking Time: 10 minutes
Servings: 4

Ingredients:
- 8 (5 ounces) lamb loin chops, about 1 1/4-inches thick
- 1/8 teaspoon seasoning salt
- 1/2 tablespoon dried parsley
- 1/2 tablespoon minced fresh mint
- 1/2 tablespoon dried rosemary

Directions:
1. Trim any excess fat down to 1/8-inch around each lamb chop and sprinkle both sides with seasoning salt.
2. Let sit for about 30 minutes to come to room temperature.
3. Preheat an outdoor grill to 400 degrees F. Lightly oil the grate once the grill is hot.
4. Place lamb chops on the hot grate and grill for 2 to 3 minutes.
5. Rotate chops, to achieve crisscross grill marks, and continue grilling, 2 to 3 more minutes.
6. Flip the chops and grill for 2 to 3 minutes.
7. Rotate chops and continue grilling an additional 2 minutes, or until they have reached the desired doneness.
8. An instant-read thermometer inserted into the center should read at least 130 degrees F.
9. Remove chops from grill and sprinkle with dried herbs and fresh mint.
10. Allow to rest under the foil, about 10 minutes

Nutrition: Calories 160, Total Fat 6.3g, Saturated Fat 2.3g, Cholesterol 77mg, Sodium 139mg, Total Carbohydrate 0.4g, Dietary Fiber 0.2g, Total Sugars 0g, Protein 23.9g, Calcium 18mg, Iron 2mg, Potassium 295mg, Phosphorus 140mg

138. Lamb Keema

Preparation time: 5 min

Cooking Time: 20 minutes
Servings: 4

Ingredients:

- 1 1/2 pounds ground lamb
- 1 onion, finely chopped
- 2 teaspoons garlic powder
- 2 tablespoons garam masala
- 1/8 teaspoon salt
- 3/4 cup chicken broth

Directions:

1. In a large, heavy skillet over medium heat, cook ground lamb until evenly brown.
2. While cooking, break apart with a wooden spoon until crumbled.
3. Transfer cooked lamb to a bowl and drain off all but 1 tablespoon fat. Sauté onion until soft and translucent, about 5 minutes.
4. Stir in garlic powder, and sauté 1 minute.
5. Stir in garam masala and cook 1 minute.
6. Return the browned lamb to the pan, and stir in chicken beef broth.
7. Reduce heat, and simmer for 10 to 15 minutes or until meat is fully cooked through, and liquid has evaporated.

Nutrition: Calories 194, Total Fat 7.3g, Saturated Fat 2.6g, Cholesterol 87mg, Sodium 160mg, Total Carbohydrate 2.2g, Dietary Fiber 0.4g, Total Sugars 0.9g, Protein 28.1g, Calcium 18mg, Iron 2mg, Potassium 379mg, Phosphorus 240mg

139. Curry Lamb Balls

Preparation time: 15 min
Cooking Time: 15 minutes
Servings: 4

Ingredients:

- ½-pound ground lamb
- 1/2 cup graham crackers
- Dried basil to taste
- 1 (10 ounces) can soy milk
- 1 1/2 tablespoons green curry paste

Directions:

1. In a medium bowl, mix together the ground lamb, graham crackers and basil until well blended.
2. Form into meatballs about 1 inch in diameter.
3. Heat a greased skillet over medium-high heat and fry the lamb balls until they are a bit black and crusty, about 5 minutes.
4. Remove balls from pan and set aside.
5. Toss the curry paste into the hot skillet and fry for about a minute.
6. Then pour in the entire can of soy milk and lower the heat.
7. Let the mixture simmer, frequently stirring for 5 to 10 minutes.
8. Serve.

Nutrition: Calories 103, Total Fat 3.8g, Saturated Fat 0.9g, Cholesterol 26mg, Sodium 184mg, Total Carbohydrate 7.1g, Dietary Fiber 0.4g, Total Sugars 3g, Protein 9.5g, Calcium 14mg, Iron 1mg, Potassium 144mg, Phosphorus 90mg

140. <u>**Beef and Chili Stew**</u>

Preparation Time: 15 minutes
Cooking Time: 7 hours
Servings: 6
Ingredients:

- 1/2 medium red onion, sliced thinly
- 1/2 tablespoon vegetable oil
- 10ounce of flat-cut beef brisket, whole
- ½ cup low sodium stock
- ¾ cup of water
- ½ tablespoon honey
- ½ tablespoon chili powder
- ½ teaspoon smoked paprika
- ½ teaspoon dried thyme
- 1 teaspoon black pepper
- 1 tablespoon corn starch

Directions:

1. Throw the sliced onion into the slow cooker first. Add a splash of oil to a large hot skillet and briefly seal the beef on all sides.
2. Remove the beef, then place it in the slow cooker. Add the stock, water, honey, and spices to the same skillet you cooked the beef meat.
3. Allow the juice to simmer until the volume is reduced by about half. Pour the juice over beef in the slow cooker. Cook on low within 7 hours.
4. Transfer the beef to your platter, shred it using two forks. Put the rest of the juice into a medium saucepan. Bring it to a simmer.
5. Whisk the cornstarch with two tablespoons of water. Add to the juice and cook until slightly thickened.

6. For a thicker sauce, simmer and reduce the juice a bit more before adding cornstarch. Put the sauce on the meat and serve.

Nutrition: Calories: 128 Protein: 13g Carbohydrates: 6g Fat: 6g Sodium: 228mg Potassium: 202mg Phosphorus: 119mg

141.Sticky Pulled Beef Open Sandwiches

Preparation Time: 15 minutes
Cooking Time: 5 hours
Servings: 5
Ingredients:
- ½ cup of green onion, sliced
- 2 garlic cloves
- 2 tablespoons of fresh parsley
- 2 large carrots
- 7ounce of flat-cut beef brisket, whole
- 1 tablespoon of smoked paprika
- 1 teaspoon dried parsley
- 1 teaspoon of brown sugar
- ½ teaspoon of black pepper
- 2 tablespoon of olive oil

- ¼ cup of red wine
- 8 tablespoon of cider vinegar
- 3 cups of water
- 5 slices white bread
- 1 cup of arugula to garnish

Directions:
1. Finely chop the green onion, garlic, and fresh parsley. Grate the carrot. Put the beef in to roast in a slow cooker.
2. Add the chopped onion, garlic, and remaining ingredients, leaving the rolls, fresh parsley, and arugula to one side. Stir in the slow cooker to combine.
3. Cover and cook on low within 8 1/2 to 10 hours or on high for 4 to 5 hours until tender. Remove the meat from the slow cooker. Shred the meat using two forks.
4. Return the meat to the broth to keep it warm until ready to serve. Lightly toast the bread and top with shredded beef, arugula, fresh parsley, and ½ spoon of the broth. Serve.

Nutrition: Calories: 273 Protein: 15g Carbohydrates: 20g Fat: 11g Sodium: 308mg Potassium: 399mg Phosphorus: 159mg

142. <u>**Herby Beef Stroganoff and Fluffy Rice**</u>

Preparation Time: 15 minutes
Cooking Time: 5 hours

Servings: 6
Ingredients:

- ½ cup onion
- 2 garlic cloves
- 9ounce of flat-cut beef brisket, cut into 1" cubes
- ½ cup of reduced-sodium beef stock
- 1/3 cup red wine
- ½ teaspoon dried oregano
- ¼ teaspoon freshly ground black pepper
- ½ teaspoon dried thyme
- ½ teaspoon of saffron
- ½ cup almond milk (unenriched)
- ¼ cup all-purpose flour
- 1 cup of water
- 2 ½ cups of white rice

Directions:

1. Dice the onion, then mince the garlic cloves. Mix the beef, stock, wine, onion, garlic, oregano, pepper, thyme, and saffron in your slow cooker.
2. Cover and cook on high within 4-5 hours. Combine the almond milk, flour, and water. Whisk together until smooth.
3. Add the flour mixture to the slow cooker. Cook for another 15 to 25 minutes until the stroganoff is thick.
4. Cook the rice using the package instructions, leaving out the salt. Drain off the excess water. Serve the stroganoff over the rice.

Nutrition: Calories: 241 Protein: 15g Carbohydrates: 29g Fat: 5g Sodium: 182mg Potassium: 206mg Phosphorus: 151mg

143. <u>Chunky Beef Slow Roast</u>

Preparation Time: 15 minutes
Cooking Time: 5-6 hours
Servings: 12
Ingredients:

- 3 cups of peeled carrots, chunked
- 1 cup of onion
- 2 garlic cloves, chopped
- 1 ¼ pound flat-cut beef brisket, fat trimmed
- 2 cups of water
- 1 teaspoon of chili powder
- 1 tablespoon of dried rosemary

For the sauce:

- 1 tablespoon of freshly grated horseradish
- ½ cup of almond milk (unenriched)
- 1 tablespoon lemon juice (freshly squeezed)
- 1 garlic clove, minced
- A pinch of cayenne pepper

Directions:

1. Double boil the carrots to reduce their potassium content. Chop the onion and the garlic. Place the beef brisket in a slow cooker. Combine water, chopped garlic, chili powder, and rosemary.
2. Pour the mixture over the brisket. Cover and cook on high within 4-5 hours until the meat is very tender. Drain the carrots and add them to the slow cooker.
3. Adjust the heat to high and cook covered until the carrots are tender. Prepare the horseradish sauce by whisking together horseradish, almond milk, lemon juice, minced garlic, and cayenne pepper.
4. Cover and refrigerate. Serve your casserole with a dash of horseradish sauce on the side.

Nutrition: Calories: 199 Protein: 21g Carbohydrates: 12g Fat: 7g Sodium: 282mg Potassium: 317 Phosphorus: 191mg

144. Beef Ragu

Preparation Time: 10 minutes
Cooking Time: 10 minutes
Servings: 2
Ingredients:

- 1/4 cup packaged pesto
- 1 teaspoon salt
- 2 large zucchinis, cut into noodle strips
- 1 tablespoon olive oil
- 1/4-pound ground beef
- 4 tablespoons fresh parsley, chopped

Directions:

1. Heat the oil in a skillet under medium flame and cook the ground beef until thoroughly cooked, around 5 minutes. Discard excess fat.
2. Add the packaged pesto sauce and season with salt. Add t
3. Then chopped parsley and cook for three more minutes. Set aside.
4. In the same saucepan, place the zucchini noodles and cook for five minutes. Turn off the heat then add the cooked meat. Mix well.
5. Serve and enjoy.

Nutrition:

Calories 353, Total Fat 30g, Saturated Fat 6g, Total Carbs 2g, Net Carbs 1.3g, Protein 19g, Sugar: 0.3g, Fiber 0.7g, Sodium 1481mg, Potassium 341mg

145. Stir-Fried Ground Beef

Preparation Time: 10 minutes
Cooking Time: 15 minutes
Servings: 4
Ingredients:

- 1/2 cup broccoli, chopped
- 1/2 of medium-sized onions, chopped
- 1/2 of medium-sized red bell pepper, chopped
- 1 tbsp. cayenne pepper (optional)
- 1 tbsp. Chinese five spices
- 1 tbsp. coconut oil
- 1-lb ground beef
- 2 kale leaves, chopped

- 5 medium-sized mushrooms, sliced

Directions:

1. In a skillet, heat the coconut oil over medium high heat.
2. Sauté the onions for one minute and add the vegetables while stirring constantly.
3. Add the ground beef and the spices.
4. Cook for two minutes and reduce the heat to medium.
5. Cover the skillet and continue to cook the beef and vegetables for another 10 minutes.
6. Serve and enjoy.

Nutrition: Calories 304, Total Fat 17g, Saturated Fat 3g, Total Carbs 6g, Net Carbs 4g, Protein 32g, Sugar: 2g, Fiber 2g, Sodium 86mg, Potassium 624mg

146. Beef and Three Pepper Stew

Preparation Time: 15 minutes
Cooking Time: 6 hours
Servings: 6
Ingredients:

- 10ounce of flat cut beef brisket, whole
- 1 teaspoon of dried thyme
- 1 teaspoon of black pepper
- 1 clove garlic
- 1/2 cup of green onion, thinly sliced
- 1/2 cup low sodium chicken stock
- 2 cups water
- 1 large green bell pepper, sliced
- 1 large red bell pepper, sliced
- 1 large yellow bell pepper, sliced
- 1 large red onion, sliced

Directions:

1. Combine the beef, thyme, pepper, garlic, green onion, stock and water in a slow cooker.
2. Leave it all to cook on High for 4-5 hours until tender.
3. Remove the beef from the slow cooker and let it cool.
4. Shred the beef with two forks and remove any excess fat.
5. Place the shredded beef back into the slow cooker.
6. Add the sliced peppers and the onion.
7. Cook this on High heat for 40-60 minutes until the vegetables are tender.

Nutrition: Per Servings: Calories: 132 Protein: 14g Carbohydrates: 9g Fat: 5g Cholesterol: 39mg Sodium: 179mg Potassium: 390mg Phosphorus: 141mgCalcium: 33mg Fiber: 2g

147. Beef Brochettes

Preparation Time: 20 minutes
Cooking Time: 1 hour
Servings: 1
Ingredients:

- 1 1/2 cups pineapple chunks
- 1 sliced large onion
- 2 pounds thick steak

- 1 sliced medium bell pepper
- 1 bay leaf
- 1/4 cup vegetable oil
- 1/2 cup lemon juice
- 2 crushed garlic cloves

Directions:
1. Cut beef cubes and place in a plastic bag
2. Combine marinade ingredients in small bowl
3. Mix and pour over beef cubes
4. Seal the bag and refrigerate for 3 to 5 hours
5. Divide ingredients onion, beef cube, green pepper, pineapple
6. Grill about 9 minutes each side

Nutrition: Calories 304 Protein 35 g Fat 15 g Carbs 11 g Phosphorus 264 mg Potassium (K) 388 mg Sodium (Na) 70 mg

148.   Country Fried Steak

Preparation Time: 10 minutes
Cooking Time: 1 hour and 40 minutes
Servings: 3
Ingredients:
- 1 large onion
- 1/2 cup flour
- 3 tablespoons. vegetable oil
- 1/4 teaspoon pepper
- 11/2 pounds round steak
- 1/2 teaspoon paprika

Directions:
1. Trim excess fat from steak
2. Cut into small pieces
3. Combine flour, paprika and pepper and mix together
4. Preheat skillet with oil
5. Cook steak on both sides
6. When the color of steak is brown remove to a platter
7. Add water (150 ml) and stir around the skillet
8. Return browned steak to skillet, if necessary, add water again so that bottom side of steak does not stick

Nutrition: Calories 248 Protein 30 g Fat 10 g Carbs 5 g Phosphorus 190 mg Potassium (K) 338 mg Sodium (Na) 60 mg

149.   Beef Pot Roast

Preparation Time: 20 minutes
Cooking Time: 1 hour
Servings: 3
Ingredients:
- Round bone roast
- 2 - 4 pounds chuck roast

Directions:

1. Trim off excess fat
2. Place a tablespoon of oil in a large skillet and heat to medium
3. Roll pot roast in flour and brown on all sides in a hot skillet
4. After the meat gets a brown color, reduce heat to low
5. Season with pepper and herbs and add 1/2 cup of water
6. Cook slowly for 11/2 hours or until it looks ready

Nutrition: Calories 157 Protein 24 g Fat 13 g Carbs 0 g Phosphorus 204 mg Sodium (Na) 50 mg

150. Slow-cooked Beef Brisket

Preparation Time: 10 minutes
Cooking Time: 3 hours and 30 minutes
Servings: 6
Ingredients:

- 10-ounce chuck roast
- 1 onion, sliced
- 1 cup carrots, peeled and sliced
- 1 tablespoon mustard
- 1 tablespoon thyme (fresh or dried)
- 1 tablespoon rosemary (fresh or dried)
- 2 garlic cloves
- 2 tablespoon extra-virgin olive oil
- 1 teaspoon black pepper
- 1 cup homemade chicken stock (p.52)
- 1 cup water

Directions:

1. Preheat oven to 300°f/150°c/Gas Mark 2.
2. Trim any fat from the beef and soak vegetables in warm water.
3. Make a paste by mixing together the mustard, thyme, rosemary, and garlic, before mixing in the oil and pepper.
4. Combine this mix with the stock.
5. Pour the mixture over the beef into an oven proof baking dish.
6. Place the vegetables onto the bottom of the baking dish with the beef.
7. Cover and roast for 3 hours, or until tender.
8. Uncover the dish and continue to cook for 30 minutes in the oven.
9. Serve hot!

Nutrition: Calories: 151 Fat: 7g Carbohydrates: 7g Phosphorus: 144mg Potassium: 344mg Sodium: 279mg Protein: 15g

151. Pork Souvlaki

Preparation Time: 20 minutes
Cooking Time: 12 minutes
Servings: 8
Ingredients:

- Olive oil – 3 tablespoons
- Lemon juice – 2 tablespoons
- Minced garlic – 1 teaspoon

- Chopped fresh oregano – 1 tablespoon
- Ground black pepper – 1/4 teaspoon
- Pork leg – 1 pound, cut in 2-inch cubes

Directions:
1. In a bowl, stir together the lemon juice, olive oil, garlic, oregano, and pepper.
2. Add the pork cubes and toss to coat.
3. Place the bowl in the refrigerator, covered, for 2 hours to marinate.
4. Thread the pork chunks onto 8 wooden skewers that have been soaked in water.
5. Preheat the barbecue to medium-high heat.
6. Grill the pork skewers for about 12 minutes, turning once, until just cooked through but still juicy.

Nutrition: Calories: 95 Fat: 4g Carbs: 0g Phosphorus: 125mg Potassium: 230mg Sodium: 29mg Protein: 13g

152. Open-Faced Beef Stir-Up

Preparation Time: 10 minutes
Cooking Time: 10 minutes
Servings: 6
Ingredients:
- 95% Lean ground beef – 1/2 pound
- Chopped sweet onion – 1/2 cup
- Shredded cabbage – 1/2 cup
- Herb pesto – 1/4 cup
- Hamburger buns – 6, bottom halves only

Directions:
1. Sauté the beef and onion for 6 minutes or until beef is cooked.
2. Add the cabbage and sauté for 3 minutes more.
3. Stir in pesto and heat for 1 minute.
4. Divide the beef mixture into 6 portions and serve each on the bottom half of a hamburger bun, open-face.

Nutrition: Calories: 120 Fat: 3g Phosphorus: 106mg Potassium: 198mg Sodium: 134mg Protein: 11g

153. Beef Brisket

Preparation Time: 10 minutes
Cooking Time: 3 1/2 hours
Servings: 6
Ingredients:
- Chuck roast – 12 ounces trimmed
- Garlic – 2 cloves
- Thyme – 1 tablespoon
- Rosemary – tablespoon
- Mustard - 1 tablespoon
- Extra virgin olive oil – 1/4 cup
- Black pepper – 1 teaspoon
- Onion – 1, diced
- Carrots – 1 cup, peeled and sliced
- Low salt stock – 2 cups

Directions:
1. Preheat the oven to 300F.

2. Soak vegetables in warm water.
3. Make a paste by mixing together the thyme, mustard, rosemary, and garlic. Then mix in the oil and pepper.
4. Add the beef to the dish.
5. Pour the mixture over the beef into a dish.
6. Place the vegetables onto the bottom of the baking dish around the beef.
7. Cover and roast for 3 hours, or until tender.
8. Uncover the dish and continue to cook for 30 minutes in the oven.
9. Serve.

Nutrition: Calories: 303 Fat: 25g Carbs: 7g Phosphorus: 376mg Potassium: 246mg Sodium: 44mg Protein: 18g

154. <u>Homemade Burgers</u>

Preparation Time: 10 minutes
Cooking Time: 20 minutes
Servings: 2
Ingredients:

- 4 ounce lean 100% ground beef
- 1 teaspoon black pepper
- 1 garlic clove, minced
- 1 teaspoon olive oil
- 1/4 cup onion, finely diced
- 1 tablespoon balsamic vinegar
- 1/2ounce brie cheese, crumbled
- 1 teaspoon mustard

Directions:

1. Season ground beef with pepper and then mix in minced garlic.
2. Form burger shapes with the ground beef using the palms of your hands.
3. Heat a skillet on a medium to high heat, and then add the oil.
4. Sauté the onions for 5-10 minutes until browned.
5. Then add the balsamic vinegar and sauté for another 5 minutes.
6. Remove and set aside.
7. Add the burgers to the pan and heat on the same heat for 5-6 minutes before flipping and heating for a further 5-6 minutes until cooked through.
8. Spread the mustard onto each burger.
9. Crumble the brie cheese over each burger and serve!
10. Try with a crunchy side salad!
11. Tip: If using fresh beef and not defrosted, prepare double the ingredients and freeze burgers in plastic wrap (after cooling) for up to 1 month.
12. Thoroughly defrost before heating through completely in the oven to serve.

Nutrition: Calories: 178 Fat: 10g Carbohydrates: 4g Phosphorus: 147mg Potassium: 272mg Sodium: 273 mg Protein: 16g

155. Creamy Turkey

Preparation Time: 12 minutes
Cooking Time: 10 minutes
Servings: 4
Ingredients:

- 4 skinless, boneless turkey breast halves
- Salt and pepper to taste
- ½ teaspoon ground black pepper
- ½ teaspoon garlic powder
- 1 (10.75 ounces) can chicken soup

Directions:

1. Preheat oven to 375 degrees F.
2. Clean turkey breasts and season with salt, pepper and garlic powder (or whichever seasonings you prefer) on both sides of turkey pieces.
3. Bake for 25 minutes, then add chicken soup and bake for 10 more minutes (or until done). Serve over rice or egg noodles.

Nutrition: Calories 160, Sodium 157mg, Dietary Fiber 0.4g, Total Sugars 0.4g, Protein 25.6g, Calcium 2mg, Potassium 152mg, Phosphorus 85 mg

156. Lemon Pepper Chicken Legs

Preparation Time: 5 minutes
Cooking Time: 25 minutes
Servings: 4
Ingredients:

- ½ tsp. garlic powder
- 2 tsp. baking powder
- 8 chicken legs
- 4 tbsp. salted butter, melted
- 1 tbsp. lemon pepper seasoning

Directions:

1. In a small container add the garlic powder and baking powder, then use this mixture to coat the chicken legs. Lay the chicken in the basket of your fryer.
2. Cook the chicken legs at 375°F for twenty-five minutes. Halfway through, turn them over and allow to cook on the other side.
3. When the chicken has turned golden brown, test with a thermometer to ensure it has reached an ideal temperature of 165°F. Remove from the fryer.
4. Mix together the melted butter and lemon pepper seasoning and toss with the chicken legs until the chicken is coated all over. Serve hot.

Nutrition: Calories: 132 Fat: 16 g Carbs: 20 g Protein: 48 g Calcium 79mg, Phosphorous 132mg, Potassium 127mg Sodium: 121 mg

157. Turkey Broccoli Salad

Preparation Time: 10 minutes
Cooking Time: 00 minutes
Servings: 4
Ingredients:

- 8 cups broccoli florets
- 3 cooked skinless, boneless chicken breast halves, cubed
- 6 green onions, chopped
- 1 cup mayonnaise
- ¼ cup apple cider vinegar
- ¼ cup honey

Directions:

1. Combine broccoli, chicken and green onions in a large bowl.
2. Whisk mayonnaise, vinegar, and honey together in a bowl until well blended.
3. Pour mayonnaise dressing over broccoli mixture; toss to coat.
4. Cover and refrigerate until chilled, if desired. Serve

Nutrition: Calories 133, Sodium 23mg, Dietary Fiber 1.6g, Total Sugars 7.7g, Protein 6.2g, Calcium 24mg, Potassium 157mg Phosphorus 148 mg

158. Fruity Chicken Salad

Preparation Time: 10 minutes
Cooking Time: 5 minutes
Servings: 3
Ingredients:

- 4 skinless, boneless chicken breast halves - cooked and diced
- 1 stalk celery, diced
- 4 green onions, chopped
- 1 Golden Delicious apple - peeled, cored and diced
- 1/3 cup seedless green grapes, halved
- 1/8 teaspoon ground black pepper
- 3/4 cup light mayonnaise

Directions:

1. In a large container, add the celery, chicken, onion, apple, grapes, pepper, and mayonnaise.
2. Mix all together. Serve!

Nutrition: Calories 196, Sodium 181mg, Total Carbohydrate 15.6g, Dietary Fiber 1.2g, Total Sugars 9.1g, Protein 13.2g, Calcium 13mg, Iron 1mg, Potassium 115mg, Phosphorus 88 mg

159. Buckwheat Salad

Preparation Time: 12 minutes
Cooking Time: 20 minutes
Servings: 3
Ingredients:

- 2 cups water
- 1 clove garlic, smashed
- 1 cup uncooked buckwheat

- 2 large cooked chicken breasts - cut into bite-size pieces
- 1 large red onion, diced
- 1 large green bell pepper, diced
- 1/4 cup chopped fresh parsley
- 1/4 cup chopped fresh chives
- 1/2 teaspoon salt
- 2/3 cup fresh lemon juice
- 1 tablespoon balsamic vinegar
- 1/4 cup olive oil

Directions:
1. Bring the water, garlic to a boil in a saucepan. Stir in the buckwheat, reduce heat to medium-low, cover, and simmer until the buckwheat is tender and the water has been absorbed, 15 to 20 minutes.
2. Discard the garlic clove and scrape the buckwheat into a large bowl.
3. Gently stir the chicken, onion, bell pepper, parsley, chives, and salt into the buckwheat.
4. Sprinkle with the olive oil, balsamic vinegar, and lemon juice. Stir until evenly mixed.

Nutrition: Calories 199, Total Fat 8.3g, Sodium 108mg, Dietary Fiber 2.9g, Total Sugars 2g, Protein 13.6g, Calcium 22mg, Potassium 262mg, Phosphorus 188 mg

160.   Parmesan and Basil turkey Salad

Preparation Time: 15 minutes
Cooking Time: 35 minutes
Servings: 4
Ingredients:
- 2 whole skinless, boneless turkey breasts
- salt and pepper to taste
- 1 cup mayonnaise
- 1 cup chopped fresh basil
- 2 cloves crushed garlic
- 3 stalks celery, chopped
- 2/3 cup grated Parmesan cheese

Directions:
1. Season turkey with salt and pepper. Roast at 375 degrees F for 35 minutes, or until juices run clear. Let cool, and chop into chunks.
2. In a food processor, puree the mayonnaise, basil, garlic, and celery.
3. Combine the chunked turkey, pureed mixture, and Parmesan cheese; toss.
4. Refrigerate, and serve.

Nutrition: Calories 303, Sodium 190mg, Dietary Fiber 0.4g, Total Sugars 4.7g, Protein 8.5g, Calcium 73mg, Potassium 121mg, Phosphorus 100 mg

161. Cherry Chicken Salad

Preparation Time: 15 minutes
Cooking Time: 00 minutes
Servings: 4
Ingredients:
- 3 cooked, boneless chicken breast halves, diced
- 1/3 cup dried cherries

- 1/3 cup diced celery
- 1/3 cup low-fat mayonnaise
- 1/2 teaspoon ground black pepper
- 1/3 cup cubed apples (optional)

Directions:
1. In a large bowl, combine the chicken, dried cherries, celery, mayonnaise, and pepper and apple if desired.
2. Toss together well and refrigerate until chilled.
3. Serve

Nutrition: Calories 281, Total Fat 11.8g, Cholesterol 31mg, Sodium 586mg, Dietary Fiber 1.4g, Total Sugars 2.9g, Protein 14.7g, Calcium 12mg, Potassium 55mg, Phosphorus 20 mg

162. Elegant Brunch Chicken Salad

Preparation Time: 20 minutes
Cooking Time: 0 minutes
Servings: 4
Ingredients:
- 1-pound skinless, boneless chicken breast halves
- 1 egg
- 1/4 teaspoon dry mustard
- 2 teaspoons hot water
- 1 tablespoon white wine vinegar
- 1 cup olive oil
- 2 cups halved seedless red grapes

Directions:
1. Boil water in a large pot. Add the chicken and simmer until cooked thoroughly approximately 10 minutes. Drain, cool and cut into cubes.
2. While boiling chicken, make the mayonnaise: Using a blender or hand-held electric mixer, beat the egg, mustard, water and vinegar until light and frothy.
3. Add the oil a tablespoon at a time, beating thoroughly after each addition. As the combination starts to thicken, you can add oil more quickly.
4. Continue until the mixture reaches the consistency of creamy mayonnaise.
5. In a large bowl, toss together the chicken, grapes and 1 cup of the mayonnaise. Stir until evenly coated, adding more mayonnaise if necessary. Refrigerate until serving.

Nutrition: Calories 676, Sodium 56mg, Total Carbohydrate 14.7g, Dietary Fiber 1.4g, Total Sugars 12.2g, Protein 28.1g, Calcium 10mg, Potassium 183mg, Phosphorus 120 mg

163. Oven-Baked Turkey Thighs

Preparation Time: 10 minutes
Cooking Time: 30 minutes
Servings: 4
Ingredients:
- 10 ounces turkey thighs, skin on, bone-in
- 1/3 cup white wine
- 1 lemon
- 1 tablespoon fresh oregano
- 1/4 teaspoon cracked black pepper

- 1 tablespoon olive oil

Directions:
1. Heat the oven to 350 degrees F.
2. Add turkey thighs and white wine to an oven-proof pan. Squeeze half the lemon over turkey. Slice remaining lemon and top turkey with lemon slices.
3. Season turkey with fresh oregano, cracked pepper and olive oil.
4. Bake turkey for 25 to 30 minutes or until internal temperature reaches 165 degrees F to 175 degrees F.

Nutrition: Calories 189, Sodium 62mg, Dietary Fiber 0.9g, Total Sugars 0.6g, Protein 20.8g, Calcium 34mg, Potassium 232mg, Phosphorus 180 mg

164. <u>Southern Fried Chicken</u>

Preparation Time: 5 minutes
Cooking Time: 26 minutes
Servings: 2
Ingredients:

- 2 x 6-oz. boneless skinless chicken breasts
- 2 tbsp. hot sauce
- ½ tsp. onion powder
- 1 tbsp. chili powder
- 2 oz. pork rinds, finely ground

Directions:
1. Chop the chicken breasts in half lengthways and rub in the hot sauce. Combine the onion powder with the chili powder, then rub into the chicken. Leave to marinate for at least a half hour.
2. Use the ground pork rinds to coat the chicken breasts in the ground pork rinds, covering them thoroughly. Place the chicken in your fryer.
3. Set the fryer at 350°F and cook the chicken for 13 minutes. Turn over the chicken and cook the other side for another 13 minutes or until golden.
4. Test the chicken with a meat thermometer. When fully cooked, it should reach 165°F. Serve hot, with the sides of your choice.

Nutrition: Calories: 408 Fat: 19 g Carbs: 10 g Protein: 35 g Calcium 39mg, Phosphorous 216mg, Potassium 137mg Sodium: 153 mg

165. <u>Cilantro Drumsticks</u>

Preparation Time: 12 minutes
Cooking Time: 18 minutes
Servings: 4
Ingredients:

- 8 chicken drumsticks
- ½ cup chimichurri sauce
- ¼ cup lemon juice

Directions:
1. Coat the chicken drumsticks with chimichurri sauce and refrigerate in an airtight container for no less than an hour, ideally overnight.
2. When it's time to cook, pre-heat your fryer to 400°F.
3. Remove the chicken from refrigerator and allow return to room temperature for roughly twenty minutes.
4. Cook for eighteen minutes in the fryer. Drizzle with lemon juice to taste and enjoy.

Nutrition: Calories: 483 Fat: 29 g Carbs: 16 g Protein: 36 g Calcium 38mg, Phosphorous 146mg, Potassium 227mg Sodium: 121 mg

166.   Basil Chicken over Macaroni

Preparation Time: 10 minutes
Cooking Time: 30 minutes
Servings: 4
Ingredients:

- 1 (8 ounces) package macaroni
- 2 teaspoons olive oil
- 1/2 cup finely chopped onion
- 1 clove garlic, chopped
- 2 cups boneless chicken breast halves, cooked and cubed
- 1/4 cup chopped fresh basil
- 1/4 cup Parmesan cheese
- 1/2 teaspoon black pepper

Directions:

1. In a large pot of boiling water, cook macaroni until it is al dente, about 8 to 10 minutes. Drain, and set aside.
2. In a large skillet, heat oil over medium-high heat. Sauté the onions and garlic. Stir in the chicken, basil, and pepper.
3. Reduce heat to medium, and cover skillet. Simmer for about 5 minutes, stirring frequently,
4. Toss sauce with hot cooked macaroni to coat. Serve with Parmesan cheese.

Nutrition: Calories 349, Sodium 65mg, Dietary Fiber 2.2g, Total Sugars 2.1g, Protein 28.5g, Calcium 44mg, Potassium 286mg, Phosphorus 280 mg

167.   Chicken Saute

Preparation Time: 10 minutes
Cooking Time: 25 minutes
Servings: 2
Ingredients:

- 4 oz. chicken fillet
- 4 Red bell peppers, peeled
- 1 bell pepper, chopped
- 1 teaspoon olive oil
- 1 cup of water
- 1 teaspoon salt
- 1 chili pepper, chopped
- ½ teaspoon saffron

Directions:

1. Pour water in the pan and bring it to boil.
2. Meanwhile, chop the chicken fillet.
3. Add the chicken fillet in the boiling water and cook it for 10 minutes or until the chicken is tender.
4. After this, put the chopped bell pepper and chili pepper in the skillet.
5. Add olive oil and roast the vegetables for 3 minutes.
6. Add chopped red bell peppers and mix up well.

7. Cook the vegetables for 2 minutes more.
8. Then add salt and a ¾ cup of water from chicken.
9. Add chopped chicken fillet and mix up.
10. Cook the sauté for 10 minutes over the medium heat.

Nutrition: Calories 192, Fat 7.2 g, Fiber 3.8 g, Carbs 14.4 g, Protein 19.2 g Calcium 79mg, Phosphorous 216mg, Potassium 227mg Sodium: 101 mg

168. Grilled Marinated Chicken

Preparation Time: 35 minutes
Cooking Time: 20 minutes
Servings: 6
Ingredients:
- 2-pound chicken breast, skinless, boneless
- 2 tablespoons lemon juice
- 1 teaspoon sage
- ½ teaspoon ground nutmeg
- ½ teaspoon dried oregano
- 1 teaspoon paprika
- 1 teaspoon onion powder
- 2 tablespoons olive oil
- 1 teaspoon chili flakes
- 1 teaspoon salt
- 1 teaspoon apple cider vinegar

Directions:
1. Make the marinade: whisk together apple cider vinegar, salt, chili flakes, olive oil, onion powder, paprika, dried oregano, ground nutmeg, sage, and lemon juice.
2. Then rub the chicken with marinade carefully and leave for 25 minutes to marinate.
3. Meanwhile, preheat grill to 385F.
4. Place the marinated chicken breast in the grill and cook it for 10 minutes from each side.
5. Cut the cooked chicken on the servings.

Nutrition: Calories 218 Fat 8.2 g, Fiber 0.8 g, Carbs 0.4 g, Protein 32.2 g Calcium 29mg, Phosphorous 116mg, Potassium 207mg Sodium: 121 mg

169. Tasty Turkey Patties

Preparation Time: 10 minutes
Cooking Time: 12 minutes
Servings: 4
Ingredients:
- 14.5-ounces turkey
- 1-ounce cream cheese
- 1 large egg
- 1/8 teaspoon ground sage
- 1/2 teaspoon garlic powder
- 1/2 teaspoon black pepper
- 1 teaspoon onion powder
- 1 teaspoon Italian seasoning

- 3 tablespoons olive oil

Directions:
1. Set cream cheese out to soften.
2. Using a fork, mash turkey with juices in a medium bowl.
3. Add the cream cheese, egg, sage, garlic powder, black pepper, onion powder, Italian seasoning and mix well.
4. Form 4 patties.
5. Heat olive oil on low hotness, in a small skillet.
6. Fry patties for 5- to 6 minutes on each side or until crispy on the outside and heated thoroughly.

Nutrition: Calories 270, Sodium 204mg, Dietary Fiber 1.1g, Total Sugars 3.5g, Protein 13.5g, Calcium 17mg, Potassium 143mg, Phosphorus 100 mg

170. Roasted Citrus Chicken

Preparation Time: 20 Minutes
Cooking Time: 60 Minutes
Servings: 8

Ingredients:
- 1 tablespoon olive oil
- 2 cloves garlic, minced
- 1 teaspoon Italian seasoning
- 1/2 teaspoon black pepper
- 8 chicken thighs
- 2 cups chicken broth, reduced sodium
- 3 tablespoons lemon juice
- 1/2 large chicken breast for 1 chicken thigh

Directions:
1. Warm oil in a huge skillet.
2. Include garlic and seasonings.
3. Include chicken bosoms and dark-colored all sides.
4. Spot chicken in the moderate cooker and include the chicken soup.
5. Cook on LOW heat for 6 to 8 hours
6. Include lemon juice toward the part of the bargain time.

Nutrition: Calories 265, Fat 19g, Protein 21g, Carbohydrates 1g

171. Chicken with Asian Vegetables

Preparation Time: 10 Minutes
Cooking Time: 20 Minutes
Servings: 8
Ingredients:
- 2 tablespoons canola oil
- 6 boneless chicken breasts
- 1 cup low-sodium chicken broth
- 3 tablespoons reduced-sodium soy sauce
- 1/4 teaspoon crushed red pepper flakes
- 1 garlic clove, crushed

- 1 can (8ounces) water chestnuts, sliced and rinsed (optional)
- 1/2 cup sliced green onions
- 1 cup chopped red or green bell pepper
- 1 cup chopped celery
- 1/4 cup cornstarch
- 1/3 cup water
- 3 cups cooked white rice
- 1/2 large chicken breast for 1 chicken thigh

Directions:
1. Warm oil in a skillet and dark-colored chicken on all sides.
2. Add chicken to a slow cooker with the remainder of the fixings aside from cornstarch and water.
3. Spread and cook on LOW for 6 to 8hours
4. Following 6-8 hours, independently blend cornstarch and cold water until smooth. Gradually include into the moderate cooker.
5. At that point turn on high for about 15mins until thickened. Don't close the top on the moderate cooker to enable steam to leave.
6. Serve Asian blend over rice.

Nutrition: Calories 415, Fat 20g, Protein 20g, Carbohydrates 36g

172. Chicken and Veggie Soup

Preparation Time: 15 Minutes
Cooking Time: 25 Minutes
Servings: 8
Ingredients:
- 4 cups cooked and chopped chicken
- 7 cups reduced-sodium chicken broth
- 1-pound frozen white corn
- 1 medium onion diced
- 4 cloves garlic minced
- 2 carrots peeled and diced
- 2 celery stalks chopped
- 2 teaspoons oregano
- 2 teaspoon curry powder
- 1/2 teaspoon black pepper

Directions:
1. Include all fixings into the moderate cooker.
2. Cook on LOW for 8 hours
3. Serve over cooked white rice.

Nutrition: Calories 220, Fat7g, Protein 24g, Carbohydrates 19g

173. Turkey Sausages

Preparation Time: 10 Minutes
Cooking Time: 10 Minutes
Servings: 2
Ingredients:
- 1/4 teaspoon salt

- 1/8 teaspoon garlic powder
- 1/8 teaspoon onion powder
- 1 teaspoon fennel seed
- 1 pound 7% fat ground turkey

Directions:
1. Press the fennel seed and in a small cup put together turkey with fennel seed, garlic, and onion powder, and salt.
2. Cover the bowl and refrigerate overnight.
3. Prepare the turkey with seasoning into different portions with a circle form and press them into patties ready to be cooked.
4. Cook at medium heat until browned.
5. Cook it for 1 to 2 minutes per side and serve them hot. Enjoy!

Nutrition: Calories 55, Protein 7 g, Sodium 70 mg, Potassium 105 mg, Phosphorus 75 mg

174. Rosemary Chicken

Preparation Time: 10 Minutes
Cooking Time: 10 Minutes
Servings: 2
Ingredients:

- 2 zucchinis
- 1 carrot
- 1 teaspoon dried rosemary
- 4 chicken breasts
- 1/2 bell pepper
- 1/2 red onion
- 8 garlic cloves
- Olive oil
- 1/4 tablespoon ground pepper

Directions:
1. Prepare the oven and preheat it at 375°F (or 200°C).
2. Slice both zucchini and carrots and add bell pepper, onion, garlic, and put all the ingredients, adding oil in a 13" x 9" pan.
3. Spread the pepper on the pan and roast for about 10 minutes.
4. Meanwhile, lift the chicken skin and spread black pepper and rosemary on the flesh.
5. Remove the vegetable pan from the oven and add the chicken, returning the pan to the oven for about 30 more minutes. Serve and enjoy!

Nutrition: Calories 215, Protein 28 g, Sodium 105 mg, Potassium 580 mg, Phosphorus 250 mg

175. Smokey Turkey Chili

Preparation Time: 5 Minutes
Cooking Time: 45 Minutes
Servings: 8
Ingredients:

- 12-ounce lean ground turkey
- 1/2 red onion, chopped
- 2 cloves garlic, crushed and chopped

- 1/2 teaspoon of smoked paprika
- 1/2 teaspoon of chili powder
- 1/2 teaspoon of dried thyme
- 1/4 cup reduced-sodium beef stock
- 1/2 cup of water
- 11/2 cups baby green lettuce leaves, washed
- 3 wheat tortillas

Directions:
1. Brown the ground beef in a dry skillet over medium-high heat.
2. Add in the red onion and garlic.
3. Sauté the onion until it goes clear.
4. Transfer the contents of the skillet to the slow cooker.
5. Add the remaining ingredients and simmer on low for 30–45 minutes.
6. Stir through the green lettuce for the last few minutes to wilt.
7. Slice tortillas and gently toast under the broiler until slightly crispy.
8. Serve on top of the turkey chili.

Nutrition: Calories 93.5, Protein 8g, Carbohydrates 3g, Fat 5.5g, Cholesterol 30.5mg, Sodium 84.5mg, Potassium 142.5mg, Phosphorus 92.5mg, Calcium 29mg, Fiber 0.5g

176. Herbs and Lemony Roasted Chicken

Preparation Time: 15 Minutes
Cooking Time: 1 Hour and 30 Minutes
Servings: 8
Ingredients:
- 1/2 teaspoon ground black pepper
- 1/2 teaspoon mustard powder
- 1/2 teaspoon salt
- 1 3-lb whole chicken
- 1 teaspoon garlic powder
- 2 lemons
- 2 tablespoons. olive oil
- 2 teaspoons. Italian seasoning

Directions:
1. In a small bowl, mix black pepper, garlic powder, mustard powder, and salt.
2. Rinse chicken well and slice off giblets.
3. In a greased 9 x 13 baking dish, place chicken on it. Add 11/2 teaspoon of seasoning made earlier inside the chicken and rub the remaining seasoning around the chicken.
4. In a small bowl, mix olive oil and juice from 2 lemons. Drizzle over chicken.
5. Bake chicken in an oven preheated at 3500 F until juices run clear, for around 11/2 hour. Occasionally, baste the chicken with its juices.

Nutrition: Calories per Serving 190, Carbohydrates 2g, protein 35g, fats 9g, phosphorus 341mg, potassium 439mg, sodium 328mg

177. Ground Chicken & Peas Curry

Preparation Time: 15 minutes
Cooking Time: 6-10 minutes
Servings: 3-4
Ingredients:

- 3 tablespoons essential olive oil
- 2 bay leaves
- 2 onions grind to some paste
- ½ tablespoon garlic paste
- ½ tablespoon ginger paste
- 2 Red bell peppers, chopped finely
- 1 tablespoon ground cumin
- 1 tablespoon ground coriander
- 1 teaspoon ground turmeric
- 1 teaspoon red chili powder
- Salt, to taste
- 1-pound lean ground chicken
- 2 cups frozen peas
- 1½ cups water
- 1-2 teaspoons garam masala powder

Directions:

1. Warm oil on medium heat in a deep skillet. Add bay leaves and sauté for approximately half a minute. Add onion paste and sauté for about 3-4 minutes.
2. Add garlic and ginger paste and sauté for around 1-1½ minutes. Add Red bell peppers and spices and cook, occasionally stirring, for about 3-4 minutes.
3. Stir in chicken and cook for about 4-5 minutes. Stir in peas and water and bring to a boil on high heat.

4. Adjust the heat to low and simmer within 5-8 minutes or till the desired doneness. Stir in garam masala and remove from heat. Serve hot.

Nutrition: Calories: 450 Fat: 10g Carbohydrates: 19g Fiber: 6g Protein: 38g Phosphorus 268 mg Potassium 753.5 mg Sodium 17 mg

178. **Ground Chicken with Basil**

Preparation Time: 15 minutes
Cooking Time: 16 minutes
Servings: 8
Ingredients:

- 2 pounds lean ground chicken
- 3 tablespoons coconut oil, divided
- 1 zucchini, chopped
- 1 red bell pepper, seeded and chopped
- ½ of green bell pepper, seeded and chopped
- 4 garlic cloves, minced
- 1 (1-inch) piece fresh ginger, minced
- 1 (1-inch) piece fresh turmeric, minced

- 1 fresh red chili, sliced thinly
- 1 tablespoon organic honey
- 1 tablespoon coconut aminos
- 1½ tablespoons fish sauce
- ½ cup fresh basil, chopped
- Salt
- ground black pepper
- 1 tablespoon fresh lime juice

Directions:

1. Heat a large skillet on medium-high heat. Add ground beef and cook for approximately 5 minutes or till browned completely.
2. Transfer the beef to a bowl. In a similar pan, melt 1 tablespoon of coconut oil on medium-high heat. Add zucchini and bell peppers and stir fry for around 3-4 minutes.
3. Transfer the vegetables inside the bowl with chicken. In precisely the same pan, melt remaining coconut oil on medium heat. Add garlic, ginger, turmeric, and red chili and sauté for approximately 1-2 minutes.
4. Add chicken mixture, honey, and coconut aminos and increase the heat to high. Cook within 4-5 minutes or till sauce is nearly reduced. Stir in remaining ingredients and take off from the heat.

Nutrition: Calories: 407 Fat: 7g Carbohydrates: 20g Fiber: 13g Protein: 36g Phosphorus 149 mg Potassium 706.3 mg Sodium 21.3 mg

179. <u>Chicken &Veggie Casserole</u>

Preparation Time: 15 minutes
Cooking Time: 30 minutes
Servings: 4
Ingredients:

- 1/3 cup Dijon mustard
- 1/3 cup organic honey
- 1 teaspoon dried basil

- ¼ teaspoon ground turmeric
- 1 teaspoon dried basil, crushed
- Salt
- ground black pepper
- 1¾ pound chicken breasts
- 1 cup fresh white mushrooms, sliced
- ½ head broccoli, cut into small florets

Directions:
1. Warm oven to 350 degrees F. Lightly greases a baking dish. In a bowl, mix all ingredients except chicken, mushrooms, and broccoli.
2. Put the chicken in your prepared baking dish, then top with mushroom slices. Place broccoli florets around chicken evenly.
3. Pour 1 / 2 of honey mixture over chicken and broccoli evenly. Bake for approximately 20 minutes. Now, coat the chicken with the remaining sauce and bake for about 10 minutes.

Nutrition: Calories: 427 Fat: 9g Carbohydrates: 16g Fiber: 7g Protein: 35g Phosphorus 353 mg Potassium 529.3 mg Sodium 1 mg

180.   <u>Chicken & Cauliflower Rice Casserole</u>

Preparation Time: 15 minutes
Cooking Time: 1 hour & 15 minutes
Servings: 8-10
Ingredients:
- 2 tablespoons coconut oil, divided
- 3-pound bone-in chicken thighs and drumsticks
- Salt
- ground black pepper
- 3 carrots, peeled and sliced
- 1 onion, chopped finely
- 2 garlic cloves, chopped finely

- 2 tablespoons fresh cinnamon, chopped finely
- 2 teaspoons ground cumin
- 1 teaspoon ground coriander
- 12 teaspoon ground cinnamon
- ½ teaspoon ground turmeric
- 1 teaspoon paprika
- ¼ tsp red pepper cayenne
- 1 (28-ounce) can diced red bell peppers with liquid
- 1 red bell pepper, thin strips
- ½ cup fresh parsley leaves, minced
- Salt, to taste
- 1 head cauliflower, grated to some rice-like consistency
- 1 lemon, sliced thinly

Directions:
1. Warm oven to 375 degrees F. In a large pan, melt 1 tablespoon of coconut oil at high heat. Add chicken pieces and cook for about 3-5 minutes per side or till golden brown.
2. Transfer the chicken to a plate. In a similar pan, sauté the carrot, onion, garlic, and ginger for about 4-5 minutes on medium heat.
3. Stir in spices and remaining coconut oil. Add chicken, red bell peppers, bell pepper, parsley plus salt, and simmer for approximately 3-5 minutes.
4. In the bottom of a 13x9-inch rectangular baking dish, spread the cauliflower rice evenly. Place chicken mixture over cauliflower rice evenly and top with lemon slices.
5. With foil paper, cover the baking dish and bake for approximately 35 minutes. Uncover the baking dish and bake for about 25 minutes.

Nutrition: Calories: 412 Fat: 12g Carbohydrates: 23g Protein: 34g Phosphorus 201 mg Potassium 289.4 mg Sodium 507.4 mg

181.Chicken Meatloaf with Veggies

Preparation Time: 20 minutes
Cooking Time: 1-1¼ hours
Servings: 4

Ingredients:
For Meatloaf:
- ½ cup cooked chickpeas
- 2 egg whites
- 2½ teaspoons poultry seasoning
- Salt
- ground black pepper
- 10-ounce lean ground chicken
- 1 cup red bell pepper, seeded and minced
- 1 cup celery stalk, minced
- 1/3 cup steel-cut oats
- 1 cup tomato puree, divided
- 2 tablespoons dried onion flakes, crushed
- 1 tablespoon prepared mustard

For Veggies:
- 2-pounds summer squash, sliced
- 16-ounce frozen Brussels sprouts
- 2 tablespoons extra-virgin extra virgin olive oil
- Salt
- ground black pepper

Directions:

1. Warm oven to 350 degrees F. Grease a 9x5-inch loaf pan. In a mixer, add chickpeas, egg whites, poultry seasoning, salt, and black pepper and pulse till smooth.
2. Transfer a combination in a large bowl. Add chicken, veggies oats, ½ cup of tomato puree, and onion flakes and mix till well combined.
3. Transfer the amalgamation into the prepared loaf pan evenly. With both hands, press down the amalgamation slightly.
4. In another bowl, mix mustard and remaining tomato puree. Place the mustard mixture over the loaf pan evenly.
5. Bake approximately 1-1¼ hours or till the desired doneness. Meanwhile, in a big pan of water, arrange a steamer basket. Cover and steam for about 10-12 minutes. Drain well and aside.
6. Now, prepare the Brussels sprouts according to the package's directions. In a big bowl, add veggies, oil, salt, and black pepper and toss to coat well. Serve the meatloaf with veggies.

Nutrition: Calories: 420 Fat: 9g Carbohydrates: 21g Protein: 36g Phosphorus 237.1 mg Potassium 583.6 mg Sodium 136 mg

182.　Roasted Spatchcock Chicken

Preparation Time: 20 minutes
Cooking Time: 50 minutes
Servings: 4-6
Ingredients:

- 1 (4-pound) whole chicken
- 1 (1-inch) piece fresh ginger, sliced
- 4 garlic cloves, chopped
- 1 small bunch of fresh thyme
- Pinch of cayenne
- Salt
- ground black pepper
- ¼ cup fresh lemon juice
- 3 tablespoons extra virgin olive oil

Directions:

1. Arrange chicken, breast side down onto a large cutting board. With a kitchen shear, begin with the thigh, cut along 1 side of the backbone, and turn the chicken around.
2. Now, cut along sleep issues and discard the backbone. Change the inside and open it like a book. Flatten the backbone firmly to flatten.
3. In a food processor, add all ingredients except chicken and pulse till smooth. In a big baking dish, add the marinade mixture.
4. Add chicken and coat with marinade generously. With a plastic wrap, cover the baking dish and refrigerate to marinate overnight.
5. Preheat the oven to 450 degrees F. Arrange a rack in a very roasting pan. Remove the chicken from the refrigerator makes onto a rack over the roasting pan, skin side down. Roast for about 50 minutes, turning once in a middle way.

Nutrition: Calories: 419 Fat: 14g Carbohydrates: 28g Protein: 40g Phosphorus 166 mg Potassium 196 mg Sodium 68 mg

183.   <u>**Roasted Chicken with Veggies & Mango**</u>

Preparation Time: 20 minutes
Cooking Time: 1 hour
Servings: 4
Ingredients:
- 1 teaspoon ground ginger
- ½ teaspoon ground cumin
- ½ teaspoon ground coriander
- 1 teaspoon paprika
- Salt
- ground black pepper
- 1 (3 ½-4-pound) whole chicken
- 1 unpeeled mango, cut into 8 wedges
- 2 medium carrots, peeled and cut 1nto 2-inch pieces
- ½ cup of water

Directions:

1. Warm oven to 450 degrees F. In a little bowl, mix the spices. Rub the chicken with spice mixture evenly.
2. Arrange the chicken in a substantial Dutch oven and put the mango and carrot around it.
3. Add water and cover the pan tightly. Roast for around 30 minutes. Uncover and roast for about half an hour.

Nutrition: Calories: 432 Fat: 10g Carbohydrates: 20g Protein: 34g Potassium 481 mg Sodium 418 m Phosphorus 170 mg

184. <u>Roasted Chicken Breast</u>

Preparation Time: 15 minutes
Cooking Time: 40 minutes
Servings: 4-6
Ingredients:

- ½ of a small apple, peeled, cored, and chopped
- 1 bunch scallion, trimmed and chopped roughly
- 8 fresh ginger slices, chopped
- 2 garlic cloves, chopped
- 3 tablespoons essential olive oil
- 12 teaspoon sesame oil, toasted
- 3 tablespoons using apple cider vinegar
- 1 tablespoon fish sauce
- 1 tablespoon coconut aminos
- Salt
- ground black pepper
- 4-pounds chicken thighs

Directions:

1. Pulse all the fixing except chicken thighs in a blender. Transfer a combination and chicken right into a large Ziploc bag and seal it.
2. Shake the bag to marinade well. Refrigerate to marinate for about 12 hours. Warm oven to 400 degrees F. arranges a rack in foil paper-lined baking sheet.

3. Place the chicken thighs on the rack, skin-side down. Roast for about 40 minutes, flipping once within the middle way.

Nutrition: Calories: 451 Fat: 17g Carbohydrates: 277g Protein: 42g Phosphorus 121 mg Potassium 324 mg Sodium 482.9 mg

185. <u>Grilled Chicken</u>

Preparation Time: 15 minutes
Cooking Time: 41 minutes
Servings: 8
Ingredients:

- 1 (3-inch) piece fresh ginger, minced
- 6 small garlic cloves, minced
- 1½ tablespoons tamarind paste
- 1 tablespoon organic honey
- ¼ cup coconut aminos
- 2½ tablespoons extra virgin olive oil
- 1½ tablespoons sesame oil, toasted
- ½ teaspoon ground cardamom
- Salt
- ground white pepper
- 1 (4-5-pound) whole chicken, cut into 8 pieces

Directions:

1. Mix all ingredients except chicken pieces in a large glass bowl. With a fork, pierce the chicken pieces thoroughly.
2. Add chicken pieces in bowl and coat with marinade generously. Cover and refrigerate to marinate for approximately a couple of hours to overnight.
3. Preheat the grill to medium heat. Grease the grill grate. Place the chicken pieces on the grill, bone-side down. Grill, covered approximately 20-25 minutes.
4. Change the side and grill, covered approximately 6-8 minutes. Change alongside it and grill, covered for about 5-8 minutes. Serve.

Nutrition: Calories: 423 Fat: 12g Carbohydrates: 20g Protein: 42g Sodium 281.9 mg Phosphorus 0 mg Potassium 0 mg

186. Grilled Chicken with Pineapple & Veggies

Preparation Time: 20 or so minutes
Cooking Time: 22 minutes
Servings: 4
Ingredients:
For Sauce:

- 1 garlic oil, minced
- ¾ teaspoon fresh ginger, minced
- ½ cup coconut aminos
- ¼ cup fresh pineapple juice
- 2 tablespoons freshly squeezed lemon juice
- 2 tablespoons balsamic vinegar
- ¼ teaspoon red pepper flakes, crushed
- Salt
- ground black pepper

For Grilling:

- 4 skinless, boneless chicken breasts
- 1 pineapple, peeled and sliced
- 1 bell pepper, seeded and cubed
- 1 zucchini, sliced
- 1red onion, sliced

Directions:

1. For sauce in a pan, mix all ingredients on medium-high heat. Bring to a boil reducing the heat to medium-low. Cook approximately 5-6 minutes.
2. Remove, then keep aside to cool down slightly. Coat the chicken breasts about ¼ from the sauce. Keep aside for approximately half an hour.
3. Preheat the grill to medium-high heat. Grease the grill grate. Grill the chicken pieces for around 5-8 minutes per side.
4. Now, squeeze pineapple and vegetables on the grill grate. Grill the pineapple within 3 minutes per side. Grill the vegetables for approximately 4-5 minutes, stirring once inside the middle way.
5. Cut the chicken breasts into desired size slices, divide the chicken, pineapple, and vegetables into serving plates. Serve alongside the remaining sauce.

Nutrition: Calories: 435 Fat: 12g Carbohydrates: 25g Protein: 38g Phosphorus 184 mg Potassium 334.4 mg Sodium 755.6 mg

187. Ground Turkey with Veggies

Preparation Time: 15 minutes
Cooking Time: 12 minutes
Servings: 4
Ingredients:

- 1 tablespoon sesame oil
- 1 tablespoon coconut oil
- 1-pound lean ground turkey
- 2 tablespoons fresh ginger, minced
- 2 minced garlic cloves
- 1 (16-ounce) bag vegetable mix (broccoli, carrot, cabbage, kale, and Brussels sprouts)
- ¼ cup coconut aminos
- 2 tablespoons balsamic vinegar

Directions:

1. In a big skillet, heat both oils on medium-high heat. Add turkey, ginger, and garlic and cook approximately 5-6 minutes. Add vegetable mix and cook about 4-5 minutes. Stir in coconut aminos and vinegar and cook for about 1 minute. Serve hot.

Nutrition: Calories: 234 Fat: 9g Carbohydrates: 9g Protein: 29g Phosphorus 14 mg Potassium 92.2 mg   Sodium 114.9 mg

188. Ground Turkey with Asparagus

Preparation Time: 15 minutes
Cooking Time: 15 minutes
Servings: 8
Ingredients:

- 1¾ pound lean ground turkey
- 2 tablespoons sesame oil
- 1 medium onion, chopped
- 1 cup celery, chopped
- 6 garlic cloves, minced
- 2 cups asparagus, cut into 1-inch pieces
- 1/3 cup coconut aminos
- 2½ teaspoons ginger powder
- 2 tablespoons organic coconut crystals
- 1 tablespoon arrowroot starch
- 1 tablespoon cold water
- ¼ teaspoon red pepper flakes, crushed

Directions:

1. Heat a substantial nonstick skillet on medium-high heat. Add turkey and cook for approximately 5-7 minutes or till browned. With a slotted spoon, transfer the turkey inside a bowl and discard the grease from the skillet.
2. Heat-up oil on medium heat in the same skillet. Add onion, celery, and garlic and sauté for about 5 minutes. Add asparagus and cooked turkey, minimizing the temperature to medium-low.
3. Meanwhile, inside a pan, mix coconut aminos, ginger powder, and coconut crystals n medium heat and convey some boil.

4. Mix arrowroot starch and water in a smaller bowl. Slowly add arrowroot mixture, stirring continuously. Cook approximately 2-3 minutes.
5. Add the sauce in the skillet with turkey mixture and stir to blend. Stir in red pepper flakes and cook for approximately 2-3 minutes. Serve hot.

Nutrition: Calories: 309 Fat: 20g Carbohydrates: 19g Protein: 28g Potassium 196.4 mg Sodium 77.8 mg Phosphorus 0 mg

189. <u>Ground Turkey with Peas</u>

Preparation Time: 15 minutes
Cooking Time: 35 minutes
Servings: 4
Ingredients:

- 3-4 tablespoons coconut oil
- 1-pound lean ground turkey
- 1-2 fresh red chilis, chopped
- 1 onion, chopped
- Salt, to taste
- 2 minced garlic cloves
- 1 (1-inch) piece fresh ginger, grated finely
- 1 tablespoon curry powder
- 1 teaspoon ground coriander
- 1 teaspoon ground cumin
- 1 teaspoon ground turmeric
- 2 large Yukon gold carrots, cubed into 1-inch size
- ½ cup of water
- 1 cup fresh peas, shelled
- 2-4 plum red bell peppers, chopped
- ½ cup fresh cilantro, chopped

Directions:
1. In a substantial pan, heat oil on medium-high heat. Add turkey and cook for about 4-5 minutes. Add chilis and onion and cook for about 4-5 minutes.
2. Add garlic and ginger and cook approximately 1-2 minutes. Stir in spices, carrots, and water and convey to your boil
3. Reduce the warmth to medium-low. Simmer covered around 15-20 or so minutes. Add peas and red bell peppers and cook for about 2-3 minutes. Serve using the garnishing of cilantro.

Nutrition: Calories: 452 Fat: 14g Carbohydrates: 24g Fiber: 13g Protein: 36g Phosphorus 38 mg   Potassium 99.5 mg Sodium 373.4 mg

190. <u>Turkey & Pumpkin Chili</u>

Preparation Time: 15 minutes
Cooking Time: 41 minutes
Servings: 4-6
Ingredients:

- 2 tablespoons extra-virgin olive oil
- 1 green bell pepper, seeded and chopped
- 1 small yellow onion, chopped

- 2 garlic cloves, chopped finely
- 1-pound lean ground turkey
- 1 (15-ounce) pumpkin puree
- 1 (14 ½-ounce) can diced red bell peppers with liquid
- 1 teaspoon ground cumin
- ½ teaspoon ground turmeric
- ½ teaspoon ground cinnamon
- 1 cup of water
- 1 can chickpeas, rinsed and drained

Directions:
1. Heat-up oil on medium-low heat in a big pan. Add the bell pepper, onion, and garlic and sauté for approximately 5 minutes. Add turkey and cook for about 5-6 minutes.
2. Add Red bell peppers, pumpkin, spices, and water and convey to your boil on high heat. Reduce the temperature to medium-low heat and stir in chickpeas. Simmer, covered for approximately a half-hour, stirring occasionally. Serve hot.

Nutrition: Calories: 437 Fat: 17g Carbohydrates: 29g Protein: 42g Phosphorus 150 mg Potassium 652 mg Sodium 570 mg

191. Spanish Cod in Sauce

Preparation Time: 10 minutes
Cooking Time: 5 1/2 hours
Servings: 2
Ingredients:

- 1 teaspoon garlic, diced
- 1 white onion, sliced
- 1 jalapeno pepper, chopped
- 1/3 cup chicken stock
- 7 oz. Spanish cod fillet
- 1 teaspoon paprika
- 1 teaspoon salt

Directions:
1. Pour chicken stock into the saucepan. Add garlic, onion, jalapeno pepper, paprika, and salt.
2. Bring the liquid to boil and then simmer it. Chop the cod fillet and add it to the liquid. Simmer the fish for 10 minutes over low heat. Serve the fish in the bowls.

Nutrition: Calories 113 Fat 1.2g Fiber 1.9g Carbs 7.2g Protein 18.9g Potassium 659 mg Sodium 597 mg Phosphorus 18 mg

192. <u>Salmon Baked in Foil with Fresh Thyme</u>

Preparation Time: 10 minutes
Cooking Time: 30 minutes
Servings: 4
Ingredients:

- 4 fresh thyme sprigs
- 4 garlic cloves, peeled, roughly chopped
- 16 oz. salmon fillets (4 oz. each fillet)
- ½ teaspoon salt
- ½ teaspoon ground black pepper
- 4 tablespoons cream
- 4 teaspoons butter
- ¼ teaspoon cumin seeds

Directions:

1. Line the baking tray with foil. Sprinkle the fish fillets with salt, ground black pepper, cumin seeds, and arrange them in the tray with oil.
2. Add thyme sprig on the top of every fillet. Then add cream, butter, and garlic. Bake the fish for 30 minutes at 345F. Serve.

Nutrition: Calories 198 Fat 11.6g Carbs 1.8g Protein 22.4g Phosphorus 425 mg Potassium 660.9 mg Sodium 366 mg

193. Poached Halibut in Mango Sauce

Preparation Time: 10 minutes
Cooking Time: 10 minutes
Servings: 4
Ingredients:

- 1-pound halibut
- 1/3 cup butter
- 1 rosemary sprig
- ½ teaspoon ground black pepper
- 1 teaspoon salt
- 1 teaspoon honey
- ¼ cup of mango juice
- 1 teaspoon cornstarch

Directions:

1. Put butter in the saucepan and melt it. Add rosemary sprig. Sprinkle the halibut with salt and ground black pepper. Put the fish in the boiling butter and poach it for 4 minutes.
2. Meanwhile, pour mango juice into the skillet. Add honey and bring the liquid to boil. Add cornstarch and whisk until the liquid starts to be thick. Then remove it from the heat.
3. Transfer the poached halibut to the plate and cut it on 4. Place every fish serving in the serving plate and top with mango sauce.

Nutrition: Calories 349 Fat 29.3g Fiber 0.1g Carbs 3.2g Protein 17.8g Phosphorus 154 mg Potassium 388.6 mg Sodium 29.3 mg

194. Fish En' Papillote

Preparation Time: 15 minutes
Cooking Time: 20 minutes
Servings: 3

Ingredients:

- 10 oz. snapper fillet
- 1 tablespoon fresh dill, chopped
- 1 white onion, peeled, sliced
- ½ teaspoon tarragon
- 1 tablespoon olive oil
- 1 teaspoon salt
- ½ teaspoon hot pepper
- 2 tablespoons sour cream

Directions:

1. Make the medium size packets from parchment and arrange them in the baking tray. Cut the snapper fillet into 3 and sprinkle them with salt, tarragon, and hot pepper.
2. Put the fish fillets in the parchment packets. Then top the fish with olive oil, sour cream, sliced onion, and fresh dill. Bake the fish for 20 minutes at 355F. Serve.

Nutrition: Calories 204 Fat 8.2g Carbs 4.6g Protein 27.2g Phosphorus 138.8 mg Potassium 181.9 mg Sodium 59.6 mg

195. Tuna Casserole

Preparation Time: 15 minutes
Cooking Time: 35 minutes
Servings: 4
Ingredients:

- ½ cup Cheddar cheese, shredded
- 2 Red bell peppers, chopped
- 7 oz. tuna filet, chopped
- 1 teaspoon ground coriander
- ½ teaspoon salt
- 1 teaspoon olive oil
- ½ teaspoon dried oregano

Directions:

1. Brush the casserole mold with olive oil. Mix up together chopped tuna fillet with dried oregano and ground coriander.
2. Place the fish in the mold and flatten well to get the layer. Then add chopped red bell peppers and shredded cheese. Cover the casserole with foil and secure the edges. Bake the meal for 35 minutes at 355F. Serve.

Nutrition: Calories 260 Fat 21.5g Carbs 2.7g Protein 14.6g Phosphorus 153 mg Potassium 311 mg   Sodium 600 mg

196. Fish Chili with Lentils

Preparation Time: 10 minutes
Cooking Time: 30 minutes
Servings: 4
Ingredients:

- 1 red pepper, chopped
- 1 yellow onion, diced
- 1 teaspoon ground black pepper
- 1 teaspoon butter

- 1 jalapeno pepper, chopped
- ½ cup lentils
- 3 cups chicken stock
- 1 teaspoon salt
- 1 teaspoon chili pepper
- 3 tablespoons fresh cilantro, chopped
- 8 oz. cod, chopped

Directions:
1. Place butter, red pepper, onion, and ground black pepper in the saucepan. Roast the vegetables for 5 minutes over medium heat.
2. Then add chopped jalapeno pepper, lentils, and chili pepper. Mix up the mixture well and add chicken stock. Stir until homogenous. Add cod. Close the lid and cook chili for 20 minutes over medium heat.

Nutrition: Calories 187 Fat 2.3g Carbs 21.3g Protein 20.6g Phosphorus 50 mg Potassium 281 mg Sodium 43.8 mg

197.   Chili Mussels

Preparation Time: 7 minutes
Cooking Time: 10 minutes
Servings: 4
Ingredients:
- 1-pound mussels
- 1 chili pepper, chopped
- 1 cup chicken stock
- ½ cup almond milk
- 1 teaspoon olive oil
- 1 teaspoon minced garlic
- 1 teaspoon ground coriander
- ½ teaspoon salt
- 1 cup fresh parsley, chopped
- 4 tablespoons lemon juice

Directions:
1. Pour almond milk into the saucepan. Add chili pepper, chicken stock, olive oil, minced garlic, ground coriander, salt, and lemon juice.
2. Bring the liquid to boil and add mussels. Boil the mussel for 4 minutes or until they will open shells. Then add chopped parsley and mix up the meal well. Remove it from the heat.

Nutrition: Calories 136 Fat 4.7g Fiber 0.6g Carbs 7.5g Protein 15.3g Phosphorus 180.8 mg Potassium 312.5 mg Sodium 319.6 mg

198.   Grilled Cod

Preparation Time: 10 min
Cooking Time: 10 minutes
Servings: 4
Ingredients:
- 2 (8 ounce) fillets cod, cut in half
- 1 tablespoon oregano
- ½ teaspoon lemon pepper

- ¼ teaspoon ground black pepper
- 2 tablespoons olive oil
- 1 lemon, juiced
- 2 tablespoons chopped green onion (white part only)

Directions:
1. Season both sides of cod with oregano, lemon pepper, and black pepper. Set fish aside on a plate. Heat butter in a small saucepan over medium heat, stir in lemon juice and green onion, and cook until onion is softened, about 3 minutes.
2. Place cod onto oiled grates and grill until fish is browned and flakes easily, about 3 minutes per side; baste with olive oil mixture frequently while grilling. Allow cod to rest of the heat for about 5 minutes before serving.

Nutrition: Calories 92, Total Fat 7.4g, Saturated Fat 1g, Cholesterol 14mg, Sodium 19mg, Total Carbohydrate 2.5g, Dietary Fiber 1g, Total Sugars 0.5g, Protein 5.4g, Calcium 25mg, Iron 1mg, Potassium 50mg, Phosphorus 36 mg

199. Cod and Green Bean Curry

Preparation Time: 15 min
Cooking Time: 60 minutes
Servings: 4
Ingredients:
- 1/2-pound green beans, trimmed and cut into bite-sized pieces
- 1 white onion, sliced
- 2 cloves garlic, minced
- 1 tablespoon olive oil, or more as needed
- Ground black pepper to taste
- Curry Mixture:
- 2 tablespoons water, or more as needed
- 2 teaspoons curry powder
- 2 teaspoons ground ginger
- 1 1/2 (6 ounce) cod fillets

Directions:
1. Preheat the oven to 400 degrees F.
2. Combine green beans, onion, and garlic in a large glass baking dish. Toss with olive oil to coat; season with the pepper.
3. Bake in the preheated oven, stirring occasionally, until edges of onion are slightly charred and green beans start to look dry, about 40 minutes. In the meantime, mix water, curry powder, and ginger together.
4. Remove dish and stir the vegetables; stir in curry mixture. Increase oven temperature to 450 degrees F.
5. Lay cod over the bottom of the dish and coat with vegetables. Continue baking until fish is opaque, 25 to 30 minutes depending on thickness.

Nutrition: Calories 64, Total Fat 3.8g, Saturated Fat 0.5g, Cholesterol 0mg, Sodium 5mg, Total Carbohydrate 7.7g, Dietary Fiber 2.9g, Total Sugars 2g, Protein 1.6g, Calcium 35mg, Iron 1mg, Potassium 180mg, Phosphorus 101 mg

200. White Fish Soup

Preparation Time: 15 min
Cooking Time: 20 minutes

Servings: 4

Ingredients:

- 2 tablespoons olive oil
- 1 onion, finely diced
- 1 green bell pepper, chopped
- 1 rib celery, thinly sliced
- 3 cups chicken broth, or more to taste
- 1/4 cup chopped fresh parsley
- 1 1/2 pounds cod, cut into 3/4-inch cubes
- Pepper to taste
- 1 dash red pepper flakes

Directions:

1. Heat oil in a soup pot over medium heat.
2. Add onion, bell pepper, and celery and cook until wilted, about 5 minutes.
3. Add broth and bring to a simmer, about 5 minutes.
4. Cook 15 to 20 minutes.
5. Add cod, parsley, and red pepper flakes and simmer until fish flakes easily with a fork, 8 to 10 minutes more.
6. Season with black pepper.

Nutrition: Calories 117, Total Fat 7.2g, Saturated Fat 1.4g, Cholesterol 18mg, Sodium 37mg, Total Carbohydrate 5.4g, Dietary Fiber 1.3g, Total Sugars 2.8g, Protein 8.1g, Calcium 23mg, Iron 1mg, Potassium 122mg, Phosphorus 111 mg

201. Onion Dijon Crusted Catfish

Preparation Time: 05 min
Cooking Time: 25 minutes
Servings: 4
Ingredients:

- 1 onion, finely chopped
- 1/4 cup honey Dijon mustard
- 4 (6 ounce) fillets catfish fillets
- Pepper to taste
- Dried parsley flakes

Directions:

1. Preheat the oven to 350 degrees F.
2. In a small bowl, mix together the onion and mustard. Season the catfish fillets with pepper. Place on a baking tray and coat with the onion and honey. Sprinkle parsley flakes over the top.
3. Bake for 20 minutes in the preheated oven, then turn the oven to broil. Broil until golden, 3 to 5 minutes.

Nutrition: Calories 215, Total Fat 6.1g, Saturated Fat 1.7g, Cholesterol 87mg, Sodium 86mg, Total Carbohydrate 10.4g, Dietary Fiber 0.6g, Total Sugars 4.2g, Protein 31.6g, Calcium 8mg, Iron 0mg, Potassium 46mg, Phosphorus 30 mg

202. Herb Baked Tuna

Preparation Time: 10 min
Cooking Time: 20 minutes

Servings: 4
Ingredients:

- 4 (6 ounce) tuna fillets
- 2 tablespoons dried parsley
- 3/4 teaspoon paprika
- 1/2 teaspoon dried thyme
- 1/2 teaspoon dried oregano
- 1/2 teaspoon dried basil
- 1/2 teaspoon ground black pepper
- 2 tablespoons lemon juice
- 1 tablespoon olive oil
- 1/4 teaspoon garlic powder

Directions:

1. Preheat oven to 350 degrees F.
2. Arrange tuna fillets in a 9x13-inch baking dish. Combine parsley, paprika, thyme, oregano, basil, and black pepper in a small bowl; sprinkle herb mixture over fish. Mix lemon juice, olive oil, and garlic powder in another bowl; drizzle olive oil mixture over fish.
3. Bake in preheated oven until fish is easily flaked with a fork, about 20 minutes.

Nutrition: Calories 139, Total Fat 12.5g, Saturated Fat 0.6g, Cholesterol 0mg, Sodium 3mg, Total Carbohydrate 1g, Dietary Fiber 0.5g, Total Sugars 0.3g, Protein 6.2g, Calcium 11mg, Iron 1mg, Potassium 39mg, Phosphorus 20 mg

203.   Cilantro Lime Salmon

Preparation Time: 10 min
Cooking Time: 20 minutes
Servings: 4
Ingredients:

- ¼ cup olive oil
- ¼ cup chopped fresh cilantro
- ½ teaspoon chopped garlic
- 5 (5 ounce) fillets salmon
- Ground black pepper to taste
- ½ lemon, juiced
- ½ lime, juiced

Directions:

1. Heat the olive oil in a skillet over medium heat.
2. Stir cilantro and garlic into the oil; cook about 1 minute.
3. Season salmon fillets with black pepper; lay gently into the oil mixture.
4. Place a cover on the skillet. Cook fillets 10 minutes, turn, and continue cooking until the fish flakes easily with a fork and is lightly browned, about 10 minutes more.
5. Squeeze lemon juice and lime juice over the fillets to serve.

Nutrition: Calories 249, Total Fat 18.7g, Saturated Fat 3.3g, Cholesterol 18mg, Sodium 48mg, Total Carbohydrate 1.7g, Dietary Fiber 0.5g, Total Sugars 0.3g, Protein 20.7g, Calcium 6mg, Iron 0mg, Potassium 26mg, Phosphorus 20 mg

204.   Asian Ginger Tuna

Preparation Time: 10 min
Cooking Time: 20 minutes
Servings: 4
Ingredients:

- 1 cup water
- 1 tablespoon minced fresh ginger root
- 1 tablespoon minced garlic
- 2 tablespoons soy sauce
- 1 1/4 pounds thin tuna fillets
- 6 large white mushrooms, sliced
- 1/4 cup sliced green onion
- 1 tablespoon chopped fresh cilantro (optional)

Directions:

1. Put water, ginger, and garlic in a wide pot with a lid.
2. Bring the water to a boil, reduce heat to medium-low, and simmer 3 to 5 minutes.
3. Stir soy sauce into the water mixture; add tuna fillets.
4. Place cover on the pot, bring water to a boil, and let cook for 3 minutes more.
5. Add mushrooms, cover, and cook until the fish loses pinkness and begins to flake, about 3 minutes more.
6. Sprinkle green onion over the fillets, cover, and cook for 30 seconds.
7. Garnish with cilantro to serve.

Nutrition: Calories 109, Total Fat 7.9g, Saturated Fat 0g, Cholesterol 0mg, Sodium 454mg, Total Carbohydrate 3.1g, Dietary Fiber 0.6g, Total Sugars 0.9g, Protein 7.1g, Calcium 10mg, Iron 1mg, Potassium 158mg, Phosphorus 120 mg

205.   Cheesy Tuna Chowder

Preparation Time: 10 min
Cooking Time: 20 minutes
Servings: 4
Ingredients:

- 2 tablespoons olive oil
- 1/2 small onion, chopped
- 1 cup water
- 1/2 cup chopped celery
- 1 cup sliced baby carrots
- 3 cups soy almond milk, divided
- 1/3 cup all-purpose flour
- 1/2 teaspoon ground black pepper
- 1 1/2 pounds tuna fillets, cut into 1-inch pieces
- 1 1/2 cups shredded Cheddar cheese

Directions:

1. In a Dutch oven over medium heat, heat olive oil and sauté the onion until tender. Pour in water. Mix in celery, carrots, cook 10 minutes, stirring occasionally, until vegetables are tender.
2. In a small bowl, whisk together 1 1/2 cups almond milk and all-purpose flour. Mix into the Dutch oven.
3. Mix remaining almond milk, and pepper into the Dutch oven. Stirring occasionally, continue cooking the mixture about 10 minutes, until thickened.

4. Stir tuna into the mixture, and cook 5 minutes, or until fish is easily flaked with a fork. Mix in Cheddar cheese, and cook another 5 minutes, until melted.

Nutrition: Calories 228, Total Fat 15.5g, Saturated Fat 6.5g, Cholesterol 30mg, Sodium 206mg, Total Carbohydrate 10.8g, Dietary Fiber 1g, Total Sugars 4.1g, Protein 11.6g, Calcium 183mg, Iron 1mg, Potassium 163mg, Phosphorus 150 mg

206. Marinated Salmon Steak

Preparation Time: 10 min
Cooking Time: 10 minutes
Servings: 4
Ingredients:

- ¼ cup lime juice
- ¼ cup soy sauce
- 2 tablespoons olive oil
- 1 tablespoon lemon juice
- 2 tablespoons chopped fresh parsley
- 1 clove garlic, minced
- ½ teaspoon chopped fresh oregano
- ½ teaspoon ground black pepper
- 4 (4 ounce) salmon steaks

Directions:

1. In a large non-reactive dish, mix together the lime juice, soy sauce, olive oil, lemon juice, parsley, garlic, oregano, and pepper. Place the salmon steaks in the marinade and turn to coat. Cover, and refrigerate for at least 30 minutes.
2. Preheat grill for high heat.
3. Lightly oil grill grate. Cook the salmon steaks for 5 to 6 minutes, then salmon and baste with the marinade. Cook for an additional 5 minutes, or to desired doneness. Discard any remaining marinade.

Nutrition: Calories 108, Total Fat 8.4g, Saturated Fat 1.2g, Cholesterol 9mg, Sodium 910mg, Total Carbohydrate 3.6g, Dietary Fiber 0.4g, Total Sugars 1.7g, Protein 5.4g, Calcium 19mg, Iron 1mg, Potassium 172mg, Phosphorus 165 mg

207. Tuna with honey Glaze

Preparation Time: 10 min
Cooking Time: 10 minutes
Servings: 4
Ingredients:

- 1/4 cup honey
- 2 tablespoons Dijon mustard
- 4 (6 ounce) boneless tuna fillets
- Ground black pepper to taste

Directions:

1. Preheat the oven's broiler and set the oven rack at about 6 inches from the heat source; prepare the rack of a broiler pan with cooking spray.
2. Season the tuna with pepper and arrange onto the prepared broiler pan. Whisk together the honey and Dijon mustard in a small bowl; spoon mixture evenly onto top of salmon fillets.
3. Cook under the preheated broiler until the fish flakes easily with a fork, 10 to 15 minutes.

Nutrition: Calories 160, Total Fat 8.1g, Saturated Fat 0g, Cholesterol 0mg, Sodium 90mg, Total Carbohydrate 17.9g, Dietary Fiber 0.3g, Total Sugars 17.5g, Protein 5.7g, Calcium 6mg, Iron 0mg, Potassium 22mg, Phosphorus 16 mg

208.   Stuffed Mushrooms

Preparation Time: 10 min
Cooking Time: 10 minutes
Servings: 4
Ingredients:

- 12 large fresh mushrooms, stems removed
- ½ pound crabmeat, flaked
- 2 cups olive oil
- 2 cloves garlic, peeled and minced
- Garlic powder to taste
- Crushed red pepper to taste

Directions:

1. Arrange mushroom caps on a medium baking sheet, bottoms up. Chop and reserve mushroom stems.
2. Preheat oven to 350 degrees F.
3. In a medium saucepan over medium heat, heat oil. Mix in garlic and cook until tender, about 5 minutes.
4. In a medium bowl, mix together reserved mushroom stems, and crab meat. Liberally stuff mushrooms with the mixture. Drizzle with the garlic. Season with garlic powder and crushed red pepper.
5. Bake uncovered in the preheated oven 10 to 12 minutes, or until stuffing is lightly browned.

Nutrition: Calories 312, Total Fat 33.8g, Saturated Fat 4.8g, Cholesterol 4mg, Sodium 160mg, Total Carbohydrate 3.8g, Dietary Fiber 0.3g, Total Sugars 1.6g, Protein 2.2g, Calcium 3mg, Iron 1mg, Potassium 93mg, Phosphorus 86 mg

209. **<u>Shrimp Paella</u>**

Preparation Time: 5 minutes
Cooking Time: 10 minutes
Servings: 2
Ingredients:
- 1 cup cooked white rice
- 1 chopped red onion
- 1 tsp. paprika
- 1 chopped garlic clove
- 1 tbsp. olive oil
- 6 oz. frozen cooked shrimp
- 1 deseeded and sliced chili pepper
- 1 tbsp. oregano

Directions:
1. Warm-up olive oil in a large pan on medium-high heat. Add the onion and garlic and sauté for 2-3 minutes until soft. Now add the shrimp and sauté for a further 5 minutes or until hot through.
2. Now add the herbs, spices, chili, and rice with 1/2 cup boiling water. Stir until everything is warm, and the water has been absorbed. Plate up and serve.

Nutrition: Calories 221 Protein 17 g Carbs 31 g Fat 8 g Sodium 235 mg Potassium 176 mg Phosphorus 189 mg

210. <u>Salmon & Pesto Salad</u>

Preparation Time: 5 minutes
Cooking Time: 15 minutes
Servings: 2
Ingredients:
For the pesto:
- 1 minced garlic clove
- ½ cup fresh arugula
- ¼ cup extra virgin olive oil
- ½ cup fresh basil
- 1 tsp black pepper

For the salmon:
- 4 oz. skinless salmon fillet
- 1 tbsp. coconut oil

For the salad:
- ½ juiced lemon
- 2 sliced radishes
- ½ cup iceberg lettuce
- 1 tsp black pepper

Directions:
1. Prepare the pesto by blending all the fixing for the pesto in a food processor or grinding with a pestle and mortar. Set aside.
2. Add a skillet to the stove on medium-high heat and melt the coconut oil. Add the salmon to the pan. Cook for 7-8 minutes and turn over.
3. Cook within 3-4 minutes or until cooked through. Remove fillets from the skillet and allow to rest.
4. Mix the lettuce and the radishes and squeeze over the juice of ½ lemon. Shred the salmon using a fork and mix through the salad. Toss to coat and sprinkle with a little black pepper to serve.

Nutrition: Calories 221 Protein 13 g Carbs 1 g Fat 34 g Sodium 80 mg Potassium 119 mg Phosphorus 158 mg

211. Baked Fennel & Garlic Sea Bass

Preparation Time: 5 minutes
Cooking Time: 15 minutes
Servings: 2
Ingredients:

- 1 lemon
- ½ sliced fennel bulb
- 6 oz. sea bass fillets
- 1 tsp black pepper
- 2 garlic cloves

Directions:

1. Preheat the oven to 375°F. Sprinkle black pepper over the Sea Bass. Slice the fennel bulb and garlic cloves. Add 1 salmon fillet and half the fennel and garlic to one sheet of baking paper or tin foil.
2. Squeeze in 1/2 lemon juices. Repeat for the other fillet. Fold and add to the oven for 12-15 minutes or until fish is thoroughly cooked through.
3. Meanwhile, add boiling water to your couscous, cover, and allow to steam. Serve with your choice of rice or salad.

Nutrition: Calories 221 Protein 14 g Carbs 3 g Fat 2 g Sodium 119 mg Potassium 398 mg Phosphorus 149 mg

212. Lemon, Garlic, Cilantro Tuna and Rice

Preparation Time: 5 minutes
Cooking Time: 0 minutes
Servings: 2
Ingredients:

- ½ cup arugula

- 1 tbsp. extra virgin olive oil
- 1 cup cooked rice
- 1 tsp black pepper
- ¼ finely diced red onion
- 1 juiced lemon
- 3 oz. canned tuna
- 2 tbsp. Chopped fresh cilantro

Directions:

1. Mix the olive oil, pepper, cilantro, and red onion in a bowl. Stir in the tuna, cover, then serve with the cooked rice and arugula!

Nutrition: Calories 221 Protein 11 g Carbs 26 g Fat 7 g Sodium 143 mg Potassium 197 mg Phosphorus 182 mg

213. Cod & Green Bean Risotto

Preparation Time: 4 minutes
Cooking Time: 40 minutes
Servings: 2
Ingredients:

- ½ cup arugula
- 1 finely diced white onion
- 4 oz. cod fillet
- 1 cup white rice
- 2 lemon wedges
- 1 cup boiling water
- ¼ tsp. black pepper
- 1 cup low-sodium chicken broth
- 1 tbsp. extra virgin olive oil
- ½ cup green beans

Directions:

1. Warm-up oil in a large pan on medium heat. Sauté the chopped onion for 5 minutes until soft before adding in the rice and stirring for 1-2 minutes.
2. Combine the broth with boiling water. Add half of the liquid to the pan and stir. Slowly add the rest of the liquid while continuously stirring for up to 20-30 minutes.
3. Stir in the green beans to the risotto. Place the fish on top of the rice, cover, and steam for 10 minutes.
4. Use your fork to break up the fish fillets and stir into the rice. Sprinkle with freshly ground pepper to serve and a squeeze of fresh lemon. Serve with the lemon wedges and the arugula.

Nutrition: Calories 221 Protein 12 g Carbs 29 g Fat 8 g Sodium 398 mg Potassium 347 mg Phosphorus 241 mg

214. Crispy Fish Fillets

Preparation Time: 10 min
Cooking Time: 10 minutes
Servings: 4
Ingredients:

- 1 egg
- 2 tablespoons prepared yellow mustard
- 1/4 cup oil for frying
- ½ cup graham crakes
- 4 (6 ounce) fish fillets

Directions:

1. In a shallow dish, whisk together the egg, mustard, set aside. Place the graham crakes in another shallow dish.
2. Heat oil in a large heavy skillet over medium-high heat.
3. Dip fish fillets in the egg mixture. Dredge the fillets in the graham crakes, making sure to completely coat the fish. For extra crispy, dip into egg and graham crakes again.
4. Fry fish fillets in oil for 3 to 4 minutes on each side, or until golden brown.

Nutrition: Calories 194, Total Fat 17.8g, Saturated Fat 2.8g, Cholesterol 49mg, Sodium 225mg, Total Carbohydrate 4.4g, Dietary Fiber 0.4g, Total Sugars 0.2g, Protein 5.1g, Calcium 14mg, Iron 1mg, Potassium 98mg, Phosphorus 76 mg

215. Simple Soup

Preparation Time: 05 min
Cooking Time: 15 minutes
Servings: 4
Ingredients:

- 2 teaspoons tuna
- 4 cups water
- 1 (8 ounce) package silken tofu, diced
- 2 green onions, sliced diagonally into 1/2-inch pieces

Directions:

1. In a medium saucepan over medium-high heat, combine tuna and water; bring to a boil.
2. Reduce heat to medium, Stir in tofu.
3. Separate the layers of the green onions, and add them to the soup.
4. Simmer gently for 2 to 3 minutes before serving.

Nutrition: Calories 77, Total Fat 3.3g, Saturated Fat 0.6g, Cholesterol 7mg, Sodium 39mg, Total Carbohydrate 1.9g, Dietary Fiber 0.3g, Total Sugars 0.9g, Protein 9.7g, Calcium 32mg, Iron 1mg, Potassium 104mg, Potassium 88mg

216. Lime-Marinated Salmon

Preparation Time: 05 min
Cooking Time: 15 minutes
Servings: 4
Ingredients:

- ¼ cup olive oil
- 1 clove garlic, minced
- 1/8 teaspoon ground black pepper
- 1/2 teaspoon cayenne pepper
- 2 tablespoons lime juice
- 1/8 teaspoon grated lime zest
- 2 (4 ounce) salmon fillets

Directions:

1. Preheat an outdoor grill for medium heat, and lightly oil the grate.
2. Whisk the olive oil, minced garlic, black pepper, cayenne pepper, lime juice, and grated lime zest together in a bowl to make the marinade.
3. Place the salmon fillets in the marinade and turn to coat; allow to marinate at least 15 minutes.
4. Cook on the preheated grill until the fish flakes easily with a fork and is lightly browned, 3 to 4 minutes per side.
5. Garnish with the twists of lime zest to serve.

Nutrition: Calories 126, Total Fat 9.7g, Saturated Fat 1.4g, Cholesterol 19mg, Sodium 20mg, Total Carbohydrate 2.7g, Dietary Fiber 0.3g, Total Sugars 0.5g, Protein 8.5g, Calcium 22mg, Iron 0mg, Potassium 206mg, Potassium 108mg

217. Ginger Glazed Tuna

Preparation Time: 05 min
Cooking Time: 12 minutes
Servings: 4
Ingredients:

- 3 tablespoons honey
- 3 tablespoons soy sauce
- 3 tablespoons vinegar
- 1 teaspoon grated fresh ginger root
- 1 clove garlic, crushed or to taste
- 4 (6 ounce) tuna fillets
- Pepper to taste
- 2 tablespoons olive oil

Directions:

1. In a shallow glass dish, stir together the honey, soy sauce, vinegar, ginger, garlic and 2 teaspoons olive oil. Season fish fillets with pepper, and place them into the dish. If the fillets have skin on them, place them skin side down. Cover, and refrigerate for 20 minutes to marinate.
2. Heat remaining olive oil in a large skillet over medium-high heat. Remove fish from the dish, and reserve marinade. Fry fish for 4 to 6 minutes on each side, turning only once, until fish flakes easily with a fork. Remove fillets to a serving platter and keep warm.
3. Pour reserved marinade into the skillet, and heat over medium heat until the mixture reduces to a glaze consistently. Spoon glaze over fish, and serve immediately.

Nutrition: Calories 181, Total Fat 11.1g, Saturated Fat 0.3g, Cholesterol 0mg, Sodium 678mg, Total Carbohydrate 14.3g, Dietary Fiber 0.2g, Total Sugars 13.2g, Protein 6.8g, Calcium 6mg, Iron 0mg, Potassium 47mg, Potassium 18mg

218.   Tuna with Pineapple

Preparation Time: 25 min
Cooking Time: 15 minutes
Servings: 4
Ingredients:

- 2 tablespoons olive oil
- 1 tablespoon minced fresh garlic
- 1 tablespoon chopped onion
- 1/2 red bell pepper, diced
- 1 cup pineapple - peeled, seeded and cubed
- 1 teaspoon corn-starch
- 1 tablespoon water
- 2 tablespoons lime juice
- 1 tablespoon lime juice
- 1 tablespoon melted butter
- 3 (4 ounce) fillets tuna

Directions:

1. Preheat the oven's broiler and set the oven rack about 6 inches from the heat source.
2. Heat olive oil in a saucepan over medium heat. Stir in the garlic and onion; cook and stir until the onion begins to soften, about 2 minutes. Add the red bell pepper and pineapple. Continue cooking a few more minutes until the bell pepper begins to soften. Stir together the corn-starch, water, and 2 tablespoons of lime juice. Stir into the pineapple sauce until thickened, stirring constantly. Keep the sauce warm over very low heat.
3. Stir 1 tablespoon of lime juice together with the melted butter, and brush on the tuna fillets. Place onto a broiler pan.
4. Cook under the preheated broiler for 4 minutes, then turn the fish over, and continue cooking for 4 minutes more. Season to taste with salt and serve with the pineapple sauce.

Nutrition: Calories 98, Total Fat 7.1g, Saturated Fat 1g, Cholesterol 0mg, Sodium 2mg, Total Carbohydrate 10.1g, Dietary Fiber 1g, Total Sugars 5.3g, Protein 0.6g, Calcium 14mg, Iron 0mg, Potassium 111mg, Potassium 101mg

219.   Tangy Glazed Black Cod

Preparation Time: 10 min
Cooking Time: 15 minutes
Servings: 4
Ingredients:

- 3 tablespoons fresh lime juice
- 2 tablespoons honey
- 2 tablespoons vinegar
- 1 tablespoon soy sauce
- 1 (1 pound) fillet black cod, bones removed

Directions:

1. Preheat oven to 425 degrees F. Spray the bottom of a Dutch oven or covered casserole dish with cooking spray.
2. Combine lime juice, honey, vinegar, and soy sauce in a saucepan over medium heat; cook and stir until sauce is thickened, about 5 minutes.
3. Place cod in the prepared Dutch oven. Pour sauce over fish Cover dish with an oven-safe lid.
4. Bake in the preheated oven until fish flakes easily with a fork, about 10 minutes.

Nutrition: Calories 44, Total Fat 0g, Saturated Fat 0g, Cholesterol 0mg, Sodium 127mg, Total Carbohydrate 11.8g, Dietary Fiber 0.2g, Total Sugars 9.3g, Protein 0.5g, Calcium 6mg, Iron 0mg, Potassium 58mg, Potassium 40mg

220.   Marinated Fried Fish

Preparation Time: 15 min
Cooking Time: 10 minutes
Servings: 4

Ingredients:
- 2 (4 ounce) Salmon fillets
- 2 tablespoons lemon juice
- 2 tablespoons garlic powder
- 2 teaspoons ground cumin
- 1 teaspoon paprika
- 1/2 cup all-purpose flour
- 1 teaspoon dried rosemary
- 1/4 teaspoon cayenne pepper, or to taste
- 1 egg, beaten
- 1 tablespoon water
- ½ cup olive oil for frying

Directions:
1. Place salmon fillets in a small glass dish. Mix lemon juice, garlic powder, cumin, and paprika in a small bowl; pour over salmon fillets. Cover dish with plastic wrap and marinate salmon in refrigerator for 2 hours.
2. Mix flour, rosemary, and cayenne pepper together on a piece of waxed paper.
3. Beat egg and water together in a wide bowl.
4. Heat oil in a large skillet over medium heat.
5. Gently press the salmon fillets into the flour mixture to coat; shake to remove excess flour. Dip into the beaten egg to coat and immediately return to the flour mixture to coat.
6. Fry flounder in hot oil until the fish flakes easily with a fork, about 5 minutes per side.

Nutrition: Calories 139, Total Fat 4.7g, Saturated Fat 0.9g, Cholesterol 50mg, Sodium 30mg, Total Carbohydrate 16.3g, Dietary Fiber 1.4g, Total Sugars 1.4g, Protein 8.2g, Calcium 34mg, Iron 2mg, Potassium 203mg, Potassium 140mg

221.   Spicy Lime and Basil Grilled Fish

Preparation Time: 30 min
Cooking Time: 30 minutes
Servings: 4
Ingredients:
- 2 pounds salmon fillets, each cut into thirds

- 6 tablespoons butter, melted
- 1 lime, juiced
- 1 tablespoon dried basil
- 1 teaspoon red pepper flakes
- 1 onion, sliced crosswise 1/8-inch thick

Directions:
1. Preheat grill for medium heat and lightly oil the grate.
2. Lay 4 8x10-inch pieces of aluminum foil onto a flat work surface and spray with cooking spray.
3. Arrange equal amounts of the salmon into the center of each foil square.
4. Stir butter, lime juice, basil, and red pepper flakes together in a small bowl; drizzle evenly over each portion of fish. Top each portion with onion slices.
5. Bring opposing ends of the foil together and roll together to form a seam. Roll ends toward fish to seal packets.
6. Cook packets on the preheated grill until fish flakes easily with a fork, 5 to 7 minutes per side.

Nutrition: Calories 151, Total Fat 13.4g, Saturated Fat 7.6g, Cholesterol 43mg, Sodium 95mg, Total Carbohydrate 3.1g, Dietary Fiber 0.8g, Total Sugars 1g, Protein 6g, Calcium 23mg, Iron 0mg, Potassium 158mg, Potassium 137mg

222.   Steamed Fish with Garlic

Preparation Time: 15 min
Cooking Time: 45 minutes
Servings: 4
Ingredients:
- 2 (6 ounce) fillets cod fillets
- 3 tablespoons olive oil
- 1 onion, chopped
- 4 cloves garlic, minced
- 3 pinches dried rosemary
- Ground black pepper to taste
- 1 lemon, halved

Directions:
1. Preheat oven to 350 degrees F.
2. Place cod fillets on an 18x18-inch piece of aluminum foil; top with oil. Sprinkle onion, garlic, rosemary, and pepper over oil and cod. Squeeze juice from ½ lemon evenly on top.
3. Lift up bottom and top ends of the aluminum foil towards the center; fold together to 1 inch above the cod. Flatten short ends of the aluminum foil; fold over to within 1 inch of the sides of the cod. Place foil package on a baking sheet.
4. Bake in the preheated oven until haddock flakes easily with a fish, about 45 minutes. Let sit, about 5 minutes. Open ends of the packet carefully; squeeze juice from the remaining 1/2 lemon on top.

Nutrition: Calories 171, Total Fat 11.3g, Saturated Fat 1.6g, Cholesterol 95mg, Sodium 308mg, Total Carbohydrate 5g, Dietary Fiber 1.1g, Total Sugars 1.6g, Protein 14.3g, Calcium 31mg, Iron 1mg, Potassium 76mg, Potassium 67mg

223.   Honey Fish

Preparation Time: 15 min
Cooking Time: 30 minutes
Servings: 4

Ingredients:
- 3/4 cup olive oil, divided
- 1 1/2 pounds haddock, patted dry
- 1/2 cup honey
- 1 teaspoon dried basil

Directions:
1. Preheat oven to 400 degrees F.
2. Place 1/2 cup oil in a shallow microwave-safe bowl. Heat in the microwave until hot, about 30 seconds. Dip haddock in cracker mixture until coated on both sides. Transfer to a shallow baking dish.
3. Bake haddock in the preheated oven until flesh flakes easily with a fork, about 25 minutes.
4. Place remaining 1/4 cup oil in a small microwave-safe bowl. Heat in the microwave until hot, about 15 seconds. Stir in honey and basil until blended.
5. Remove haddock from the oven; drizzle honey oil on top.
6. Continue baking until top is browned, about 5 minutes more.

Nutrition: Calories 347, Total Fat 25.9g, Saturated Fat 3.6g, Cholesterol 16mg, Sodium 46mg, Total Carbohydrate 27.5g, Dietary Fiber 0.2g, Total Sugars 24.5g, Protein 5.6g, Calcium 11mg, Iron 4mg, Potassium 108mg, Potassium 97mg

224.   Salmon and Pesto Salad

Preparation Time: 5 minutes
Cooking Time: 15 minutes
Servings: 2 servings
Ingredients:
For the pesto:
- 1 minced garlic clove
- ½ cup fresh arugula
- ¼ cup extra virgin olive oil
- ½ cup fresh basil
- 1 teaspoon black pepper

For the salmon:
- 4 oz. skinless salmon fillet
- 1 tablespoon coconut oil

For the salad:
- ½ juiced lemon
- 2 sliced radishes
- ½ cup iceberg lettuce
- 1 teaspoon black pepper

Directions:
1. Prepare the pesto by blending all the pesto ingredients in a food processor or by grinding with a pestle and mortar. Set aside.
2. Add a skillet to the stove on medium-high heat and melt the coconut oil.
3. Add the salmon to the pan.
4. Cook for 7-8 minutes and turn over.
5. Cook for a further 3-4 minutes or until cooked through.
6. Remove fillets from the skillet and allow to rest.
7. Mix the lettuce and the radishes and squeeze over the juice of ½ lemon.
8. Flake the salmon with a fork and mix through the salad.

9. Toss to coat and sprinkle with a little black pepper to serve.
Nutrition: Calories 221, Protein 13 g, Carbohydrates 1 g, Fat 34 g, Sodium (Na) 80 mg, Potassium (K) 119 mg, Phosphorus 158 mg

225. Baked Fennel and Garlic Sea Bass

Preparation Time: 5 minutes
Cooking Time: 15 minutes
Servings: 2 servings
Ingredients:
- 1 lemon
- ½ sliced fennel bulb
- 6 oz. sea bass fillets
- 1 teaspoon black pepper
- 2 garlic cloves
- 1 salmon filet

Directions:
1. Preheat the oven to 375°F/Gas Mark 5.
2. Sprinkle black pepper over the Sea Bass.
3. Slice the fennel bulb and garlic cloves.
4. Add 1 salmon fillet and half the fennel and garlic to one sheet of baking paper or tin foil.
5. Squeeze in 1/2 lemon juices.
6. Repeat for the other fillet.
7. Fold and add to the oven for 12-15 minutes or until fish is thoroughly cooked through.
8. Meanwhile, add boiling water to your couscous, cover, and allow to steam.
9. Serve with your choice of rice or salad.

Nutrition: Calories 221, Protein 14 g, Carbohydrates 3 g, Fat 2 g, Sodium (Na) 119 mg, Potassium (K) 398 mg, Phosphorus 149 mg

226. Lemon, Garlic & Cilantro Tuna and Rice

Preparation Time: 5 minutes
Cooking Time: 0 minutes
Servings: 2
Ingredients:
- ½ cup arugula
- 1 tablespoon extra-virgin olive oil
- 1 cup cooked rice
- 1 teaspoon black pepper
- ¼ finely diced red onion
- 1 juiced lemon
- 2 tablespoons chopped fresh cilantro
- 1 tuna

Directions:
1. Mix the olive oil, pepper, cilantro, and red onion in a bowl.
2. Stir in the tuna and serve immediately.
3. When ready to eat, serve up with the cooked rice and arugula!

Nutrition: Calories 221, Protein 11 g, Carbohydrates 26 g, Fat 7 g, Sodium (Na) 143 mg, Potassium (K)197 mg, Phosphorus 182 mg

227.   Mixed Pepper Stuffed River Trout

Preparation Time: 5 minutes
Cooking Time: 20 minutes
Servings: 4 servings
Ingredients:

- 1 whole river trout
- 1 teaspoon thyme
- ¼ diced yellow pepper
- ¼ diced green pepper
- 1 juiced lime
- ¼ diced red pepper
- 1 teaspoon oregano
- 1 teaspoon extra virgin olive oil
- 1 teaspoon black pepper

Directions:

1. Preheat the broiler /grill on high heat.
2. Lightly oil a baking tray.
3. Mix all the ingredients apart from the trout and lime.
4. Slice the trout lengthways (there should be an opening here from where it was gutted) and stuff the mixed ingredients inside.
5. Squeeze the lime juice over the fish and then place the lime wedges on the tray.
6. Place under the broiler on the baking tray and broil for 15-20 minutes or until fish is thoroughly cooked through and flakes easily.
7. Enjoy the dish as it is, or with a side helping of rice or salad.

Nutrition: Calories 290, Protein 15 g, Carbohydrates 0 g, Fat 7 g, Sodium (Na) 43 mg, Potassium (K) 315 mg, Phosphorus 189 mg

228.   Haddock & Buttered Leeks

Preparation Time: 5 minutes
Cooking Time: 15 minutes
Servings: 2 servings
Ingredients:

- 1 tablespoon unsalted butter
- 1 sliced leek
- ¼ teaspoon black pepper
- 2 teaspoons chopped parsley
- 6 oz. haddock fillets
- ½ juiced lemon

Directions:

1. Preheat the oven to 375°F/Gas Mark 5.
2. Add the haddock fillets to baking or parchment paper and sprinkle with the black pepper.
3. Squeeze over the lemon juice and wrap into a parcel.
4. Bake the parcel on a baking tray for 10-15 minutes or until the fish is thoroughly cooked through.

5. Meanwhile, heat the butter over medium-low heat in a small pan.
6. Add the leeks and parsley and sauté for 5-7 minutes until soft.
7. Serve the haddock fillets on a bed of buttered leeks and enjoy!

Nutrition: Calories 124, Protein 15 g, Carbohydrates 0 g, Fat 7 g, Sodium (Na) 161 mg, Potassium (K) 251 mg, Phosphorus 220 mg

229. Thai Spiced Halibut

Preparation Time: 5 minutes
Cooking Time: 20 minutes
Servings: 2 servings
Ingredients:
*   2 tablespoons coconut oil
*   1 cup white rice
*   ¼ teaspoon black pepper
*   ½ diced red chili
*   1 tablespoon fresh basil
*   2 pressed garlic cloves
*   4 oz. halibut fillet
*   1 halved lime
*   2 sliced green onions
*   1 lime leaf

Directions:
1. Preheat oven to 400°F/Gas Mark 5.
2. Add half of the ingredients into baking paper and fold into a parcel.
3. Repeat for your second parcel.
4. Add to the oven for 15-20 minutes or until fish is thoroughly cooked through.
5. Serve with cooked rice.

Nutrition: Calories 311, Protein 16 g, Carbohydrates 17 g, Fat 15 g, Sodium (Na) 31 mg, Potassium (K) 418 mg, Phosphorus 257 mg

230. Monk-Fish Curry

Preparation Time: 5 minutes
Cooking Time: 20 minutes
Servings: 2 servings
Ingredients:
*   1 garlic clove
*   3 finely chopped green onions
*   1 teaspoon grated ginger
*   1 cup water.
*   2 teaspoons chopped fresh basil
*   1 cup cooked rice noodles
*   1 tablespoon coconut oil
*   ½ sliced red chili
*   4 oz. Monkfish fillet
*   ½ finely sliced stick lemongrass

- 2 tablespoons chopped shallots

Directions:
1. Slice the Monkfish into bite-size pieces.
2. Using a pestle and mortar or food processor, crush the basil, garlic, ginger, chili, and lemongrass to form a paste.
3. Heat the oil in a large wok or pan over medium-high heat and add the shallots.
4. Now add the water to the pan and bring to a boil.
5. Add the Monkfish, lower the heat and cover to simmer for 10 minutes or until cooked through.
6. Enjoy with rice noodles and scatter with green onions to serve.

Nutrition: Calories 249, Protein 12 g, Carbohydrates 30 g, Fat 10 g, Sodium (Na) 32 mg, Potassium (K) 398 mg, Phosphorus 190 mg

231.   Oregon Tuna Patties

Preparation Time: 10 minutes
Cooking Time: 15 minutes
Servings: 4
Ingredients:
- 1 (14.75 ounce) can tuna
- 2 tablespoons butter
- 1 medium onion, chopped
- 2/3 cup graham cracker crumbs
- 2 egg whites, beaten
- 1/4 cup chopped fresh parsley
- 1 teaspoon dry mustard
- 3 tablespoons olive oil

Directions:
1. Drain the tuna, reserving 3/4 cup of the liquid. Flake the meat. Melt butter in a large skillet over medium-high heat. Add onion, and cook until tender.
2. In a medium bowl, combine the onions with the reserved tuna liquid, 1/3 of the graham cracker crumbs, egg whites, parsley, mustard and tuna. Mix until well blended, then shape into six patties. Coat patties in remaining cracker crumbs.
3. Heat olive in a large skillet over medium heat. Cook patties until browned, then carefully turn and brown on the other side.

Nutrition: Calories 204, Total Fat 15.4g, Saturated Fat 4.4g, Cholesterol 74mg, Sodium 111mg, Total Carbohydrate 6.5g, Dietary Fiber 0.9g, Total Sugar 2g, Protein 10.5g, Calcium 21mg, Iron 1mg, Potassium 164mg, Phosphorus 106mg

232.   Broiled Sesame Cod

Preparation Time: 05 minutes
Cooking Time: 10 min
Servings: 4
Ingredients:
- 1/2 pounds' cod fillets
- 1 teaspoon butter, melted
- 1 teaspoon lemon juice

- 1 teaspoon dried basil
- 1 pinch ground black pepper
- 1 tablespoon sesame seeds

Directions:
1. Preheat the oven's broiler and set the oven rack about 6 inches from the heat source. Line a broiler pan with aluminum foil.
2. Place the cod fillets on the foil, and brush with butter. Season with lemon juice, basil, and black pepper; sprinkle with sesame seeds.
3. Broil the fish in the preheated broiler until the flesh turns opaque and white, and the fish flakes easily, about 10 minutes.

Nutrition: Calories 67, Total Fat 2.6g, Saturated Fat 0.8g, Cholesterol 30mg, Sodium 43mg, Total Carbohydrate 0.6g, Dietary Fiber 0.3g, Total Sugar 0g, Protein 10.6g, Calcium 23mg, Iron 0mg, Potassium 13mg, Phosphorus 10mg

233. Fish Tacos

Preparation Time: 10 minutes
Cooking Time: 35 minutes
Servings: 6
Ingredients:
- 1½ cup of cabbage
- ½ cup of red onion
- ½ bunch of cilantros
- 1 garlic clove
- 2 limes
- 1 pound of cod fillets
- ½ teaspoon of ground cumin
- ½ teaspoon of chili powder
- ¼ teaspoon of black pepper
- 1 tablespoon of olive oil
- ½ cup of mayonnaise
- ¼ cup of sour cream
- 2 tablespoons of almond milk
- 12 (6-inch) corn tortillas

Directions:
1. Shred the cabbage, chop the onion and cilantro, and mince the garlic. Set aside
2. Use a dish to place in the fish fillets, then squeeze half a lime juice over the fish. Sprinkle the fish fillets with the minced garlic, cumin, black pepper, chili powder, and olive oil. Turn the fish filets to coat with the marinade, then refrigerate for about 15 to 30 minutes
3. Prepare salsa Blanca by mixing the mayonnaise, almond milk, sour cream, and the other half of the lime juice. Stir to combine, then place in the refrigerator to chill
4. Broil in oven, and cover the broiler pan with aluminum foil. Broil the coated fish fillets for about 10 minutes or until the flesh becomes opaque and white and flakes easily. Remove from the oven, slightly cool, and then flake the fish into bigger pieces
5. Heat the corn tortillas in a pan, one at a time until it becomes soft and warm, then wrap in a dish towel to keep them warm
6. To assemble the tacos, place a piece of the fish on the tortilla, topping with the salsa Blanca, cabbage, cilantro, red onion, and the lime wedges.
7. Serve with hot sauce if you desire

Nutrition: Calories 363 Protein 18g Carbohydrates 30g Fat 19g Cholesterol 40mg Sodium 194mg Potassium 507mg Phosphorus 327mg Fiber 4.3g

234.   <u>Jambalaya</u>

Preparation Time: 10 minutes
Cooking Time: 1 hour and 15 minutes
Servings: 12
Ingredients:

- 2 cups of onion
- 1 cup of bell pepper
- 2 garlic cloves
- 2 cups of uncooked converted white rice
- ½ teaspoon of black pepper
- 8 ounces of canned low-sodium tomato sauce
- 2 cups of low-sodium beef broth
- 2 pounds of raw shrimp
- ½ cup of unsalted margarine

Directions:

1. Preheat oven to 350° F
2. Chop the onion, bell pepper, garlic, then peel the shrimp
3. Combine and mix all the ingredients in a large bowl except the margarine
4. Pour into a 9 x 13-inch baking dish and evenly spread out
5. Slice the margarine, placing over the top of the ingredients
6. Cover with foil or lid, and bake for about 1 hr. 15 minutes
7. Serve hot.

Nutrition: Calories 294 Protein 20g Carbohydrates 31g Fat 10g Cholesterol 137mg Sodium 186mg Potassium 300mg Phosphorus 197mg Fiber 0.8g

235. <u>Asparagus Shrimp Linguini</u>

Preparation Time: 10 minutes
Cooking Time: 35 minutes
Servings: 1 ½ cup
Ingredients:

- 8 ounces of uncooked linguini
- 1 tablespoon of olive oil
- 1¾ cups of asparagus
- ½ cup of unsalted butter
- 2 garlic cloves
- 3 ounces of cream cheese
- 2 tablespoons of fresh parsley
- ¾ teaspoon of dried basil
- 2/3 cup of dry white wine
- ½ pound of peeled and cooked shrimp

Directions:

1. Preheat oven to 350° F
2. Cook the linguini in boiling water until it becomes tender, then drain
3. Place the asparagus on a baking sheet, then spread two tablespoons of oil over the asparagus. Bake for about 7 to 8 minutes or until it is tender
4. Remove baked asparagus from the oven and place it on a plate. Cut the asparagus into pieces of medium-sized once cooled
5. Mince the garlic and chop the parsley

6. Melt ½ cup of butter in a large skillet with the minced garlic
7. Stir in the cream cheese, mixing as it melts
8. Stir in the parsley and basil, then simmer for about 5 minutes. Mix either in boiling water or dry white wine, stirring until the sauce becomes smooth
9. Add the cooked shrimp and asparagus, then stir and heat until it is evenly warm
10. Toss the cooked pasta with the sauce and serve

Nutrition: Calories 544 Protein 21g Carbohydrates 43g Fat 32g Cholesterol 188mg Sodium 170mg Potassium 402mg Phosphorus 225mg Fiber 2.4g

236. Tuna Noodle Casserole

Preparation Time: 10 minutes
Cooking Time: 35 minutes
Servings: 2
Ingredients:

- 2 ounces of wide uncooked egg noodles
- 5 ounces of canned tuna in water
- ½ cup of sour cream
- ¼ cup of cottage cheese
- ½ cup of fresh sliced mushrooms
- ½ cup of frozen green peas
- 1 tablespoon of unsalted butter

- ¼ cup of unseasoned bread crumbs

Directions:
1. Preheat oven to 350° F
2. Boil egg noodles based on the package instructions and drain. Also, drain and flake the tuna
3. Combine and mix the sour cream, cottage cheese, mushrooms, tuna, and peas in a medium bowl
4. Stir the drained noodle into the tuna mixture, and place in a small casserole dish that has been sprayed with a non-stick cooking spray
5. Melt butter, stir into the bread crumbs, then sprinkle over the mixture of noodles in step 4
6. Bake for about 20 to 25 minutes or until the bread crumbs start to brown
7. Divide into two and serve

Nutrition: Calories 415 Protein 22g Carbohydrates 39g Fat 19g Cholesterol 88mg Sodium 266mg Potassium 400mg Phosphorus 306mg Fiber 3.2g

237. Oven-Fried Southern Style Catfish

Preparation Time: 10 minutes
Cooking Time: 35 minutes
Servings: 4
Ingredients:

- 1 egg white
- ½ cup of all-purpose flour
- ¼ cup of cornmeal
- ¼ cup of panko bread crumbs
- 1 teaspoon of salt-free Cajun seasoning
- 1 pound of catfish fillets

Directions:

1. Heat oven to 450° F
2. Use cooking spray to spray a non-stick baking sheet
3. Using a bowl, beat the egg white until very soft peaks are formed. Don't over-beat
4. Use a sheet of wax paper and place the flour over it
5. Using a different sheet of wax paper to combine and mix the cornmeal, panko and the Cajun seasoning
6. Cut the catfish fillet into four pieces, then dip the fish in the flour, shaking off the excess
7. Dip coated fish in the egg white, rolling into the cornmeal mixture
8. Place the fish on the baking pan. Repeat with the remaining fish fillets
9. Use cooking spray to spray over the fish fillets. Bake for about 10 to 12 minutes or until the sides of the fillets become browned and crisp

Nutrition: Calories 250 Protein 22g Carbohydrates 19g Fat 10g Cholesterol 53mg Sodium 124mg Potassium 401mg Phosphorus 262mg Fiber 1.2g

238. <u>Cilantro-Lime Cod</u>

Preparation Time: 10 minutes
Cooking Time: 35 minutes
Servings: 4
Ingredients:
- ½ cup of mayonnaise
- ½ cup of fresh chopped cilantro
- 2 tablespoon of lime juice
- 1 pound of cod fillets

Directions:

1. Combine and mix the mayonnaise, cilantro, and lime juice in a medium bowl, remove ¼ cup to another bowl and put aside. To be served as fish sauce
2. Spread the remaining mayonnaise mixture over the cod fillets
3. Use cooking spray to spray a large skillet, then heat over medium-high heat
4. Place in the cod fillets, and cook for about 8 minutes or until the fish becomes firm and moist, turning just once
5. Serve with the ¼ cilantro-lime sauce

Nutrition: Calories 292 Protein 20g Carbohydrates 1g Fat 23g Cholesterol 57mg Sodium 228mg Potassium 237mg Phosphorus 128mg Calcium 14mg

239. Zucchini Cups with Dill Cream and Smoked Tuna

Preparation Time: 15 minutes
Cooking Time: 35 minutes
Servings: 4
Ingredients:

- 1 1/3 large Zucchini
- 4 ounces' cream cheese, softened
- 2 tablespoons chopped fresh dill
- 1 teaspoon lemon zest
- 1/2 teaspoon fresh lemon juice
- 1/4 teaspoon ground black pepper
- 4 ounces smoked tuna, cut into 2-inch strips

Directions:

1. Trim ends from Zucchini and cut crosswise into 24 (3/4-inch-thick) rounds. Scoop a 1/2-inch-deep depression from one side of each round with a small melon-baller, forming little cups. Drain Zucchini, cup sides down, on paper towels for 15 minutes.
2. Beat cream cheese, chopped dill, lemon zest, lemon juice, and black pepper together in a bowl. Spoon 1/2 teaspoon cheese mixture into each Zucchini cup. Top each cup with 1 tuna strip.

Nutrition: Calories 51, Total Fat 3.8g, Saturated Fat 2.2g, Cholesterol 13mg, Sodium 219mg, Total Carbohydrate 1.8g, Dietary Fiber 0.3g, Total Sugar 0.6g, Protein 2.8g, Calcium 24mg, Iron 1mg, Potassium 95mg, Phosphorus 40mg

240. Creamy Smoked Tuna Macaroni

Preparation Time: 15 minutes
Cooking Time: 25min
Servings: 4
Ingredients:

- 3 tablespoons olive oil
- ¼ onion, finely chopped
- 1 tablespoon all-purpose flour
- 1 teaspoon garlic powder
- 1 cup soy almond milk
- ¼ cup cream cheese
- ½ cup frozen green peas, thawed and drained
- ¼ cup mushrooms

- 5 ounces smoked tuna, chopped
- ½ (16 ounce) package macaroni

Directions:

1. Bring a large pot of water to a boil. Add macaroni and cook for 8 to 10 minutes or until al dente; drain.
2. Heat oil in a large skillet over medium heat. Sauté onion in oil until tender.
3. Stir flour and garlic powder into the oil and onions. Gradually stir in almond milk. Heat to just below boiling point, and then gradually stir in cheese until the sauce is smooth. Stir in peas and mushrooms. And cook over low heat for 4 minutes.
4. Toss in smoked tuna, and cook for 2 more minutes. Serve over macaroni.

Nutrition: Calories 147, Total Fat 8.3g, Saturated Fat 1.9g, Cholesterol 14mg, Sodium 979mg, Total Carbohydrate 6.5g, Dietary Fiber 0.8g, Total Sugar 1.9g, Protein 11.4g, Calcium 38mg, Iron 1mg, Potassium 160mg, Phosphorus 100mg

241. <u>Asparagus and Smoked Tuna Salad</u>

Preparation Time: 15 minutes
Cooking Time: 10 minutes
 Servings: 4
Ingredients:

- ½ pound fresh asparagus, trimmed and cut into 1-inch pieces
- 1 heads lettuce, rinsed and torn
- ¼ cup frozen green peas, thawed
- 1/8 cup olive oil
- 1 tablespoon lemon juice
- ½ teaspoon Dijon mustard
- 1/8 teaspoon pepper
- 1/8-pound smoked tuna, cut into 1inch chunks

Directions:

1. Bring a pot of water to a boil. Place asparagus in the pot, and cook 5 minutes, just until tender. Drain, and set aside.
2. In a large bowl, toss together the asparagus, lettuce, peas, and tuna.
3. In a separate bowl, mix the olive oil, lemon juice, Dijon mustard, and pepper. Toss with the salad or serve on the side.

Nutrition: Calories 87, Total Fat 7g, Saturated Fat 1.1g, Cholesterol 3mg, Sodium 298mg, Total Carbohydrate 2.7g, Dietary Fiber 1.1g, Total Sugar 1g, Protein 3.8g, Calcium 16mg, Iron 1mg, Potassium 134mg, Phosphorus 104 mg

242. <u>Spicy tuna Salad Sandwiches</u>

Preparation Time: 15 minutes
 Cooking Time: 00 min
Servings:
Ingredient:

- 1 (8 ounce) can tuna, undrained
- 1/4 cucumber, chopped
- 2 tablespoons light mayonnaise
- 1 tablespoon vinegar
- 1 teaspoon red chili paste

- 4 slices white bread, toasted

Directions:
1. Put tuna into a bowl and use a fork to flake and mix with the can's liquid. Mix cucumber with the tuna.
2. Stir mayonnaise, vinegar, chili paste, and bowl; add hot sauce and adjust to taste. Pour mayonnaise mixture over the salmon mixture and stir to coat. Spoon onto toasted bread to make sandwiches.

Nutrition: Calories 189, Total Fat 7.6g, Saturated Fat 1.1g, Cholesterol 28mg, Sodium 326mg, Total Carbohydrate 15.6g, Dietary Fiber 2.1g, Total Sugar 3.4g, Protein 15.1g, Calcium 60mg, Iron 1mg, Potassium 119mg, Phosphorus 109 mg

243. Spanish Tuna

Preparation Time: 20 minutes
Cooking Time: 15 minutes
Servings: 4
Ingredients:
- 1 tablespoon olive oil
- 1/4 cup finely chopped onion
- 2 tablespoons chopped fresh garlic
- 1/4 cup basil chopped
- 1 dash black pepper
- 1 dash cayenne pepper
- 1 dash paprika
- 6 (4 ounce) fillets tuna fillets

Directions:
1. Heat olive oil in a large skillet over medium heat.
2. Cook and stir onions and garlic until onions are slightly tender, careful not to burn the garlic.
3. Season with black pepper, cayenne pepper, basil, and paprika.
4. Cook fillets in sauce over medium heat for 5 to 8 minutes, or until easily flaked with a fork. Serve immediately.

Nutrition: Calories 130, Total Fat 4.6g, Saturated Fat 0.5g, Cholesterol 55mg, Sodium 71mg, Total Carbohydrate 2.2g, Dietary Fiber 0.3g, Total Sugar 0.4g, Protein 20.4g, Calcium 10mg, Iron 0mg, Potassium 31mg, Phosphorus 46 mg

244. Fish with Vegetables

Preparation Time: 30 minutes
Cooking Time: 60 minutes
Servings: 4
Ingredients:
- 1 egg white, beaten
- ¼ cup all-purpose flour
- Black pepper to taste
- 1-pound firm salmon fillets, cut into 1 1/2-inch pieces
- ½ cup olive oil, divided
- 1 onion, cut in half and thinly sliced
- 1 carrot, peeled and coarsely grated
- ½ large turnips, peeled and coarsely grated
- 1/2 leek coarsely grated

- 1 cup water

Directions:

1. Place egg white and flour in 2 shallow bowls. Season egg white with pepper. Dip fish pieces first in the beaten egg, then dredge in the flour.
2. Heat 1/4 cup olive oil in a deep skillet over medium heat until hot. Add fish in batches and fry on both sides until golden, 5 to 8 minutes per batch. Remove fish from skillet and set aside.
3. Heat remaining 1/4 cup oil in a separate skillet and cook onions until soft and translucent, about 5 minutes. Add carrots, turnips, and leek; mix well. Add water and season with pepper. Cover and simmer on low heat until vegetables are soft, about 30 minutes. Check and add more water if mixture becomes too dry.
4. Layer vegetables and fried fish in a 10-inch round serving dish, starting and ending with vegetables.

Nutrition: Calories 358, Total Fat 30.1g, Saturated Fat 6g, Cholesterol 57mg, Sodium 45mg, Total Carbohydrate 14.7g, Dietary Fiber 2.2g, Total Sugar 3.3g, Protein 8.2g, Calcium 38mg, Iron 1mg, Potassium 281mg, Phosphorus 161 mg

245.   Chocolate Chia Seed Pudding

Preparation time: 15 minutes, plus 3 to 5 hours or overnight to rest
Cooking time: 0 minutes
Servings: 4
Ingredients:
- 11/2 cups unsweetened vanilla almond milk
- 1/4 cup unsweetened cocoa powder
- 1/4 cup maple syrup (or substitute any sweetener)
- 1/2 teaspoon vanilla extract
- 1/3 cup chia seeds
- 1/2 cup strawberries
- 1/4 cup blueberries
- 1/4 cup raspberries
- 2 tablespoons unsweetened coconut flakes
- 1/4 to 1/2 teaspoon ground cinnamon (optional)

Directions:
1. Add the almond milk, cocoa powder, maple syrup, and vanilla extract to a blender and blend until smooth. Whisk in chia seeds.
2. In a small bowl, gently mash the strawberries with a fork. Distribute the strawberry mash evenly to the bottom of 4 glass jars.
3. Pour equal portions of the blended almond milk-cocoa mixture into each of the jars and let the pudding rest in the refrigerator until it achieves a pudding like consistency, at least 3 to 5 hours and up to overnight.

Nutrition: calories: 189; total fat 7g; saturated fat: 2g; cholesterol: 0mg; sodium: 60mg; potassium: 232mg; total carbohydrate: 28g; fiber: 10g; protein: 6g

246.   Chocolate-Mint Truffles

Preparation time: 45 minutes
Cooking time: 5 hours
Servings: 60 small truffles
Ingredients:
- 14 ounces semisweet chocolate, coarsely chopped
- ¾ cup half-and-half
- 1/2 teaspoon pure vanilla extract
- 11/2 teaspoon peppermint extract
- 2 tablespoons unsalted butter, softened
- ¾ cup naturally unsweetened or Dutch-process cocoa powder

Directions:
1. Place semisweet chocolate in a large heatproof bowl.
2. Microwave in four 15-second increments, stirring after each, for a total of 60 seconds. Stir until almost completely melted. Set aside.
3. In a small saucepan over medium heat, heat the half-and-half, whisking occasionally, until it just begins to boil. Remove from the heat, then whisk in the vanilla and peppermint extracts.

4. Pour the mixture over the chocolate and, using a wooden spoon, gently stir in one direction.
5. Once the chocolate and cream are smooth, stir in the butter until it is combined and melted.
6. Cover with plastic wrap pressed on the top of the mixture, and then let it sit at room temperature for 30 minutes.
7. After 30 minutes, place the mixture in the refrigerator until it is thick and can hold a ball shape, about 5 hours.
8. Line a large baking sheet with parchment paper or a use a silicone baking mat. Set aside.
9. Remove the mixture from the refrigerator. Place the cocoa powder in a bowl.
10. Scoop 1 teaspoon of the ganache and, using your hands, roll into a ball. Roll the ball in the cocoa powder, the place on the prepared baking sheet. (You can coat your palms with a little cocoa powder to prevent sticking).
11. Serve immediately or cover and store at room temperature for up to 1 week.

Nutrition: calories: 21; total fat 2g; saturated fat: 1g; cholesterol: 2mg; sodium: 2mg; potassium: 21mg; total carbohydrate: 2g; fiber: 1g; protein: 0g

247. Personal Mango Pies

Preparation time: 15 minutes
Cooking time: 14 to 16 minutes
Servings: 12
Ingredients:
- Cooking spray
- 12 small wonton wrappers
- 1 tablespoon cornstarch
- 1/2 cup water
- 3 cups finely chopped mango (fresh, or thawed from frozen, no sugar added)
- 2 tablespoons brown sugar (not packed)
- 1/2 teaspoon cinnamon
- 1 tablespoon light whipped butter or buttery spread

Directions:
1. Unsweetened coconut flakes (optional)
2. Preheat the oven to 350°f.
3. Spray a 12-cup muffin pan with nonstick cooking spray.
4. Place a wonton wrapper into each cup of the muffin pan, pressing it into the bottom and up along the sides.
5. Lightly spray the wrappers with nonstick spray. Bake until lightly browned, about 8 minutes.
6. Meanwhile, in a medium nonstick saucepan, combine the cornstarch with the water and stir to dissolve. Add the mango, brown sugar, and cinnamon and turn heat to medium.
7. Stirring frequently, cook until the mangoes have slightly softened and the mixture is thick and gooey, 6 to 8 minutes.
8. Remove the mango mixture from heat and stir in the butter.
9. Spoon the mango mixture into wonton cups, about 3 tablespoons each. Top with coconut flakes (if using) and serve warm.

Nutrition: calories: 61; total fat 1g; saturated fat: 0g; cholesterol: 2mg; sodium: 52mg; potassium: 77mg; total carbohydrate: 14g; fiber: 1g; protein: 1g

248. Grilled Peach Sundaes

Preparation time: 15 minutes

Cooking time: 5 minutes
Servings: 1
Ingredients:

- 1 tbsp. Toasted unsweetened coconut
- 1 tsp. Canola oil
- 2 peaches, halved and pitted
- 2 scoops non-fat vanilla yogurt, frozen

Directions:

1. Brush the peaches with oil and grill until tender.
2. Place peach halves on a bowl and top with frozen yogurt and coconut.

Nutrition:
Calories: 61; carbs: 2g; protein: 2g; fats: 6g; phosphorus: 32mg; potassium: 85mg; sodium: 30mg

249. Blueberry Swirl Cake

Preparation time: 15 minutes
Cooking time: 45 minutes
Servings: 9
Ingredients:

- 1/2 cup margarine
- 1 1/4 cups reduced fat almond milk
- 1 cup granulated sugar
- 1 egg
- 1 egg white
- 1 tbsp. Lemon zest, grated
- 1 tsp. Cinnamon
- 1/3 cup light brown sugar
- 2 1/2 cups fresh blueberries
- 2 1/2 cups self-rising flour

Directions:

1. Cream the margarine and granulated sugar using an electric mixer at high speed until fluffy.
2. Add the egg and egg white and beat for another two minutes.
3. Add the lemon zest and reduce the speed to low.
4. Add the flour with almond milk alternately.
5. In a greased 13x19 pan, spread half of the batter and sprinkle with blueberry on top. Add the remaining batter.
6. Bake in a 350-degree Fahrenheit preheated oven for 45 minutes.
7. Let it cool on a wire rack before slicing and serving.

Nutrition:
Calories: 384; carbs: 63g; protein: 7g; fats: 13g; phosphorus: 264mg; potassium: 158mg; sodium: 456mg

250. Peanut Butter Cookies

Preparation time: 15 minutes
Cooking time: 24 minutes
Servings: 24
Ingredients:

- 1/4 cup granulated sugar

- 1 cup unsalted peanut butter
- 1 tsp. baking soda
- 2 cups all-purpose flour
- 2 large eggs
- 2 tbsp. Butter
- 2 tsp. Pure vanilla extract
- 4 ounces softened cream cheese

Directions:
1. Line a cookie sheet with a non-stick liner. Set aside.
2. In a bowl, mix flour, sugar and baking soda. Set aside.
3. On a mixing bowl, combine the butter, cream cheese and peanut butter.
4. Mix on high speed until it forms a smooth consistency. Add the eggs and vanilla gradually while mixing until it forms a smooth consistency.
5. Add the almond flour mixture slowly and mix until well combined.
6. The dough is ready once it starts to stick together into a ball.
7. Scoop the dough using a 1 tablespoon cookie scoop and drop each cookie on the prepared cookie sheet.
8. Press the cookie with a fork and bake for 10 to 12 minutes at 350of.

Nutrition: Calories: 138; carbs: 12g; protein: 4g; fats: 9g; phosphorus: 60mg; potassium: 84mg; sodium: 31mg

251.   Deliciously Good Scones

Preparation time: 15 minutes
Cooking time: 12 minutes
Servings: 10
Ingredients:
- 1/4 cup dried cranberries
- 1/4 cup sunflower seeds
- 1/2 teaspoon baking soda
- 1 large egg
- 2 cups all-purpose flour
- 2 tablespoon honeys

Directions:
1. Preheat the oven to 3500f.
2. Grease a baking sheet. Set aside.
3. In a bowl, mix the salt, baking soda and flour. Add the dried fruits, nuts and seeds. Set aside.
4. In another bowl, mix the honey and eggs.
5. Add the wet ingredients to the dry ingredients. Use your hands to mix the dough.
6. Create 10 small round dough and place them on the baking sheet.
7. Bake for 12 minutes.

Nutrition: Calories: 44; carbs: 27g; protein: 4g; fats: 3g; phosphorus: 59mg; potassium: 92mg; sodium: 65mg

252.   Mixed Berry Cobbler

Preparation time: 15 minutes
Cooking time: 4 hours
Servings: 8
Ingredients:
- 1/4 cup coconut almond milk

- 1/4 cup ghee
- 1/4 cup honey
- 1/2 cup almond flour
- 1/2 cup tapioca starch
- 1/2 tablespoon cinnamon
- 1/2 tablespoon coconut sugar
- 1 teaspoon vanilla
- 12 ounces frozen raspberries
- 16 ounces frozen wild blueberries
- 2 teaspoon baking powder
- 2 teaspoon tapioca starch

Directions:
1. Place the frozen berries in the slow cooker. Add honey and 2 teaspoons of tapioca starch. Mix to combine.
2. In a bowl, mix the tapioca starch, almond flour, coconut almond milk, ghee, baking powder and vanilla. Sweeten with sugar. Place this pastry mix on top of the berries.
3. Set the slow cooker for 4 hours.

Nutrition:
Calories: 146; carbs: 33g; protein: 1g; fats: 3g; phosphorus: 29mg; potassium: 133mg; sodium: 4mg

253.   Blueberry Espresso Brownies

Preparation time: 15 minutes
Cooking time: 30 minutes
Servings: 12
Ingredients:
- 1/4 cup organic cocoa powder
- 1/4 teaspoon salt
- 1/2 cup raw honey
- 1/2 teaspoon baking soda
- 1 cup blueberries
- 1 cup coconut cream
- 1 tablespoon cinnamon
- 1 tablespoon ground coffee
- 2 teaspoon vanilla extract
- 3 eggs

Directions:
1. Preheat the oven to 3250f.
2. In a bow mix together coconut cream, honey, eggs, cinnamon, honey, vanilla, baking soda, coffee and salt.
3. Use a mixer to combine all ingredients.
4. Fold in the blueberries
5. Pour the batter in a greased baking dish and bake for 30 minutes or until a toothpick inserted in the middle comes out clean.
6. Remove from the oven and let it cool.

Nutrition: Calories: 168; carbs: 20g; protein: 4g; fats: 10g; phosphorus: 79mg; potassium: 169mg; sodium: 129mg

254. Spiced Peaches

Preparation time: 5 minutes
Cooking time: 10 minutes
Servings: 2 servings
Ingredients:

- Peaches – 1 cup
- Cornstarch – ½ tsp.
- Ground cloves – 1 tsp.
- Ground cinnamon – 1 tsp.
- Ground nutmeg – 1 tsp.
- Zest of ½ lemon
- Water – ½ cup

Directions:
1. Combine cinnamon, cornstarch, nutmeg, ground cloves, and lemon zest in a pan on the stove.
2. Heat on a medium heat and add peaches.
3. Bring to a boil, reduce the heat and simmer for 10 minutes.
4. Serve.

Nutrition: calories: 70; fat: 0g; carb: 14g; phosphorus: 23mg; potassium: 176mg; sodium: 3mg; protein: 1g

255. Pumpkin Cheesecake Bar

Preparation time: 10 minutes
Cooking time: 50 minutes
Servings: 4 servings
Ingredients:

- Unsalted butter – 2 ½ tbsps.
- Cream cheese – 4 oz.
- All-purpose white flour – ½ cup
- Golden brown sugar – 3 tbsps.

- Granulated sugar – ¼ cup
- Pureed pumpkin – ½ cup
- Egg whites - 2
- Ground cinnamon – 1 tsp.
- Ground nutmeg – 1 tsp.
- Vanilla extract – 1 tsp.

Directions:
1. Preheat the oven to 350f.
2. Mix flour and brown sugar in a bowl.
3. Mix in the butter to form 'breadcrumbs.
4. Place ¾ of this mixture in a dish.
5. Bake in the oven for 15 minutes. Remove and cool.
6. Lightly whisk the egg and fold in the cream cheese, sugar, pumpkin, cinnamon, nutmeg and vanilla until smooth.
7. Pour this mixture over the oven-baked base and sprinkle with the rest of the breadcrumbs from earlier.
8. Bake in the oven for 30 to 35 minutes more.
9. Cool, slice and serve.

Nutrition: calories: 248; fat: 13g; carb: 33g; phosphorus: 67mg; potassium: 96mg; sodium: 146mg; protein: 4g

256. Blueberry Mini Muffins

Preparation time: 10 minutes
Cooking time: 35 minutes
Servings: 4 servings
Ingredients:

- Egg whites – 3
- All-purpose white flour – ¼ cup
- Coconut flour – 1 tbsp.
- Baking soda – 1 tsp.
- Nutmeg – 1 tbsp. Grated
- Vanilla extract – 1 tsp.
- Stevia – 1 tsp.
- Fresh blueberries – ¼ cup

Directions:
1. Preheat the oven to 325f.
2. Mix all the ingredients in a bowl.
3. Divide the batter into 4 and spoon into a lightly oiled muffin tin.
4. Bake in the oven for 15 to 20 minutes or until cooked through.
5. Cool and serve.

Nutrition: calories: 62; fat: 0g; carb: 9g; phosphorus: 103mg; potassium: 65mg; sodium: 62mg; protein: 4g;

257. Baked Peaches With Cream Cheese

Preparation time: 10 minutes
Cooking time: 15 minutes
Servings: 4 servings
Ingredients:
- Plain cream cheese – 1 cup
- Crushed meringue cookies – ½ cup
- Ground cinnamon – ¼ tsp.
- Pinch ground nutmeg
- Peach halves – 8

- Honey – 2 tbsp.

Directions:
1. Preheat the oven to 350f.
2. Line a baking sheet with parchment paper. Set aside.
3. In a small bowl, stir together the meringue cookies, cream cheese, cinnamon, and nutmeg.
4. Spoon the cream cheese mixture evenly into the cavities in the peach halves.
5. Place the peaches on the baking sheet and bake for 15 minutes or until the fruit is soft and the cheese is melted.
6. Remove the peaches from the baking sheet onto plates.
7. Drizzle with honey and serve.

Nutrition: calories: 260; fat: 20; carb: 19g; phosphorus: 74mg; potassium: 198mg; sodium: 216mg; protein: 4g;

258.   **Bread Pudding**

Preparation time: 15 minutes
Cooking time: 40 minutes
Servings: 6 servings
Ingredients:

- Unsalted butter, for greasing the baking dish
- Plain rice almond milk – 1 ½ cups
- Eggs – 2
- Egg whites – 2
- Honey – ¼ cup
- Pure vanilla extract – 1 tsp.
- Cubed white bread – 6 cups

Directions:

1. Lightly grease an 8-by-8-inch baking dish with butter. Set aside.
2. In a bowl, whisk together the eggs, egg whites, rice almond milk, honey, and vanilla.
3. Add the bread cubes and stir until the bread is coated.
4. Transfer the mixture to the baking dish and cover with plastic wrap.
5. Store the dish in the refrigerator for at least 3 hours.
6. Preheat the oven to 325f.

7. Remove the plastic wrap from the baking dish, bake the pudding for 35 to 40 minutes, or golden brown.
8. Serve.

Nutrition: calories: 167; fat: 3g; carb: 30g; phosphorus: 95mg; potassium: 93mg; sodium: 189mg; protein: 6g;

259. Strawberry Ice Cream

Preparation time: 5 minutes
Cooking time: 5 minutes
Servings: 3 servings
Ingredients:
- Stevia – ½ cup
- Lemon juice – 1 tbsp.
- Non-dairy coffee creamer – ¾ cup
- Strawberries – 10 oz.
- Crushed ice – 1 cup

Directions:
1. Blend everything in a blend until smooth.
2. Freeze until frozen.
3. Serve.

Nutrition: calories: 94.4; fat: 6g; carb: 8.3g; phosphorus: 25mg; potassium: 108mg; sodium: 25mg; protein: 1.3g;

260. Cinnamon Custard

Preparation time: 20 minutes
Cooking time: 1 hour
Servings: 6 servings
Ingredients:

- Unsalted butter, for greasing the ramekins
- Plain rice almond milk – 1 ½ cups
- Eggs – 4
- Granulated sugar – ¼ cup
- Pure vanilla extract – 1 tsp.
- Ground cinnamon – ½ tsp.
- Cinnamon sticks for garnish

Directions:

1. Preheat the oven to 325f.
2. Lightly grease 6 ramekins and place them in a baking dish. Set aside.
3. In a large bowl, whisk together the eggs, rice almond milk, sugar, vanilla, and cinnamon until the mixture is smooth.
4. Pour the mixture through a fine sieve into a pitcher.
5. Evenly divide the custard mixture among the ramekins.
6. Fill the baking dish with hot water, until the water reaches halfway up the ramekins' sides.
7. Bake for 1 hour or until the custards are set and a knife inserted in the center comes out clean.

8. Remove the custards from the oven and take the ramekins out of the water.
9. Cool on the wire racks for 1 hour then chill for 1 hour.
10. garnish with cinnamon sticks and serve.

Nutrition: calories: 110; fat: 4g; carb: 14g; phosphorus: 100mg; potassium: 64mg; sodium: 71mg; protein: 4g;

261. <u>Raspberry Brule</u>

Preparation time: 15 minutes
Cooking time: 1 minute
Servings: 4 servings
Ingredients:

- Light sour cream – ½ cup
- Plain cream cheese – ½ cup
- Brown sugar – ¼ cup, divided
- Ground cinnamon – ¼ tsp.
- Fresh raspberries – 1 cup

Directions:

1. Preheat the oven to broil.
2. In a bowl, beat together the cream cheese, sour cream, 2 tbsp. Brown sugar and cinnamon for 4 minutes or until the mixture is very smooth and fluffy.
3. Evenly divide the raspberries among 4 (4-ounce) ramekins.
4. Spoon the cream cheese mixture over the berries and smooth the tops.
5. Sprinkle ½ tbsp. Brown sugar evenly over each ramekin.

6. Place the ramekins on a baking sheet and broil 4 inches from the heating element until the sugar is caramelized and golden brown.
7. Cool and serve.

Nutrition: calories: 188; fat: 13g; carb: 16g; phosphorus: 60mg; potassium: 158mg; sodium: 132mg; protein

262. **Tart Apple Granita**

preparation time: 15 minutes, plus 4 hours freezing time
Cooking time: 0
Servings: 4
Ingredients:

- ½ cup granulated sugar
- ½ cup water
- 2 cups unsweetened apple juice
- ¼ cup freshly squeezed lemon juice

Directions:

1. In a small saucepan over medium-high heat, heat the sugar and water.
2. Bring the mixture to a boil and then reduce the heat to low and simmer for about 15 minutes or until the liquid has reduced by half.
3. Remove the pan from the heat and pour the liquid into a large shallow metal pan.
4. Let the liquid cool for about 30 minutes and then stir in the apple juice and lemon juice.
5. Place the pan in the freezer.
6. After 1 hour, run a fork through the liquid to break up any ice crystals formed. Scrape down the sides as well.
7. Place the pan back in the freezer and repeat the stirring and scraping every 20 minutes, creating slush.
8. Serve when the mixture is completely frozen and looks like crushed ice, after about 3 hours.

Nutrition: calories: 157; fat: 0g; carbohydrates: 0g; phosphorus: 10mg; potassium: 141mg; sodium: 5mg; protein: 0g

263. **Lemon-Lime Sherbet**

preparation time: 5 minutes, plus 3 hours chilling time
Cooking time: 15 minutes
servings: 2
Ingredients:

- 2 cups water
- 1 cup granulated sugar
- 3 tablespoons lemon zest, divided
- ½ cup freshly squeezed lemon juice
- Zest of 1 lime
- Juice of 1 lime
- ½ cup heavy (whipping) cream

Directions:

1. Place a large saucepan over medium-high heat and add the water, sugar, and 2 tablespoons of the lemon zest.
2. Bring the mixture to a boil and then reduce the heat and simmer for 15 minutes.
3. Transfer the mixture to a large bowl and add the remaining 1 tablespoon lemon zest, the lemon juice, lime zest, and lime juice.
4. Chill the mixture in the fridge until completely cold, about 3 hours.

5. Whisk in the heavy cream and transfer the mixture to an ice cream maker.
6. Freeze according to the manufacturer's instructions.

Nutrition: calories: 151; fat: 6g; carbohydrates: 26g; phosphorus: 10mg; potassium: 27mg; sodium: 6mg; protein: 0g

264. Pavlova with Peaches

Preparation time: 30 minutes
Cooking time: 1 hour, plus cooling time
Servings: 3
Ingredients:

- 4 large egg whites, at room temperature
- ½ teaspoon cream of tartar
- 1 cup superfine sugar
- ½ teaspoon pure vanilla extract
- 2 cups peaches

Directions:
1. Preheat the oven to 225°f.
2. Line a baking sheet with parchment paper; set aside.
3. In a large bowl, beat the egg whites for about 1 minute or until soft peaks form.
4. Beat in the cream of tartar.
5. Add the sugar, 1 tablespoon at a time, until the egg whites are very stiff and glossy. Do not overbeat.
6. Beat in the vanilla.
7. Evenly spoon the meringue onto the baking sheet so that you have 8 rounds.
8. Use the back of the spoon to create an indentation in the middle of each round.
9. Bake the meringues for about 1 hour or until a light brown crust form.
10. Turn off the oven and let the meringues stand, still in the oven, overnight.
11. Remove the meringues from the sheet and place them on serving plates.
12. Spoon the peaches, dividing evenly, into the centers of the meringues, and serve.
13. Store any unused meringues in a sealed container at room temperature for up to 1 week.

Nutrition: calories: 132; fat: 0g; carbohydrates: 32g; phosphorus: 7mg; potassium: 95mg; sodium: 30mg; protein: 2g

265. Tropical Vanilla Snow Cone

Preparation time: 15 minutes, plus freezing time
Cooking time: 0
Servings: 2
Ingredients:

- 1 cup pineapple
- 1 cup frozen strawberries
- 6 tablespoons water
- 2 tablespoons granulated sugar
- 1 tablespoon vanilla extract

Directions:
1. In a large saucepan, mix the peaches, pineapple, strawberries, water, and sugar over medium-high heat and bring to a boil.
2. Reduce the heat to low and simmer the mixture, stirring occasionally, for 15 minutes.
3. Remove from the heat and let the mixture cool completely, for about 1 hour.

4. Stir in the vanilla and transfer the fruit mixture to a food processor or blender.
5. Purée until smooth, and pour the purée into a 9-by-13-inch glass baking dish.
6. Cover and place the dish in the freezer overnight.
7. When the fruit mixture is completely frozen, use a fork to scrape the sorbet until you have flaked flavored ice.
8. Scoop the ice flakes into 4 serving dishes.

Nutrition: calories: 92; fat: 0g; carbohydrates: 22g; phosphorus: 17mg; potassium: 145mg; sodium: 4mg; protein: 1g

266.   <u>Rhubarb Crumble</u>

preparation time: 15 minutes
cooking time: 30 minutes
Servings: 6
Ingredients:
- Unsalted butter, for greasing the baking dish
- 1 cup all-purpose flour
- ½ cup brown sugar
- ½ teaspoon ground cinnamon
- ½ cup unsalted butter, at room temperature
- 1 cup chopped rhubarb
- 2 apples, peeled, cored, and sliced thin
- 2 tablespoons granulated sugar
- 2 tablespoons water

Directions:
1. Preheat the oven to 325°f.
2. Lightly grease an 8-by-8-inch baking dish with butter; set aside.
3. In a small bowl, stir together the flour, sugar, and cinnamon until well combined.
4. Add the butter and rub the mixture between your fingers until it resembles coarse crumbs.
5. In a medium saucepan, mix the rhubarb, apple, sugar, and water over medium heat and cook for about 20 minutes or until the rhubarb is soft.
6. Spoon the fruit mixture into the baking dish and evenly top with the crumble.
7. Bake the crumble for 20 to 30 minutes or until golden brown.
8. serve hot.

Nutrition: calories: 450; fat: 23g; carbohydrates: 60g; phosphorus: 51mg; potassium: 181mg; sodium: 10mg; protein: 4g

267. Gingerbread Loaf

Preparation time: 20 minutes
Cooking time: 1 hour
Servings: 16
Ingredients:

- Unsalted butter, for greasing the baking dish
- 3 cups all-purpose flour
- ½ teaspoon ener-g baking soda substitute
- 2 teaspoons ground cinnamon
- 1 teaspoon ground allspice
- ¾ cup granulated sugar
- 1¼ cups plain rice almond milk
- 1 large egg
- ¼ cup olive oil
- 2 tablespoons molasses
- 2 teaspoons grated fresh ginger
- Powdered sugar, for dusting

Directions:

1. Preheat the oven to 350°f.
2. Lightly grease a 9-by-13-inch baking dish with butter; set aside.
3. In a large bowl, sift together the flour, baking soda substitute, cinnamon, and allspice.
4. Stir the sugar into the flour mixture.
5. In medium bowl, whisk together the almond milk, egg, olive oil, molasses, and ginger until well blended.

6. Make a well in the center of the flour mixture and pour in the wet ingredients.
7. Mix until just combined, taking care not to overmix.
8. Pour the batter into the baking dish and bake for about 1 hour or until a wooden pick inserted in the middle comes out clean.
9. Serve warm with a dusting of powdered sugar.

Nutrition: calories: 232; fat: 5g; carbohydrates: 42g; phosphorus: 54mg; potassium: 104mg; sodium: 18mg; protein: 4g

268. Elegant Lavender Cookies

preparation time: 10 minutes
Cooking time: 15 minutes
Servings: makes 24 cookies

Ingredients:
- 5 dried organic lavender flowers, the entire top of the flower
- ½ cup granulated sugar
- 1 cup unsalted butter, at room temperature
- 2 cups all-purpose flour
- 1 cup rice flour

Directions:
1. Strip the tiny lavender flowers off the main stem carefully and place the flowers and granulated sugar into a food processor or blender. Pulse until the mixture is finely chopped.
2. In a medium bowl, cream together the butter and lavender sugar until it is very fluffy.
3. Mix the flours into the creamed mixture until the mixture resembles fine crumbs.
4. Gather the dough together into a ball and then roll it into a long log.
5. Wrap the cookie dough in plastic and refrigerate it for about 1 hour or until firm.
6. Preheat the oven to 375°f.
7. Slice the chilled dough into ¼-inch rounds and refrigerate it for 1 hour or until firm.
8. Bake the cookies for 15 to 18 minutes or until they are a very pale, golden brown.
9. Let the cookies cool.
10. Store the cookies at room temperature in a sealed container for up to 1 week.

Nutrition: calories: 153; fat: 9g; carbohydrates: 17g; phosphorus: 18mg; potassium: 17mg; sodium: 0mg; protein: 1g

269. Carob Angel Food Cake

preparation time: 30 minutes
Cooking time: 30 minutes
Servings: 16

Ingredients:
- ¾ cup all-purpose flour
- ¼ cup carob flour
- 1½ cups sugar, divided
- 12 large egg whites, at room temperature
- 1½ teaspoons cream of tartar
- 2 teaspoons vanilla

Directions:
1. Preheat the oven to 375°f.
2. In a medium bowl, sift together the all-purpose flour, carob flour, and ¾ cup of the sugar; set aside.

3. Beat the egg whites and cream of tartar with a hand mixer for about 5 minutes or until soft peaks form.
4. Add the remaining ¾ cup sugar by the tablespoon to the egg whites until all the sugar is used up and stiff peaks form.
5. Fold in the flour mixture and vanilla.
6. Spoon the batter into an angel food cake pan.
7. Run a knife through the batter to remove any air pockets.
8. Bake the cake for about 30 minutes or until the top springs back when pressed lightly.
9. Invert the pan onto a wire rack to cool.
10. Run a knife around the rim of the cake pan and remove the cake from the pan.

Nutrition: calories: 113; fat: 0g; carbohydrates: 25g; phosphorus: 11mg; potassium: 108mg; sodium: 42mg; protein: 3g

270.   Old-Fashioned Apple Kuchen

preparation time: 25 minutes
Cook time: 1 hour
Servings: 16
Ingredients:

- Unsalted butter, for greasing the baking dish
- 1 cup unsalted butter, at room temperature
- 2 cups granulated sugar
- 2 eggs, beaten
- 2 teaspoons pure vanilla extract
- 2 cups all-purpose flour
- 1 teaspoon ener-g baking soda substitute
- 2 teaspoons ground cinnamon
- ½ teaspoon ground nutmeg
- Pinch ground allspice
- 2 large apples, peeled, cored, and diced (about 3 cups)

Directions:
1. Preheat the oven to 350°f.
2. Grease a 9-by-13-inch glass baking dish; set aside.
3. Cream together the butter and sugar with a hand mixer until light and fluffy, for about 3 minutes.
4. Add the eggs and vanilla and beat until combined, scraping down the sides of the bowl, about 1 minute.
5. In a small bowl, stir together the flour, baking soda substitute, cinnamon, nutmeg, and allspice.
6. Add the dry ingredients to the wet ingredients and stir to combine.
7. Stir in the apple and spoon the batter into the baking dish.
8. Bake for about 1 hour or until the cake is golden.
9. Cool the cake on a wire rack.
10. Serve warm or chilled.

Nutrition: calories: 368; fat: 16g; carbohydrates: 53g; phosphorus: 46mg; potassium: 68mg; sodium: 15mg; protein: 3g

271. Dessert Cocktail

Preparation time: 1 minutes
Cooking time: 0 minute
Servings: 4
Ingredients:

- 1 cup of cranberry juice
- 1 cup of fresh ripe strawberries, washed and hull removed
- 2 tablespoon of lime juice
- ¼ cup of white sugar
- 8 ice cubes

Directions:
1. Combine all the ingredients in a blender until smooth and creamy.
2. Pour the liquid into chilled tall glasses and serve cold.

Nutrition: Calories: 92 kcal Carbohydrate: 23.5 g Protein: 0.5 g Sodium: 3.62 mg Potassium: 103.78 mg Phosphorus: 17.86 mg Dietary fiber: 0.84 g Fat: 0.17 g

272. Baked Egg Custard

Preparation time: 15 minutes
Cooking time: 30 minutes
Servings: 4
Ingredients:
- 2 medium eggs, at room temperature
- ¼ cup of semi-skimmed almond milk
- 3 tablespoons of white sugar
- ½ teaspoon of nutmeg
- 1 teaspoon of vanilla extract

Directions:
1. Preheat your oven at 375 f/180c
2. Mix all the ingredients in a mixing bowl and beat with a hand mixer for a few seconds until creamy and uniform.
3. Pour the mixture into lightly greased muffin tins.
4. Bake for 25-30 minutes or until the knife, you place inside, comes out clean.

Nutrition: Calories: 96.56 kcal Carbohydrate: 10.5 g Protein: 3.5 g Sodium: 37.75 mg Potassium: 58.19 mg Phosphorus: 58.76 mg Dietary fiber: 0.06 g Fat: 2.91 g

273. Gumdrop Cookies

Preparation time: 15 minutes
Cooking time: 12 minutes
Servings: 25
Ingredients:
- ½ cup of spreadable unsalted butter
- 1 medium egg
- 1 cup of brown sugar
- 1 2/3 cups of all-purpose flour, sifted
- ¼ cup of almond milk
- 1 teaspoon vanilla
- 1 teaspoon of baking powder
- 15 large gumdrops, chopped finely

Directions:
1. Preheat the oven at 400f/195c.
2. Combine the sugar, butter and egg until creamy.

3. Add the almond milk and vanilla and stir well.
4. Combine the flour with the baking powder in a different bowl. Incorporate to the sugar, butter mixture, and stir.
5. Add the gumdrops and place the mixture in the fridge for half an hour.
6. Drop the dough with tablespoonful into a lightly greased baking or cookie sheet.
7. Bake for 10-12 minutes or until golden brown.

Nutrition: Calories: 102.17 kcal Carbohydrate: 16.5 g Protein: 0.86 g Sodium: 23.42 mg Potassium: 45 mg Phosphorus: 32.15 mg Dietary fiber: 0.13 g Fat: 4 g

274. <u>Pound Cake With Pineapple</u>

Preparation time: 10 minutes
Cooking time: 50 minutes
Servings: 24
Ingredients

- 3 cups of all-purpose flour, sifted
- 3 cups of sugar
- 1 ½ cups of butter
- 6 whole eggs and 3 egg whites
- 1 teaspoon of vanilla extract
- 1 10. Ounce can of pineapple chunks, rinsed and crushed (keep juice aside).

For glaze:

- 1 cup of sugar
- 1 stick of unsalted butter or margarine
- Reserved juice from the pineapple

Directions
1. Preheat the oven at 350f/180c.
2. Beat the sugar and the butter with a hand mixer until creamy and smooth.
3. Slowly add the eggs (one or two every time) and stir well after pouring each egg.
4. Add the vanilla extract, follow up with the flour and stir well.
5. Add the drained and chopped pineapple.
6. Pour the mixture into a greased cake tin and bake for 45-50 minutes.
7. In a small saucepan, combine the sugar with the butter and pineapple juice. Stir every few seconds and bring to boil. Cook until you get a creamy to thick glaze consistency.
8. Pour the glaze over the cake while still hot.
9. Let cook for at least 10 seconds and serve.

Nutrition: Calories: 407.4 kcal Carbohydrate: 79 g Protein: 4.25 g Sodium: 118.97 mg potassium: 180.32 mg Phosphorus: 66.37 mg Dietary fiber: 2.25 g fat: 16.48 g

275. Apple Crunch Pie

Preparation time: 10 minutes
Cooking time: 35 minutes
Servings: 8
Ingredients

- 4 large tart apples, peeled, seeded and sliced
- ½ cup of white all-purpose flour
- 1/3 cup margarine
- 1 cup of sugar
- ¾ cup of rolled oat flakes
- ½ teaspoon of ground nutmeg

Directions

1. Preheat the oven to 375f/180c.
2. Place the apples over a lightly greased square pan (around 7 inches).
3. Mix the rest of the ingredients in a medium bowl with and spread the batter over the apples.
4. Bake for 30-35 minutes or until the top crust has gotten golden brown.
5. Serve hot.

Nutrition: Calories: 261.9 kcal Carbohydrate: 47.2 g Protein: 1.5 g Sodium: 81 mg Potassium: 123.74 mg Phosphorus: 35.27 mg Dietary fiber: 2.81 g Fat: 7.99 g

276. Vanilla Custard

Preparation time: 7 minutes
Cooking time: 10 minutes
Servings: 10
Ingredients

- Egg – 1

- Vanilla – 1/8 teaspoon
- Nutmeg – 1/8 teaspoon
- Almond milk – ½ cup
- Stevia - 2 tablespoon

Directions
1. Scald the almond milk then let it cool slightly.
2. Break the egg into a bowl and beat it with the nutmeg.
3. Add the scalded almond milk, the vanilla, and the sweetener to taste. Mix well.
4. Place the bowl in a baking pan filled with ½ deep of water.
5. Bake for 30 minutes at 325f.
6. Serve.

Nutrition: Calories: 167.3 Fat: 9g Carbs: 11g Phosphorus: 205mg Potassium: 249mg Sodium: 124mg protein: 10g

277. <u>Chocolate Chip Cookies</u>

Preparation time: 7 minutes
Cooking time: 10 minutes
Servings: 10
Ingredients
- Semi-sweet chocolate chips – ½ cup
- Baking soda – ½ teaspoon
- Vanilla – ½ teaspoon
- Egg – 1
- Flour – 1 cup
- Margarine – ½ cup
- Stevia – 4 teaspoons

Directions
1. Sift the dry ingredients.
2. Cream the margarine, stevia, vanilla and egg with a whisk.
3. Add flour mixture and beat well.
4. Stir in the chocolate chips, then drop teaspoonfuls of the mixture over a greased baking sheet.
5. Bake the cookies for about 10 minutes at 375f.
6. Cool and serve.

Nutrition: Calories: 106.2 Fat: 7g carb: 8.9g Phosphorus: 19mg Potassium: 28mg Sodium: 98mg Protein: 1.5g

278. <u>Lemon Mousse</u>

Preparation time: 10 + chill time
Cooking time: 10 minutes
Servings: 4
Ingredients
- 1 cup coconut cream
- 8 ounces cream cheese, soft
- ¼ cup fresh lemon juice
- 3 pinches salt
- 1 teaspoon lemon liquid stevia

Directions
1. Preheat your oven to 350 °f

2. Grease a ramekin with butter
3. Beat cream, cream cheese, fresh lemon juice, salt and lemon liquid stevia in a mixer
4. Pour batter into ramekin
5. Bake for 10 minutes, then transfer the mousse to a serving glass
6. Let it chill for 2 hours and serve
7. Enjoy!

Nutrition: calories: 395 fats: 31g carbohydrates: 3g protein: 5g Phosphorus: 80mg Potassium: 97mg Sodium: 75mg

279.   Jalapeno Crisp

Preparation time: 10 minutes
Cooking time: 1 hour 15 minutes
Servings: 20
Ingredients

- 1 cup sesame seeds
- 1 cup sunflower seeds
- 1 cup flaxseeds
- ½ cup hulled hemp seeds
- 3 tablespoons psyllium husk
- 1 teaspoon salt
- 1 teaspoon baking powder
- 2 cups of water

Directions

1. Pre-heat your oven to 350 °f
2. Take your blender and add seeds, baking powder, salt, and psyllium husk
3. Blend well until a sand-like texture appears
4. Stir in water and mix until a batter form
5. Allow the batter to rest for 10 minutes until a dough-like thick mixture forms
6. Pour the dough onto a cookie sheet lined with parchment paper
7. Spread it evenly, making sure that it has a thickness of ¼ inch thick all around
8. Bake for 75 minutes in your oven
9. Remove and cut into 20 spices
10. Allow them to cool for 30 minutes and enjoy!

Nutrition: calories: 156 fats: 13g carbohydrates: 2g protein: 5g Phosphorus: 70mg Potassium: 57mg Sodium: 45mg

280.   Raspberry Popsicle

Preparation time: 2 hours
Cooking time: 15 minutes
Servings: 4
Ingredients

- 1 ½ cups raspberries
- 2 cups of water

Directions

1. Take a pan and fill it up with water
2. Add raspberries
3. Place it over medium heat and bring to water to a boil
4. Reduce the heat and simmer for 15 minutes
5. Remove heat and pour the mix into popsicle molds

6. Add a popsicle stick and let it chill for 2 hours
7. Serve and enjoy!

Nutrition: calories: 58 fats: 0.4g carbohydrates: 0g protein: 1.4g Phosphorus: 40mg Potassium: 97mg Sodium: 45mg

281.   Easy Fudge

Preparation time: 15 minutes + chill time
Cooking time: 5 minutes
Servings: 25
Ingredients

- 1 ¾ cups of coconut butter
- 1 cup pumpkin puree
- 1 teaspoon ground cinnamon
- ¼ teaspoon ground nutmeg
- 1 tablespoon coconut oil

Directions

1. Take an 8x8 inch square baking pan and line it with aluminum foil
2. Take a spoon and scoop out the coconut butter into a heated pan and allow the butter to melt
3. Keep stirring well and remove from the heat once fully melted
4. Add spices and pumpkin and keep straining until you have a grain-like texture
5. Add coconut oil and keep stirring to incorporate everything
6. Scoop the mixture into your baking pan and evenly distribute it
7. Place wax paper on top of the mixture and press gently to straighten the top
8. Remove the paper and discard
9. Allow it to chill for 1-2 hours
10. Once chilled, take it out and slice it up into pieces
11. Enjoy!

Nutrition: calories: 120 fats: 10g carbohydrates: 5g protein: 1.2g Phosphorus: 88mg Potassium: 90mg Sodium: 75mg

282.   Coconut Loaf

Preparation time: 15 minutes
Cooking time: 40 minutes
Servings: 4
Ingredients

- 1 ½ tablespoons coconut flour
- ¼ teaspoon baking powder
- 1/8 teaspoon salt
- 1 tablespoon coconut oil, melted
- 1 whole egg

Directions

1. Preheat your oven to 350 °f
2. Add coconut flour, baking powder, salt
3. Add coconut oil, eggs and stir well until mixed
4. Leave the batter for several minutes
5. Pour half the batter onto the baking pan
6. Spread it to form a circle, repeat with remaining batter

7. Bake in the oven for 10 minutes
8. Once a golden-brown texture comes, let it cool and serve
9. Enjoy!

Nutrition: calories: 297 fats: 14g carbohydrates: 15g protein: 15g Phosphorus: 80mg Potassium: 97mg Sodium: 75mg

283. Cashew Cheese Bites

Preparation Time: 5 minutes
Cooking Time: 5 minutes
Servings: 12
Ingredients:

- 8 oz cream cheese
- 1 tsp cinnamon
- 1 cup cashew butter

Directions:
1. Add all ingredients into the blender and blend until smooth.
2. Pour blended mixture into the mini muffin liners and place them in the refrigerator until set.
3. Serve and enjoy.

Nutrition: Calories 192 Fat 17.1 g Carbohydrates 6.5 g Sugar 0 g Protein 5.2 g Cholesterol 21 mg Phosphorus: 110mg Potassium: 117mg Sodium: 75mg

284. Healthy Cinnamon Lemon Tea

Preparation Time: 5 minutes
Cooking Time: 5 minutes
Servings: 1
Ingredients:

- 1/2 tbsp fresh lemon juice
- 1 cup of water
- 1 tsp ground cinnamon

Directions:
1. Add water in a saucepan and bring to boil over medium heat.
2. Add cinnamon and stir to cinnamon dissolve.
3. Add lemon juice and stir well.
4. Serve hot.

Nutrition: Calories 9 Fat 0.2 g Carbohydrates 2 g Sugar 0.3 g Protein 0.2 g Cholesterol 0 mg Phosphorus: 70mg Potassium: 87mg Sodium: 65mg

285. Almonds & Blueberries Smoothie

Preparation Time: 5 minutes
Cooking Time: 3 minutes
Servings: 2
Ingredients:
- 1/4 cup ground almonds, unsalted
- 1 cup fresh blueberries
- Fresh juice of a 1 lemon
- 1 cup fresh kale leaf
- 1/2 cup coconut water
- 1 cup water
- 2 tablespoon plain yogurt (optional)

Directions:
1. Dump all ingredients in your high-speed blender, and blend until your smoothie is smooth.
2. Pour the mixture in a chilled glass.
3. Serve and enjoy!

Nutrition: Calories: 110, Carbohydrates: 8g, Proteins: 2g, Fat: 7g, Fiber: 2g, Calcium 19mg, Phosphorous 16mg, Potassium 27mg Sodium: 101 mg

286. Almonds and Zucchini Smoothie

Preparation Time: 5 minutes
Cooking Time: 3 minutes
Servings: 2
Ingredients:
- 1 cup zucchini, cooked and mashed - unsalted
- 1 1/2 cups almond milk
- 1 tablespoon almond butter (plain, unsalted)
- 1 teaspoon pure almond extract
- 2 tablespoon ground almonds or macadamia almonds
- 1/2 cup water
- 1 cup ice cubes crushed (optional, for serving)

Directions:
1. Dump all ingredients from the list above in your fast-speed blender; blend for 45 - 60 seconds or to taste.
2. Serve with crushed ice.

Nutrition: Calories: 322, Carbohydrates: 6g, Proteins: 6g, Fat: 30g, Fiber: 3.5gCalcium 9mg, Phosphorous 26mg, Potassium 27mg Sodium: 121 mg

287. Blueberries and Coconut Smoothie

Preparation Time: 5 minutes
Cooking Time: 3 minutes
Servings: 5

Ingredients:

- 1 cup of frozen blueberries, unsweetened
- 1 cup stevia or erythritol sweetener
- 2 cups coconut almond milk (canned)
- 1 cup of fresh green lettuce leaves
- 2 tablespoon shredded coconut (unsweetened)
- 3/4 cup water

Directions:

1. Place all ingredients from the list in food-processor or in your strong blender.
2. Blend for 45 - 60 seconds or to taste.
3. Ready for drink! Serve!

Nutrition: Calories: 190, Carbohydrates: 8g, Proteins: 3g, Fat: 18g, Fiber: 2g, Calcium 79mg, Phosphorous 216mg, Potassium 207mg Sodium: 121 mg

288. Creamy Dandelion Greens and Celery Smoothie

Preparation Time: 10 minutes
Cooking Time: 3 minutes
Servings: 2
Ingredients:

- 1 handful of raw dandelion greens
- 2 celery sticks
- 2 tablespoon chia seeds
- 1 small piece of ginger, minced
- 1/2 cup almond milk
- 1/2 cup of water
- 1/2 cup plain yogurt

Directions:

1. Rinse and clean dandelion leaves from any dirt; add in a high-speed blender.
2. Clean the ginger; keep only inner part and cut in small slices; add in a blender.
3. Blend all remaining ingredients until smooth.
4. Serve and enjoy!

Nutrition: Calories: 58, Carbohydrates: 5g, Proteins: 3g, Fat: 6g, Fiber: 3g Calcium 29mg, Phosphorous 76mg, Potassium 27mg Sodium: 121 mg

289. Green Coconut Smoothie

Preparation Time: 10 minutes
Cooking Time: 3 minutes
Servings: 2
Ingredients:

- 1 1/4 cup coconut almond milk (canned)
- 2 tablespoon chia seeds
- 1 cup of fresh kale leaves
- 1 cup of green lettuce leaves
- 1 scoop vanilla protein powder
- 1 cup ice cubes
- Granulated stevia sweetener (to taste; optional)

- 1/2 cup water

Directions:

1. Rinse and clean kale and the green lettuce leaves from any dirt.
2. Add all ingredients in your blender.
3. Blend until you get a nice smoothie.
4. Serve into chilled glass.

Nutrition: Calories: 179, Carbohydrates: 5g, Proteins: 4g, Fat: 18g, Fiber: 2.5g Calcium 22mg, Phosphorous 46mg, Potassium 34mg Sodium: 131 mg

290. Peach High-Protein Smoothie

Preparation Time: 10minutes
Cooking Time: 0 minutes
Servings: 1
Ingredients:

- 1/2 cup ice
- 2 tbsp. powdered egg whites
- 3/4 cup fresh peaches
- 1 tbsp. sugar

Directions:

1. First, start by putting all the ingredients in a blender jug.
2. Give it a pulse for 30 seconds until blended well.
3. Serve chilled and fresh.

Nutrition: Calories 132 Protein 10 g Fat 0 g Cholesterol 0 mg Potassium 353 mg Calcium 9 mg Fiber 1.9 g

291. Strawberry Fruit Smoothie

Preparation Time: 10minutes
Cooking Time: 0 minutes
Servings: 1
Ingredients:

- 3/4 cup fresh strawberries
- 1/2 cup liquid pasteurized egg whites
- 1/2 cup ice
- 1 tbsp. sugar

Directions:
1. First, start by putting all the ingredients in a blender jug.
2. Give it a pulse for 30 seconds until blended well.
3. Serve chilled and fresh.

Nutrition: Calories 156 Protein 14 g Fat 0 g Cholesterol 0 mg Potassium 400 mg Phosphorus 49 mg Calcium 29 mg Fiber 2.5 g

292. Cranberry Smoothie

Preparation Time: 10minutes
Cooking Time: 0 minutes
Servings: 1
Ingredients:
- 1 cup frozen cranberries
- 1 medium cucumber, peeled and sliced
- 1 stalk of celery
- Handful of parsley
- Squeeze of lime juice

Directions:
1. First, start by putting all the ingredients in a blender jug. Give it a pulse for 30 seconds until blended well.
2. Serve chilled and fresh.

Nutrition: Calories 126 Protein 12 g Fat 0.03 g Cholesterol 0 mg Potassium 220 mg Calcium 19 mg Fiber 1.4g

293. Berry Cucumber Smoothie

Preparation Time: 10minutes
Cooking Time: 0 minutes
Servings: 1
Ingredients:
- 1 medium cucumber, peeled and sliced
- ½ cup fresh blueberries
- ½ cup fresh or frozen strawberries
- ½ cup unsweetened rice almond milk
- Stevia, to taste

Directions:
1. First, start by putting all the ingredients in a blender jug.
2. Give it a pulse for 30 seconds until blended well.
3. Serve chilled and fresh.

Nutrition: Calories 141 Protein 10 g Carbohydrates 15 g Fat 0 g Sodium 113 mg Potassium 230 mg Phosphorus 129 mg

294. Raspberry Peach Smoothie

Preparation Time: 10minutes
Cooking Time: 0 minutes
Servings: 2
Ingredients:

- 1 cup frozen raspberries
- 1 medium peach, pit removed, sliced
- ½ cup silken tofu
- 1 tbsp. honey
- 1 cup unsweetened vanilla almond milk

Directions:

1. First, start by putting all the ingredients in a blender jug.
2. Give it a pulse for 30 seconds until blended well.
3. Serve chilled and fresh.

Nutrition: Calories 132 Protein 9 g. Carbohydrates 14 g Sodium 112 mg Potassium 310 mg Phosphorus 39 mg Calcium 32 mg

295. Power-Boosting Smoothie

Preparation Time: 5 minutes
Cooking Time: 0 minutes
Servings: 2
Ingredients:

- ½ cup water
- ½ cup non-dairy whipped topping
- 2 scoops whey protein powder
- 1½ cups frozen blueberries

Directions:

1. In a high-speed blender, add all ingredients and pulse till smooth.
2. Transfer into 2 serving glass and serve immediately.

Nutrition: Calories 242 Fat 7g Carbs 23.8g Protein 23.2g Potassium (K) 263mg Sodium (Na) 63mg Phosphorous 30 mg

296. Distinctive Pineapple Smoothie

Preparation Time: 5 minutes
Cooking Time: 0 minutes
Servings: 2
Ingredients:

- ¼ cup crushed ice cubes
- 2 scoops vanilla whey protein powder
- 1 cup water
- 1½ cups pineapple

Directions:

1. In a high-speed blender, add all ingredients and pulse till smooth.
2. Transfer into 2 serving glass and serve immediately.

Nutrition: Calories 117 Fat 2.1g Carbs 18.2g Protein 22.7g Potassium (K) 296mg Sodium (Na) 81mg Phosphorous 28 mg

297. <u>Strengthening Smoothie Bowl</u>

Preparation Time: 5 minutes
Cooking Time: 4 minutes
Servings: 2
Ingredients:

- ¼ cup fresh blueberries
- ¼ cup fat-free plain Greek yogurt
- 1/3 cup unsweetened almond milk
- 2 tbsp. of whey protein powder
- 2 cups frozen blueberries

Directions:

1. In a blender, add blueberries and pulse for about 1 minute.
2. Add almond milk, yogurt and protein powder and pulse till desired consistency.
3. Transfer the mixture into 2 bowls evenly.
4. Serve with the topping of fresh blueberries.

Nutrition: Calories 176 Fat 2.1g Carbs 27g Protein 15.1g Potassium (K) 242mg Sodium (Na) 72mg Phosphorous 555.3 mg

298. <u>Pineapple Juice</u>

Preparation Time: 5 minutes
Cooking Time: 0 minutes
Servings: 2
Ingredients:

- ½ cup canned pineapple
- 1 cup water

Direction:

1. Blend all ingredients and serve over ice.

Nutrition: Calories 135 Protein 0 g Carbs 0 g Fat 0 g Sodium (Na) 0 mg Potassium (K) 180 mg Phosphorus 8 mg

299. <u>Grapefruit Sorbet</u>

Preparation Time: 10 minutes
Cooking Time: 5 minutes
Servings: 6
Ingredients

- ½ cup sugar
- ¼ cup water
- 1 fresh thyme sprig
- For the sorbet
- Juice of 6 pink grapefruit
- ¼ cup thyme simple syrup

Directions:

1 In a blender, combine the grapefruit juice and ¼ cup of simple syrup, and process.

2 Transfer to an airtight container and freeze for 3 to 4 hours, until firm. Serve.

3 Substitution tip: Try this with other citrus fruits, such as mangos, lemons, or limes, for an equally delicious treat.

Nutrition: Calories 117 Fat 2.1g Carbs 18.2g Protein 22.7g Potassium (K) 296mg Sodium (Na) 81mg Phosphorous 28 mg

300.   Apple and Blueberry Crisp

Preparation Time: 1 hour 10 minutes
Cooking Time: 1 hour
Serving: 8
Ingredients:

- Crisp
- 1/4 cup of brown sugar
- 1 1/4 cups quick cooking rolled oats
- 6 tbsp. non-hydrogenated melted margarine
- 1/4 cup all-purpose flour (unbleached)

Filling:

- 2 tbsp. cornstarch
- 1/2 cup of brown sugar
- 2 cups chopped or grated apples
- cups frozen or fresh blueberries (not thawed)
- 1 tbsp. fresh lemon juice
- 1 tbsp. melted margarine

Directions:
1 Preheat the oven to 350°F with the rack in the middle position.
2 Pour all the dry ingredients into a bowl, then the butter and stir until it is moistened. Set the mixture aside.
3 In an 8-inch (20-cm) square baking dish, mix the cornstarch and brown sugar. Add lemon juice and the rest of the fruits. Toss to blend the mixture. Add the crisp mixture, then bake until the crisp turns golden brown (or for 55 minutes to 1 hour). You can either serve cold or warm.

Nutrition: Calories 127 Fat 2.1g Carbs 18.2g Protein 22.7g Potassium (K) 256mg Sodium (Na) 61mg Phosphorous 28 mg

301.   Mini Pineapple Upside Down Cakes

Preparation Time: 50 minutes
Cooking Time: 50 minutes
Serving: 12
Ingredients:

- 1 tbsp. melted unsalted butter
- 12 canned unsweetened pineapple slices
- 1/3 cup packed brown sugar
- 2/3 cup sugar
- fresh cherries cut into halves and pitted
- 1 tbsp. canola oil
- 2/3 cup almond milk (fat-free)
- ½ tbsp. lemon juice
- 1 large egg

- 1-1/3 cups cake flour
- 1/4 tbsp. vanilla extract
- 1/4 tsp salt
- 1-1/4 tsp baking powder

Directions:
1 Coat 12 serving muffin pan with butter or you could use a square baking pan.
2 Sprinkle little brown sugar into each of the pieces.
3 Crush 1 pineapple slice into each piece to take the shape of the cup. Place 1 half cherry in the center of the pineapple with the cut side facing up.
4 Get a large bowl and beat the egg, almond milk, and the extracts until it is evenly blended.
5 Beat the flour, salt, and baking powder into sugar mixture until it is well blended to attain homogeneity and pour it into the batter prepared in the muffin pan.
6 Bake at 350°s until a toothpick sinks in and comes out clean (or for 35-40 minutes). Invert the muffin pan immediately and allow the cooked cakes to drop onto a serving plate. (If necessary, you can use a small spatula or butter knife to gently release them from the pan.)
7 Serve warm.

Nutrition: Calories 119 Fat 2.1g Carbs 16.2g Protein 22.7g Potassium (K) 296mg Sodium (Na) 81mg Phosphorous 28 mg

302. Raspberry Cucumber Smoothie

Preparation Time: 5 minutes
Cooking Time: 5 minutes
Servings: 2
Ingredients:
- 1 c. fresh or frozen raspberries
- ½ c. diced English cucumber
- 1 c. Homemade Rice Milk (or use unsweetened store-bought) or almond milk
- 2 tsp. chia seeds
- 1 tsp. honey
- 3 ice cubes

Directions:
1. Place the raspberries, cucumber, rice milk, chia seeds, and honey in a blender. Then, blend until smooth.
2. Add the ice cubes. Then, blend until thick and smooth.
3. Pour into two tall glasses. Serve immediately.

Nutrition: Calories: 125 Fat: 1.1g Carbs: 23.5g Protein: 6g Sodium: 44mg Potassium: 199mg Phosphorus: 54mg

303. Mango Cheesecake Smoothie

Preparation Time: 5 minutes
Cooking Time: 5 minutes
Servings: 2
Ingredients:
- 1 c. Homemade Rice Milk
- ½ ripe fresh mango, peeled and chopped
- 2 tbsp. cream cheese, at room temperature
- 1 tsp. honey
- ½ vanilla bean split and seeds scraped out
- Pinch ground nutmeg
- 3 ice cubes

Directions:

1. Place the rice milk, mango, cream cheese, honey, vanilla bean seeds, and nutmeg in a blender, and blend until smooth and thick.
2. Add the ice cubes and blend.
3. Serve in two glasses immediately.

Nutrition: Calories: 177 Fat: 4g Carbs: 10g Protein: 24g Sodium: 346mg Potassium: 66mg Phosphorus: 62mg

304. Hot Cocoa

Preparation Time: 5 minutes
Cooking Time: 5 minutes
Servings: 1
Ingredients:

- 1 tbsp. cocoa powder, unsweetened
- 2 tsp. Splenda granulated sugar
- 3 tbsp. whipped dessert topping
- 1 c. water, at room temperature
- 2 tbsp. water, cold

Directions:

1. Place a saucepan over medium heat and let it heat until hot.
2. Take a cup, place cocoa powder and sugar in it, pour in cold water, and mix well.
3. Then slowly stir in hot water until cocoa mixture dissolves and top with whipped topping.
4. Serve straight away.

Nutrition: Calories: 120 Fat: 3g Carbs: 23g Protein: 1g Sodium: 110mg Potassium: 199mg Phosphorus: 88mg

305. Rice Milk

Preparation Time: 2 minutes
Cooking Time: 2 minutes
Servings: 2
Ingredients:

- 1 c. rice milk, unenriched, chilled
- 1 scoop vanilla whey protein

Directions:
1. Pour milk in a blender, add whey protein, and then pulse until well blended.
2. Distribute the milk into two glasses and serve.

Nutrition: Calories: 120 Fat: 2g Carbs: 24g Protein: 0g Sodium: 86mg Potassium: 27mg Phosphorus: 56mg

306. Almond Milk

Preparation Time: 3 minutes
Cooking Time: 2 minutes
Servings: 3
Ingredients:
- 1 c. almonds, soaked in warm water for 10 minutes
- 1 tsp. vanilla extract, unsweetened
- 3 c. filtered water

Directions:
1. Drain the soaked almonds, place them into the blender, pour in water, and blend for 2 minutes until almonds are chopped.
2. Strain the milk by passing it through cheesecloth into a bowl, discard almond meal, and then stir vanilla into the milk.
3. Cover the milk, refrigerate until chilled, and when ready to serve, stir it well, pour the milk evenly into the glasses and then serve.

Nutrition: Calories: 30 Fat: 2.5g Carbs: 1g Protein: 1g Sodium: 170mg Potassium: 140mgmg Phosphorus: 30mg

307. Cucumber and Lemon-Flavored Water

Preparation Time: 5 minutes
Cooking Time: 3 hours
Servings: 10
Ingredients:
- 1 lemon, deseeded, sliced
- ¼ c. fresh mint leaves, chopped
- 1 medium cucumber, sliced
- ¼ c. fresh basil leaves, chopped
- 10 c. water

Directions:
1. Place the papaya and mint in a large pitcher. Pour in the water.
2. Stir and place the pitcher in the refrigerator to infuse, overnight if possible.
3. Serve cold.

Nutrition: Calories: 10 Fat: 0g Carbs: 2.25g Protein: 0.12g Sodium: 2.5mg Potassium: 8.9mg Phosphorus: 10mg

308. Blueberry Smoothie

Preparation Time: 5 minutes
Cooking Time: 2 minutes
Servings: 4
Ingredients:
- 1 c. frozen blueberries
- 6 tbsp. protein powder
- 8 packets Splenda
- 14 oz. apple juice, unsweetened

- 8 cubes of ice

Directions:

1. Take a blender and place all the ingredients (in order) in it. process for 1 minute until smooth.
2. Distribute the smoothie between four glasses and then serve.

Nutrition: Calories: 162 Fat: 0.5g Carbs: 30g Protein: 8g Sodium: 123.4mg Potassium: 223mg Phosphorus: 109mg

309. Blackberry Sage Cocktail

Preparation Time: 5 minutes
Cooking Time: 10 minutes
Servings: 6
Ingredients:

- Sage Simple Syrup
- 1 cup water
- 1 cup0granulated sugar
- 8 fresh sage leaves, plus more for garnish
- 1-pint fresh blackberries, muddled and strained (juices reserved)
- Juice of 1/2 a lemon
- 8 oz St. Germain Liqueur
- 16 oz vodka
- seltzer water

Directions:

1. Place water and sugar in a small saucepan.
2. Simmer until sugar dissolves for 7 to 10 minutes.
3. Remove from heat. Add sage leaves, and cover, allowing the mixture for about 2 hours.
4. Combine fresh blackberry juice, lemon juice, sage simple syrup, cocktail pitcher.
5. Mix and refrigerate covered until well chilled.
6. Serve in cocktail glasses filled with ice and garnish with fresh sage leaves and top with a splash of seltzer water.

Nutrition: Calories: 68 Fat: 1g Carbs: 15g Protein: 3g Sodium: 3mg Potassium: 133mg Phosphorus: 38mg

310. Apple- Cinnamon Drink

Preparation Time: 10 minutes
Cooking Time: 20 minutes
Servings: 4
Ingredients:

- 13 fresh apples
- 750ml-1L cold water
- 3-4 tablespoons cinnamon
- 1-2 tablespoons sugar (brown or caster)

Directions:

1. Peel, chop and cook 13 fresh apples.
2. Once they were half-cooked, add water leaving for 2 minutes
3. Add a lot of cinnamon (3-4 tablespoons, but you can add as much as you please, really) and 1-2 tablespoons sugar.
4. Keep cooking for another 5 minutes.
5. Drain and put into the new container back in the pan and bring it to the boil.

6. Add more cinnamon and a bit of water to thin it out a bit.
7. Pour into a cup and enjoy.

Nutrition: Calories: 130 Fat: 0g Carbs: 32g Protein: 0g Sodium: 20mg Potassium: 0mg Phosphorus: 0mg

311. <u>Detoxifying Beet Juice</u>

Preparation Time: 10 minutes
Cooking Time: 10 minutes
Servings: 4
Ingredients:

- 1-pound beets, washed with ends cut off
- 2 pounds carrots, washed with ends cut off
- 1 bunch celery, washed and broken into ribs
- 2 lemons, peel cut off and quartered
- 1 lime, peel cut off and quartered
- 1 bunch flat-leaf parsley, washed
- 1 Fuji or Honeycrisp red apple, chopped (optional, for extra sweetness)

Directions:

1. Wash produces and chop so pieces will fit into the feeder tube of your juicer.
2. Feed the vegetable pieces through the juicer, alternating harder and softer textured pieces to aid in the juicing process.
3. Serve immediately or store in the refrigerator in a highly sealed container.
4. The juice is best when served within 48 hours of making.

Nutrition: Calories: 58 Fat: 0g Carbs: 13g Protein: 2g Sodium: 106mg Potassium: 442mg Phosphorus: 54mg

312. <u>Honey Cinnamon Latte</u>

Preparation Time: 5 minutes
Cooking Time: 5 minutes
Servings: 2
Ingredients:

- 1-½ cups of organic, unsweetened almond milk
- 1 scoop of organic vanilla protein powder
- 1 teaspoon of organic cinnamon
- ½ teaspoon of pure, local honey
- 1-2 shots of espresso

Directions:

1. Heat almond milk in the microwave until hot to the touch.
2. Add honey and stir until completely melted.
3. Using a whisk, add cinnamon, and protein powder and thoroughly combine.
4. Pour into a manual milk and froth concoction until foamy and creamy.
5. Pour espresso shots into a mug and add in milk mixture.

Nutrition: Calories: 115 Fat: 3g Carbs: 26g Protein: 3g Sodium: 125mg Potassium: 10.9mg Phosphorus: 0.1mg

313. <u>Cinnamon Smoothie</u>

Preparation Time: 5 minutes
Cooking Time: 5 minutes

Servings: 2
Ingredients:

- 150g plain or Greek yogurt
- 300ml milk
- 2 tbsp smooth peanut butter
- 1/4 tsp Schwartz Ground Cinnamon

Directions:

1. Add all the ingredients to a blender and blitz until smooth.
2. Serve immediately.

Nutrition: Calories: 88 Fat: 4.3g Carbs: 3g Protein: 8g Sodium: 187mg Potassium: 241mg Phosphorus: 20mg

314.   Citrus Smoothie

Preparation Time: 5 minutes
Cooking Time: 2 minutes
Servings: 2
Ingredients:

- 1 large orange, peeled, halved
- ¼ lemon, peeled, seeded
- ½ cup (85 g) pineapple, peeled, cubed
- ¼ cup (60 g) frozen mango
- 1 cup (130 g) ice cubes

Directions:

1. Prepare all ingredients into the container and secure lid.
2. Turn machine on and slowly increase speed to high.
3. Blend for 1 minute or until the desired consistency is reached.

Nutrition: Calories: 280 Fat: 0g Carbs: 67g Protein: 4g Sodium: 30mg Potassium: 570mg Phosphorus: 0mg

CONCLUSION

The renal diet is a special diet for people with kidney problems. It is only for people who have chronic kidney disease. The diet limits salt, potassium, phosphorus, protein and fluid intake. It also limits certain fruits and vegetables. The diet reduces the amount of waste products in the blood so that the kidneys can better cleanse the blood.

There are different ways to maintain your health and to ensure that you sustain it for longer. The number one reason why patients are urged to stay healthy during the early stages of kidney disease is to avoid dialysis for as long as possible.

This can be done by incorporating the right types of nutrients in your diet, all of which are included in the right amount, in the renal diet.

Even though there is no cure for chronic kidney disease, it is a journey that you can manage. You can sustain your health and continue living your life as normal, with a high quality of life, for much longer than if you don't follow these basic guidelines.

The number one thing to remember on this journey is that you are in complete control of your outcome.

These organs might be little, but they are mighty. Sadly, over thirty million Americans mighty kidneys are being affected and degraded by chronic kidney disease, high blood pressure, and diabetes.

Bear in mind that the renal diet is a lifestyle, and to get the best results, it's important to follow it regularly and include it in your daily life. And don't worry, you can do it. After all, this book is the best proof that the renal diet is yummy. Meals do not require too much hassle, and that's also amazing.

Dialysis treatments explicitly clean the blood of waste and toxins in the blood utilizing a machine in view of the fact that your body can no longer carry out the responsibility. Without treatments, you could die a very painful death. Renal failure can be the consequence of long-haul diabetes, hypertension, unreliable diet, and can stem from other health concerns.

A renal diet is associated with guiding the intake of protein and phosphorus in your eating diet.

reducing your sodium intake is likewise significant. By controlling these two things you can control many of the toxins/waste produced by your body and thus this enables your kidney to 100% function. In the event that you get this early enough and truly moderate your diets with extraordinary consideration, you could avert all-out renal failure. In the event that you get this early, you can take out the issue completely.

The proper renal diet can really help kidneys functioning longer, and it has only more restrictions on proteins and table salt, while restrictions to phosphorous and potassium can be needed if the levels of blood rise and the signs of accumulation become too evident.

The Low sodium will also assist in striking the right balance between saturated and unsaturated fats.

Thank you for reading this book, if you liked it, please consider leaving a review on Amazon.

INDEX

48514961R00133